W9-CFD-284

GREAT FALLS, MT

GREAT FALLS, MT

FAST TIMES, POST-PUNK WEIRDOS, AND A TALE OF COMING HOME AGAIN

reggie watts

Tiny
Reparations
Books

An imprint of Penguin Random House LLC
penguinrandomhouse.com

Copyright © 2023 by Reginald Watts
Penguin Random House supports copyright. Copyright fuels creativity,
encourages diverse voices, promotes free speech, and creates a vibrant culture.
Thank you for buying an authorized edition of this book and for complying with
copyright laws by not reproducing, scanning, or distributing any part of it
in any form without permission. You are supporting writers and allowing
Penguin Random House to continue to publish books for every reader.

Interior art: Grunge background © MPFphotography / Shutterstock.com

Girl Watcher
Words and Music by Ronald B. Killette and E. Wayne Pittman
Copyright © 1968 (Renewed) by Embassy Music Corporation
(BMI) and Music Sales Corporation (ASCAP)
International Copyright Secured   All Rights Reserved
Reprinted by Permission of Hal Leonard LLC

TINY REPARATIONS BOOKS with colophon is a
registered trademark of YQY, Inc.

LIBRARY OF CONGRESS CATALOGING-IN-PUBLICATION DATA
has been applied for.

ISBN (hardcover) 9780593472460
ISBN (ebook) 9780593472477

Printed in the United States of America
1st Printing

BOOK DESIGN BY KRISTIN DEL ROSARIO

While the author has made every effort to provide accurate telephone numbers, internet
addresses, and other contact information at the time of publication, neither the publisher nor
the author assumes any responsibility for errors, or for changes that occur after publication.
Further, publisher does not have any control over and does not assume any
responsibility for author or third-party websites or their content.

To Maman and Dad.

Thank you so much. You guys rule forever.

contents

· · · · · · · · · · · · ·

CONTENTS

CONTENTS

author's note

. . . .

Oh, hello!

I didn't see you there.

You must be here to read this book. Forgive me. It's my very first book, and I'm still getting the hang of these various formalities.

For example, this book is primarily a coming-of-age tale about growing up in the 1980s in my hometown of Great Falls, MT, then leaving to find my way in the world as a musician, comedian, and consummate weirdo, only to be drawn back again by personal, mystical forces that I finally try to come to terms with within these pages. This portion is what esteemed scholars and learned journals apparently refer to as "narrative."

But there is another portion of this book, and those same esteemed scholars and learned journals have notified me that that portion is best classified as "a bunch of silly ridiculousness."

I wear their pronouncement as a badge of copper.

Now, sometimes I may get confused about which portion is which. Which is real, which is imagined, which is more, which is less, and which is candy with peanut butter in the middle and also chocolate all around it. But that's just fine. And potentially delicious.

Either way, I really hope you like my book. If you don't, that's okay. I still want us to be friends. Or at least nonthreatening acquaintances who respect each other's personal space.

Thank you.

introduction
· · · · · · · · · · · · · · ·
DAY ONE

My dad and I walked down the crowded streets of Madrid to his favorite bar.

Once inside, I soaked it all in. The polished wood, the smell of cigarillos in the air, the light glinting off the brown and green bottles of cerveza and vino. Of course, I was only three and a half years old, so I stuck with something a little lighter.

"*¿Un jugo de naranja, por favor?*" I said to the bartender, standing on my tiptoes.

An orange juice. My babysitter was Spanish, so not only did I know how to speak the language, but a lot of the time that's simply what I spoke.

"I'll take a cognac, please," my dad said.

It was 1976. My dad, Charles, was a Black American air force serviceman, a Vietnam vet with big, soft brown eyes, a strong chin, and an easygoing smile. My mom, Christiane, was a strong-willed, hazel-eyed redhead from northern France. They'd met nine years earlier at a little joint in Verdun called Charlie Bar, just like my dad's name, while he was helping decommission a base nearby. He'd picked up just enough of the local language to impress the attractive friend of his best buddy's girl. Romantic gems like *"enchanté"* and

"Désirez-vous du vin?" and, knowing my dad and his way with the ladies, something like *"Le bar, c'est Charlie. Je suis Charlie. Coïncidence? Non!"*

My mom asked him where he learned to speak such good French. Cleveland, he replied.

She leaned over to her friend, her eyes locked on the handsome soldier from Ohio, and whispered, *"Il est à moi."* He is mine. To this day, she insists he was *absolument* fluent.

Then there was me. I was already on my third country. Born in Stuttgart on the base hospital, lived in Germany for almost a year, followed that with a stint in Italy, and now Spain. For reasons I still don't understand, I was born without citizenship to any country. Literally. I didn't have American citizenship, or French, or German. I was legally a Nothing. That's not something I technically understood at the time, of course—I was too young—but somehow, on some level, I absorbed the reality of my jumbled identity, and I embraced it. I was the consummate outsider. A cosmopolitan who lived in awe of the cool, colorful world that surrounded me.

So the conversation that led to my dad bringing me to my very first bar that sunny Saturday afternoon went something like this, with everyone speaking their preferred language:

MOM: Charles, *j'ai beaucoup à faire dans la maison, prends* Reggie *dehors et joue avec lui.*

DAD: What do you say, Reg? You wanna go exploring with me?

ME: *¡Sí, por favor!*

At the bar, my dad offered me his hand and boosted me onto the stool. Our spot was right by a giant window, open to the air. Now I got it. We weren't there for the drinks, not really. We were there for the environment, for the atmosphere. For the view.

We sipped away and gazed out at the teeming boulevard. The traffic, the cypress trees, the ancient cathedrals. But most of all the people. So many different types of people. Tall and short, heavy and thin, light-skinned and dark. Blue eyes, hazel eyes, blond, and brunette. Each person completely unique, each with their own quirks and mannerisms. Even the way they strolled along the sidewalk had personality.

And their voices. So many voices! Madrid was a truly international city, and I found myself engulfed by more languages than I ever knew existed. I let the sounds wash over me, fragments of sentences, of words, of conversations, like a strange sort of music.

"Was kannst du empfehlen?"

"—so che siete ai ferri corti, non me ne importa—"

"—naiz zu ezagutzeaz!"

"Το νυν εστι μεσότης τις . . ."

"—aus Würste, die einem in den Weg gelegt werden, kann man Schönes—"

"そうだね。また行きたいな!"

"Zuzen-zuzen jarrai'zazu . . ."

"لكل انسان لسان . . ."

Then I heard another kind of sound. Actual music. My dad was humming something to himself.

"What are you singing, Dad?"

"Oh," he said, "it's nothing. Just an oldie from back in the day."

"An oldie?"

He gathered himself, clearing his throat in mock seriousness, and sang in his deep voice.

I'm a girl watcher.
I'm a girl watcher.
Watching girls go by.
My, my, myyyy.

"Is that what you're doing?" I asked, wide-eyed. "Watching girls?"

"Nah," he said with a laugh. "Well . . . maybe a little bit. Your mother doesn't mind. She knows she's the only girl for me."

I smiled. I looked back at the boulevard, at all the girls walking by. My dad was right. Even though I was only a boy, I could tell there was something special about women. Something that made them vastly more interesting than men. I didn't quite understand what, not yet. But I sensed that it was related to the same swirl of voices and cultures and identities that made Europe feel so alive. Women possessed a style, a vitality, a creative force that represented everything exciting and mysterious about life. I can't tell you how I knew that, how I felt that, but I did.

Sitting in a bar in Madrid with my dad, I experienced all of that for the very first time. We sang what became our favorite song as the mishmash of languages whirled around us.

"I'm a girl watcher..."

"lui ha una capacità"

"I'm a girl watcher..."

"Bihotzean dagoena . . ."

"Watching girls go by..."

"πάμε να δούμε"

"My,"

"카페에서"

"my,"

"اما من نمی کنم"

"my."

Then, suddenly, it was over. Just like that.

I don't remember any big talk. One day we were in Spain. The next day we were gone, and I found myself in a brand-new place. A brand-new world.

I didn't know it then, but this place would become my first true home. It would shape me, mold me, help define my identity. Here, I would grow apart from the father I loved so much, even fight him, and turn to my mom as my protector and savior. I would make a new family of friends, a bunch of free-spirit, post-punk oddballs who did a lot of drugs and lived and died for each other. I would fall in love with women—all of them, and one in particular. I would play the violin and watch PBS and steal cars. I would follow my own rules, embrace society's conventions, and then demolish them for the fun of it.

This place would lay the foundation for everything I would someday become. An eccentric. An artist. A connoisseur of weed and Robitussin and old James Bond flicks. A performer who created a constantly changing mélange of music and improv and technology and just-plain-fucking-around that's so abnormal I still have no idea what exactly it is.

Most important, even now, after all these years of living in some of our country's greatest cities, of traveling the globe and performing with massive stars in front of millions of people—even now, this place is still where I always come back to.

At the time, though, all I knew about this brand-new place was that it was big and open and wide. It was very white. It was very quiet. And it was called the strangest, most exotic word I had ever heard.

Its name was Montana.

GREAT FALLS, MT

chapter one

SHOEHORNS

The reason I love shoehorns is because I hate tying shoelaces so much.

A shoehorn's design is so flawless, so efficient, so gloriously functional. You simply slip the curved horn into your shoe, then allow your foot to glide along its length, and—presto! Your foot has now been seamlessly, miraculously, simply slipped into your shoe.

It's good for your foot, because it lessens friction. It's good for your shoe, because it forestalls wear. It's good for your soul, because it eases frustration.

And now they even make these cool new kinds with extra-long handles. You just walk over to your shoes, you stay standing, you hold on to the end of your shoehorn's extra-long handle, and you guide your foot into your shoe effortlessly. They even make these little, like, hooks, so you can hang your extra-long shoehorn right by your front door.

My old shoehorn broke, so I got a new carbon-fiber shoehorn.

Sometimes I stop and I look at it, and I just think, *Yes.*

chapter two

MY OWN PRIVATE MONTANA

"Okay," my dad said. "Here we are."

Our car pulled to a stop, and I stared in wonder at the big, ugly square building.

"Maman," I asked, *"c'est notre maison?"*

"Non, Reggie," she said. *"C'est un motel."*

It was one of those classic motor lodges you see on the outskirts of towns all around America. Two-story, pay in advance, every room's door opening onto the parking lot. Perfect for road trips or illicit high school parties. And our very first stop at our new city, Great Falls, MT.

"Well," my dad said, "for now, it's the home we got."

The air force was in the process of helping us find a house in town. My dad had been assigned to serve as a master sergeant in the military police on the Malmstrom Air Force Base, but my parents didn't want to live on base. The military had actually given my dad a choice between relocating to Montana or North or South Dakota, and he and my mom chose Montana because they'd been impressed by the local schools. If my parents had to move to the States, they wanted to raise their son in a normal neighborhood, off base, with good schools, nice yards, and friendly neighbors. Sure, there would be other military families nearby, and we wouldn't be far from Malmstrom, but my parents didn't want the typical armed forces experience. They wanted Great Falls.

I got out of the car and looked around. I had just turned four—we had flown out of Madrid on my birthday, March 23, 1976—and even then, even at that young age, I was bizarrely . . . aware. Aware of everything around me, the sights, the sounds, the smells. And aware of myself. In any situation, no matter how sad or happy or intense, I would remove myself from the moment and start studying my response, observing my reaction like some kind of alien-watcher sent to Earth to figure these wacky humans out.

Like right now, even as I'm typing these words, and I'm enjoying typing these words, I'm thinking, *Ah, I'm enjoying typing these words, and isn't it interesting that people somewhere thousands of miles away from where I am right now who don't even know I'm currently typing these words will someday read these words, and to them my now will become their now, even though it's not really their now at all, it's my now and their past?* And all these thoughts are happening in my mind simultaneously in my current now, and maybe, just maybe, I've done too many perception-altering drugs in my life, except, no, I didn't do drugs back when I was four—I think?—and I was like this back then too.

So when we arrived in Great Falls and I got out of our car and gazed around, at first I felt nervous, excited, and a little apprehensive, for maybe about five seconds. Then I became *aware* that I was feeling nervous, excited, and a little apprehensive, and then I started *watching myself* feel nervous, excited, and a little apprehensive.

Huh. How fascinating. So that's *how that feels.*

I felt an odd emotional distance from both myself—and from the town. To me, this was just the latest stop in a long line of cities and bases. I'd spent my entire life on the move. It was a simple fact of life, something I was used to. So I didn't know if I'd ever feel a real connection to this place. It definitely didn't feel like my home. It felt like a giant nameless motel. Like a big blank slate. A nothing, kind of like me.

Everything about this place felt different from where I'd been before. Madrid had been dense, bustling, with people and buildings and languages piled all on top of each other. A city. A capital. Somehow this new space, Montana, felt both incredibly smaller and infinitely larger all at the same time.

The buildings I could see were tiny compared to what I was used to. The biggest one was the bank downtown with seven floors, but the rest were one, maybe two floors. Fast-food restaurants and gas stations in the sprawl around our hotel, and near the center of the city simple Craftsman houses and quaint brick storefronts all arranged on a simple grid, its broad streets dotted with linden trees. It felt like the prototypical small American town, as if a random computer simulation was like, "Let's create a real-life version of Marty McFly's hometown in *Back to the Future* and put it, I don't know . . . here?"

But at the same time, there was something about the landscape that was bigger, broader, wider—*vaster*—than anything I'd experienced in my young life. Here I was, a little boy, standing underneath a sky so huge it felt like it could swallow me up at any moment. The Montana sky stretches above you like a giant panoramic theater of nature. You can *see* entire weather systems forming and unfolding in front of you in real time. The sky is more than just present, it's eventful, more a character in the drama of your life than scenery.

Far in the distance I could see a small brown mountain range, scattered hills and plateaus. Beyond the city limits, we were surrounded by miles and miles of prairie grass dotted with farms and wheat fields. Running through the center of town was the Missouri

River, the source of the falls that gave the city its name. Then, right on the horizon, there was a massive five-hundred-foot industrial smokestack from back when the local smelter was still processing tons of ore, all the railroad lines were still jammed with trains, and people still thought Great Falls was going to be the Chicago of the West, brimming with hope and potential.

But for my parents, wearily unloading our bags in front of our motel room, the reality was more complicated. There was promise in our move to Montana, sure. The middle-class neighborhoods, the good schools, the American Dream. But for them, moving to America also meant something different, something darker. Something other than a magical dream.

In Europe, my dad had experienced a freedom he'd never felt before. He had grown up poor and Black on the streets of Cleveland. His own father had been involved in crime, running the numbers for a local gang, and he'd been murdered at a young age. So my dad had been raised by his mom and his stepfather, a strict disciplinarian who had no problem taking to my dad with his belt. And why not? It was a hard world with hard lessons to learn. Racism was everywhere. As a child, he'd been called every racial slur in the book, more times than he could remember. Life had been a constant battle. Then, the first time he left the country, he went to battle for real. Served two tours in Vietnam, then another in Algeria. All he'd known was conflict.

But once the war ended, for the first time in his life so did the struggle. He was based in cosmopolitan cities across Europe, with all the privileges afforded an American soldier. For the very first time, he wasn't a Black man in a white man's world. He wasn't constrained by any categories, any lines. He could live life unrestricted and be whoever he wanted. He could drive down the road in the classic green Firebird he'd shipped in from the States, the windows open and the wind in his hair, simply because he liked going fast. Or he could marry a white woman simply because they were in love.

When my dad traveled to my mom's village to ask her father for permission to marry his daughter—because my dad could be a traditionalist like that—my mom's dad didn't slam the door in his face. He didn't shut my dad out because he looked different. He just looked at my dad and said, "What? You don't need my permission! If you want to marry her, you can. Just ask her!"

In a sense, that's why my dad fell in love with my mom. I mean, obviously she was stunning and perfect. But beyond that, she represented a life he had never experienced back in the States. There were no women like her in Cleveland, certainly not in the part he was from. They expanded each other's horizons, going out dancing until the early hours of the morning, introducing each other to new foods and languages, immersing themselves in the music of Édith Piaf, Julio Iglesias, and Greek icon Nana Mouskouri, who herself recorded songs in twelve languages.

But even with my mom by his side, my dad knew that America would be different. Sure, things had changed by the late '70s—but they hadn't changed that much. Before I was born, my dad had taken my mom home to Ohio for a few months to meet his family. The two of them had been walking downtown, hand in hand—something they had done every day without a second thought in Spain—and a passing white man had spat at her for having the audacity to love a Black man. Spat at her! Imagine that. Your first trip to a new country and that's the kind of welcome you get.

Now, Montana wasn't exactly the inner city, and my dad would have the base nearby. But would racism in rural, red-state America really be any better than Cleveland? He doubted it.

And that wasn't the only thing he had to worry about.

This was long before anyone understood what exactly PTSD

was. Military culture at the time didn't exactly promote sharing your feelings about what you'd experienced in war. You were supposed to tough it out, keep it all in, go about your business as if nothing was wrong. And Europe had made that easier to do. Surrounded by all the exotic locales, the different cultures, the fascinating people . . . it was almost like a fantasy. It had barely felt real. What happened in Vietnam felt like a part of a different lifetime, like it had happened to someone else.

But now that he was back in the States, back to reality, my dad could feel those memories slowly start to seep back in. And he didn't know how to make it stop. He smoked a lot, and he definitely liked his drink, and the strain on his mental health slowly started to impact the rest of his health. He had his first heart surgery shortly after we moved to Great Falls, and four more all before 1982. The one good thing about all that military service, as traumatizing as it had been, was that at least he had good health care. My dad was strong, he was an active person, but that kind of intrusion—literally being opened up so doctors can fix your blocked arteries—was enough to change anyone. Slow anyone down.

My mom had her own share of burdens. Born in 1938 not far from the border with Germany, she'd grown up under Nazi occupation. She'd always been the strong one of her family, always willful, always intense. They were solidly middle-class. Her father and her brother had both been taxi drivers, but she wasn't going to let them do all the work. She got her own job making brake pads—yes, brake pads—at a local auto factory, like a French, redheaded Jennifer Beals in *Flashdance* welding away at the steel mill by day and dancing it up with foreign soldiers by night. Except my mom never needed a body double, because she had all her own moves.

She also wasn't going to let anyone tell her who she could or couldn't date. She may have represented a certain kind of exotic freedom to my dad, but her choice of him as a husband was no less significant. Like most of the women in her town, she could've easily chosen a traditional provincial lifestyle, close to her family. But she was famous for her independent streak. So when she told her dad she had agreed to marry the Black American serviceman who'd asked for her hand, her dad simply sighed and shrugged. "You know, there are plenty of Black men in France," he said. "Couldn't you at least love one of them?"

Yeah. My grandfather definitely had a way with words.

But even my mom's strength had been tested the first time her new husband had brought her to America. No one had ever spat at her before, not for any reason, much less holding hands with a Black man. She had felt my father flinch when it happened, felt his hesitation, but my mom had simply gripped his hand even tighter, set her jaw, stared straight ahead, and kept on walking.

She sensed that she would have to be the strong one now that we were in Montana. Her husband had always been charming, charismatic, and funny. But she could already feel him starting to tighten up, holding back his emotions and bottling up his trauma from the war. Trauma he'd never felt comfortable sharing with her. Then, when he got sick, when he went to the hospital, she was the one who had to take care of him. My dad would always be an amazing provider, even after the surgeries, but my mom would have to become our protector, the force that kept our family together. I was just a little boy at the time, more confused than anything. And I would be caught somewhere in between.

I took one more look at Great Falls, MT, before I went into our motel room. The traffic lights, the smokestack, the mountains in the distance. It somehow felt both incredibly foreign and bizarrely conventional. It felt disconnected. *I* felt disconnected.

Now I had to figure out who exactly I was in this new place, and how I fit in. Or whether I even wanted to in the latest town to serve as my home.

· · · · ·

The elderly lady reached down and took me by the hand. Her skin had a thin, papery feel to it. She led me to the front of her living room, next to a big TV with a rabbit-ear antenna.

"Children," she said, "quiet down now! Pay attention! I'd like you all to meet the newest member of our playgroup. Reggie, can you tell the others a little about yourself?"

The room, which had just been a jumble of activity and commotion, suddenly grew quiet. I gulped. Looked out over a sea of shag carpeting at twelve sets of staring eyes. And froze.

The little day care, run by one of our neighbors, was just up the street from our new house. The neighborhood was a perfect snapshot of '70s-style Middle America. Neat little roads dotted with pine trees and small three-bedroom ranch houses and spotless green yards, each one exactly like the next, perfect for little families like mine. It was a planned, exquisitely engineered subdivision with the streets named after the wives of the developers. Alice Drive, Beth Drive, Diana Drive. Our own beige cookie-cutter house with orange wooden shutters was located on Carol Drive. I'd sit on the sofa in our living room, staring out our big front window at the houses across the street, wondering about the kids who lived behind those closed doors.

I imagined them to be like the kids I'd seen in Mountain Dew commercials on TV, all blue eyes and long straight hair and white skin bronzed from the sun, laughing and jumping off tire swings into a sparkling body of water as they guzzled their electric-yellow liquid caffeine. That was where they spent most of their days, of course—at the river or the lake or wherever it was. But when they came home, they came here, to Alice or Beth or Diana Drive, I just knew it. Those were the new friends I dreamed of making. That was the lifestyle I dreamed of leading. That sweet Mountain Dew existence.

Of course, there were other kids on base too. Base, with its commissary, where we bought all our groceries, and its exchange, where we could get the coolest toys and electronics at an awesome discount. At base, I met a bunch of kids with backgrounds as mixed-up as mine. My dad wasn't the only soldier coming home with a wife and kid after years of service abroad, far from it. There was a half-Belgian kid, a half-Thai kid, a half-Japanese kid. Even a half-French kid like me, my buddy Didier, whose dad opened a hobby shop in a nearby town. I'd go over on weekends and we'd fly model planes in his backyard, chattering away in French the whole time. We were a generation of military kids, all on our own journeys trying to fit into a country that was supposed to be ours.

But I didn't want friends on base or in other towns. I wanted friends close to me. I had no brother or sister, my dad was gone all day working with the military police, and soon my mom got a job selling Avon. I needed a new family to hang out with every day, a family of kids my own age who lived in my own neighborhood.

But now that I was finally here, standing in front of twelve kids from around the block, this exciting new family of mine, I couldn't help noticing that they all looked kinda the same. No half-this, no half-that, no blur of different identities. None of them looked like me. And I had a feeling that none of them talked like me either.

"Reggie?" the lady said, giving me a gentle nudge. "Would you like to say hello?"

My mouth went dry. At home, I spoke French with my mom. Some English with my dad, but we were communicating less these days, just short exchanges about cleaning my room or getting ready for bed. Would these neighborhood kids understand me? What if my accent was too thick? What if my English was bad? What if they made fun of me? What if they laughed? It was like my usual self-awareness had gone into overdrive, leaving my mind reeling.

"Uh," I said, as the shining, curious eyes studied me. "*Mon* name *est*, um, Reggie. I live, um, *pas loin d'ici, dans ce quartier. Une maison* like, um, this one. And, uh . . . *Comment appelez-vous?*"

They looked back at me and blinked. *"What did he say?"*

A little hand shot up in the air.

"Hey, new kid! How old are you?"

"Um, *quatre*, I mean—"

"Hey, new kid! Where are you from?"

"Well, España, sort of, *pero también*, I mean, *mais aussi*, I mean—"

"Hey, new kid! Do you have parents?"

"*Bien sûr!* My dad *est* in l'air force, *et ma maman travaille pour* Avon!"

"Avon?" "Did the new kid say 'Avon'?" "My mom loves Avon!"

"Hey, new kid! What language are you speaking?"

"Um—"

"Hey, new kid! Are you American like us?"

"Well—"

"Hey, new kid! How do you even live here?"

"Please—"

The elderly lady placed her hands firmly but kindly on my shoulders.

"All right, everyone!" she said. "That's enough for now. I'm sure we'll learn more about Reggie as we get to know him better, okay?"

The other children gave a collective shrug. I watched as they went back to playing without me.

Back in Europe, language had felt borderless, organic. It had possessed an energy, a flow, and I simply grabbed hold and went along for the joyride. But here, in front of these twelve kids, it had become a wall, a psychic barrier.

For the first time in my life, I couldn't break through.

. . . . .

My eyes flickered open. It was dark in my bedroom, the middle of the night.

I had been having a dream where I had to go to the bathroom really bad. Finally I woke up and realized . . . Oh, I needed to go to the bathroom really bad.

I crawled out from between my sheets, felt my way to the door, and opened it. The bathroom was just down the hall, but I noticed light coming from the kitchen. It was tinted red. My mom's favorite color was red, so everything in the kitchen was red. Wallpaper, tablecloth, seat cushions. Everything.

Someone must've forgot to turn off the light, I thought. *Guess I will.*

I blinked as I walked into the brightness. My dad was sitting at the table, staring into the distance, silent.

"Dad?" I said.

He didn't respond. Didn't say a word, didn't move a muscle. I didn't understand what was happening. I only knew that somehow my dad wasn't the same person he had been in Spain. He could still be quick with a joke. He still liked driving his car on the weekends. Sometimes he and I would quietly watch *Star Trek*, just the two of us.

But the connection I had felt with him back in Europe, that special bond when we'd spend the day together, enjoying life,

singing our favorite songs, not just as father and son but as friends—
that was gone now. And I didn't know how to get it back.

"Dad?" I said. "*Ça va?* Are you okay?"

He nodded, just barely, and kept staring out at nothing.

I went and used the bathroom and climbed back into bed. I
tried and tried, but I couldn't fall back asleep.

· · · · ·

It was a hazy summer afternoon when I finally worked up the courage. I had been staring out our big living room window at the house
across the street for what felt like forever.

Once we moved into our new house, it hadn't taken long to
figure out if any kids lived across the street. Two boys, brothers,
right around my age. Just normal, average Montana kids. Brown hair,
brown eyes, easy laughs whenever they played outside together. But I
was a normal Montana kid now too, wasn't I? Brown hair, brown
eyes, an easy laugh when I played outside. And brown skin, also that.

But after my experience with the other kids at my day care, I
became a little hesitant to make other friends in my neighborhood.
It had been months since we got settled, and I still hadn't even introduced myself. I wasn't typically shy, wasn't naturally uncomfortable around other people. I just wasn't sure what to say. I worried
that the jumble of languages in my mind would confuse kids, keep
them away. Maybe once I learned some bigger words in English,
became more comfortable speaking the local language, maybe then
I could walk around to the other houses to meet some people.

Then something had happened. I had gone from being a nothing to being a something. I had gotten my American citizenship.
Once we'd gotten settled in Great Falls, my mom had made it her
mission to get me my citizenship. She had no interest in it for herself.

Even though she was married to an American service member and could've easily qualified, she refused to get anything beyond permanent residency. It was a matter of principle, she said. She was French to her core, her spirit was French, her identity was French—fiery, strong, willful—and she'd always be French, no matter where she lived. She would never change that.

Maybe that was why she was so insistent on getting me my American citizenship as soon as we got to the States. She wanted me to know that whatever language—or languages—I spoke, whatever color my skin, I belonged in this country. This was my home, this was my birthright, and no one could take that away.

The morning I took my oath at the town courthouse, I started to understand that, started to understand just what it meant to be a citizen, to have a nation of my own. My mom dressed me in a nice sweater. I had memorized the few facts I thought I needed to know. The old white guys who founded the country declared independence on July 4, 1776. I had that one down pat. And it was another old white guy who administered the Pledge of Allegiance that day, Judge Carter, a man who'd taken a liking to me and my family, who'd helped my very insistent, very strong mother expedite the citizenship process.

But when I looked around the room at the courthouse, I realized that, other than the judge, most of the other people there looked more like me. Not necessarily Black, though some were. But different shades of brown, their hair different textures, their noses different shapes, their accents something other than the usual Montana drawl. Once we took our oath, all of us would be just as American as Judge Carter or the kids on my block or anyone else in Great Falls.

Except of course my mom, because to hell with that—she was French.

With that newfound confidence, I took a deep breath, walked

out our front door, and headed across the street to see if my neighbors could come out to play.

Their house looked like ours, most of the houses in our neighborhood did. But there was something a little shabbier about their place. The grass was long and shaggy, the hedges hadn't been trimmed. The driveway was the only one in the neighborhood that wasn't paved. It was gravel, and I liked to think of their house as the Fred Flintstone House. I stepped onto their unfinished drive, and my feet made a soft crunching sound as I slowly approached their door. The curtains of their big living room window were pulled closed, but I had seen the boys playing on the porch earlier, so I knew they were home.

I pushed the doorbell and waited. Nothing. But I hadn't heard any bell, so maybe the doorbell was broken. I knocked on the aluminum frame of the screen door, and after a few seconds I heard heavy footsteps inside.

The door opened and a big man I recognized as the boys' father stood there looking down at me. He was wearing blue jeans and an old white undershirt. I was wearing suspenders. I wore a lot of suspenders back then. Suspenders and sweaters, that was my look.

"Hi there," I said in my meticulously rehearsed English. "My name is Reggie. I live across the street. Can the boys who live here come out and play with me?"

The big man frowned.

I don't remember exactly what he said after that. I just remember that he used a bunch of words I didn't know and they didn't sound very nice, and one of those words started with an *n*. Seconds later I was crying and running back across the street—*crying, I'm crying now, so this is what pain feels like, I really don't like it*—my mom had always told me to look both ways before crossing, but I didn't care. I just wanted to go home.

As soon as she heard my cries, my mother rushed out of her red kitchen and into our living room.

"Reggie, qu'est-ce quis passe?"

I told her the word our neighbor had called me.

I'd seen my mom angry before, but I'd never seen her like this. Her hazel eyes flashed a brighter shade of red than her hair. When she had been spat at in Cleveland, she had endured it with strong, quiet dignity. But that had happened to her; this was her *son*.

She grabbed my arm and marched me right back across the street. I noticed she didn't look both ways either. She pounded on the door, and the big man in the old white undershirt opened it with a smug look on his face. That didn't last long.

"Now you listen to me, you piece of white trash! Zis is just a little boy, and you talk to him zat way? Huh? Are you crazy? I'm telling you zis right now, okay—if you ever mess with zis kid again, I will come for you. I swear it! *I will come for you!*"

I had no idea my mom knew that much English.

Technically, she wasn't that physically imposing. A little over five feet tall, maybe a foot taller than I was. But you got this small bundle of pure redheaded French rage coming right at your face, and let's see how well you hold up. This dude didn't say a word. Just slammed the door.

So my mom called the cops. A few minutes later lights were flashing across the street as a couple of cops—both white, of course—knocked on my neighbor's door and had their own conversation with the man in the old white undershirt. Probably a little more polite than my mom, I guess, but with the same basic message. That he better leave me alone from here on out.

I couldn't help wondering how many other kids in our neighborhood had seen us stomping back and forth across that street. Had noticed the police reaming our neighbor out moments later. What would they think of me? Would *anyone* want to be my friend now?

Later that night, my dad came home from work. My mom told him what had happened. He shook his head and sighed. It was like all his fears about moving back to America were coming true.

"This won't be the last time, Reg," he said, looking at me. "You're gonna have to learn how to stand up for yourself. Some white kid calls you the n-word, you call him a redneck honky. Some white kid hits you, you hit them back. Harder, if you can. That's life. You better get used to it."

Now, I was just a little boy. My dad knew that. I don't think he expected me to defend myself, physically or verbally, against a grown man who was five times my size. But my father felt like he had to prepare me for the same harsh realities he had dealt with growing up. I don't think he was inherently an angry person or a fighter by nature. Years of war, of racism, of discipline at the hands of his stepfather, had all burned it into him. He'd taken up judo when he was stationed in Japan, even earned a brown belt. Our bookshelf was stacked with trophies from all the tournaments he'd won. If someone called him the n-word, he knew how to respond.

Then there was my mom. *She* was a natural fighter.

"*Si quelqu'un te derange, dis-moi,*" she whispered to me. "*JE m'en occuperai d'eux.*"

If someone gives you trouble, you tell me. I'LL take care of them.

But I knew I needed to find my own path, the same way I needed to find my own identity.

My dad was right. I did get called the n-word again. Not a lot, but it happened. To be clear, Montana isn't the uncivilized backwater so many Americans assume it to be. I've had friends from the coasts say things to me like "Wait, was it just like *Little House on the*

Prairie growing up?" First—no, it wasn't. Second—I kinda wish it was, because hanging out with Michael Landon and riding horses sounds pretty sick. But are there racists in Montana? Ignorant people who say and do stupid things? People who get so frustrated with their own disappointing lives that they take it out on others, even kids? Absolutely, just like in the rest of the world. And yeah, on occasion I had to deal with them.

But I had zero interest in telling someone off or calling them a redneck honky. Zero interest in punching someone with a judo chop, even if they deserved it. I hated arguing, and I hated confrontation. I simply wasn't a fighter. It's not who I am.

Instead, I decided to transcend my differences with others. I decided to *make* people like me, whether they wanted to or not.

I invented my very first social hack.

· · · · ·

I stepped to the front of the living room at the old lady's day care down the street, right next to the big TV. Except this time no one was holding my hand. I was on my own.

Maybe Great Falls was different from Madrid. Maybe there wasn't the culture or the architecture or the languages. Maybe I couldn't spend afternoons with my dad sipping OJ and cognac and watching the world walk by together. But even at that young age, I sensed that with all its wide, broad plains and sprawling new neighborhoods, Montana possessed a kind of openness, a kind of possibility that Europe didn't have. It had a libertarian vibe. People tended to keep to themselves, but that also allotted a certain freedom. A chance to be whatever you wanted to be.

Moving to a strange new country, starting out with an entirely clean slate—that didn't have to be a bad thing. Sure, I had no idea how long we'd be here before we moved again. Yeah, my life was full of uncertainty. But if I looked at it the right way, that uncertainty could be exciting! An adventure! Fun! I could be and do and create whatever I wanted here. Right in Great Falls!

The other kids in the day care were playing with each other, ignoring me, which is pretty much what they'd done since my very first day. But I was about to change all that.

"Hey, all you kids!" I shouted, accent and all. "*Vous aimez danser?* Then look at me!"

And then, as their eyes grew wide and their mouths dropped, I started to dance.

Now let's be honest. In real life, I was doing a funny little jig. Shuffling my feet, wiggling my little hips, and pointing my fingers in the air like a preschool John Travolta.

But in my mind?

I was gliding across that shag carpeting.

I was swooping through the air.

I was turning and twisting like Zizi Jeanmaire.

I was living free. All the lines broke down, all the barriers dissolved. For those few moments all my self-awareness lifted, my mind relaxed, and I just *was*.

Most important of all, the other kids loved it. They loved me. I felt a synchronicity with them, a closeness, a commonality. We shared the same frequency. They were clapping their hands, laughing—not at me, not even with me, but simply everywhere.

After a couple minutes of nonstop jiggling and gyrating, they weren't calling me "new kid," they were chanting my name. I sucked it up like a sponge, basking in all the joy. This was me. This was my hack.

If other people thought I was different, I wasn't going to fight them. I wasn't going to prove them wrong. I was going to prove them *right*—by being the biggest, craziest, funniest "different" they'd ever seen. You think a little Black kid is *strange*? You think someone who blends English and French and Spanish is *weird*? Well, I got news for you guys.

I was gonna be the biggest oddball in the history of Great Falls, MT.

Now . . . I just needed to figure out what exactly that meant.

chapter three

THE REGGIE-MATIC EMOTIONAL TYPEWRITER!™

Several years ago, I devised a brilliant scheme for a revolutionary, state-of-the-art, new typewriter.

Such a typewriter, forged entirely out of cast iron and human genius and duly named "The Reggie-Matic Emotional Typewriter!™ with Expressive Text Technology™ (patent pending)," would be the first of its kind. A machine that would enable the typist to express their emotional state through the mere touching of the keys. That's right, using our exclusive Expressive Text Technology™ (patent pending), the simple pressure of one's physical fingerprint upon said keys would transmit crucial, fundamental qualities of one's emotions, all depending on how hard or light you hit the pressure-sensitive keyboard.

For example:

If one is angry and wants to convey shouting in one's writing, one may (or may not) slam one's fingers down on the keys. The harder you slam, the bigger and angrier the font becomes. Just like this. RARRRRRR!

Or if one (or two or three and so on) is feeling a bit randy, a bit frisky, a trifle lustful, shall we (or they) say, one must merely stroke said keys with the tips of one's fingers, gently and soothingly and amorously, and the Reggie-Matic Emotional Typewriter!™ will produce a correspondingly *romantic*, *passionate*, **heart-throbbing** font. **Oh, baby.**

Or if one is feeling in a science-fictional sort of mood—those generally strike me on the second Wednesday of the fifth year of every third month, when I typically spend the entire day bingeing the original *Battlestar Galactica*—simply channel your natural bio-electric luminescent energy through my revolutionary new type-writer and you'll type like a cyborg.

I never got around to making the thing.

But you know. Seems like it would be kinda cool if I did.

chapter four
THE WEIRDENING

"Cling!" I bellow. ***"Cling fast to the mighty Reg-Darr the Barbarian!"***

The meek villagers of this tattered, postapocalyptic earth hang from my massive warrior legs, my burly barbarian arms, and my powerful Battle Cat back as I carry them over the crumbling ruins of our planet's broken half-moon.

"Don't let us die, Reg-Darr!" they cry.

"You're our only hope, Reg-Darr!"

"Save us, Reg-Darr!"

And with one massive step, I, **Reg-Darr the Barbarian**, heave the helpless villagers—who look suspiciously like third-grade students—over a bottomless ravine and

. . . . .

Becoming truly, ridiculously odd in a small American town wasn't going to happen by accident. But the weirdening of Reggie Watts was a complexly silly process.

I was in grade school, and as hard as I tried to be positive about my new town, Great Falls was still a foreign place to me, still a little scary at times. New faces, new buildings, a new culture. It was a lot for a kid to take in, and my parents were around less and less to help me adjust.

My dad retired from the air force when I was about ten, but my family never talked about leaving Montana. My parents had ultimately found what they'd been looking for when they'd chosen to transfer here over North or South Dakota—good schools, a community of hardworking families, a real neighborhood environment for raising their son. Sure, it wasn't perfect—they were still a mixed-race family in a mostly white town—but nothing ever would be. They'd laid down roots over the last five or six years, they'd made good lifelong friends, they went golfing on weekends and played bingo at the community center, and they had no intention of leaving. They were also busy working. A lot.

My mom had moved on from selling Avon to a full-time job cleaning and preparing base houses for all the new families arriving from overseas. She was one of the company's top cleaners, so they'd have her doing deep cleans on two or three houses a day. And once my dad left the military, he worked more, not less. His first job was at a meat processing plant on the outskirts of town called Meats Unlimited, which maybe sounds a little gross—I went there once and you could smell the meat and the blood everywhere—but you gotta remember that this was Montana, there was a real hunting culture, and I'd go to my neighbor's house and see a newly killed buck hanging from the rafters like it was nothing. With all my dad's trouble sleeping, he also decided to pick up a few late-night hours at the local 7-Eleven, just to help pass the time. He even got a gig at a fried chicken chain called the Broaster, seriously because I think he really loved the food.

So when school let out each day, I'd go straight home and hang out there alone, for hours. I was a latchkey kid, Macaulay Culkin without the wacky burglars, and I loved every minute of it. I mean, I enjoyed being social, for sure. But there was a richness I experienced by myself that I didn't find with others.

Becoming strange was more than just a social hack, it was my outlet, my intellectual and emotional refuge. I began to hone all these different interests that became something like tools in my growing Toolbox of Weird. I used those tools to craft a bizarre new reality that existed apart from Montana, a mystical space that allowed me to become whoever or whatever I wanted, a fantasyland that followed my own rules.

It also happened to be a lot of nonsensical fun.

My first tool was music. Music had always been a huge part of my upbringing. My parents raised me on the international sounds they'd come to love in Europe, jazz musicians like Coltrane, singers like Josephine Baker. My dad had once played the saxophone himself, even been part of an informal band. My mom would drop hints about it, little breadcrumbs about the life he'd once led back in Ohio before the war, but that was all I'd ever get. I'd ask my dad about it, but he was never forthcoming.

I also played an instrument. Kind of.

Back in Spain I had an instrument of my own—a little toy piano. I would do my best Ray Charles impression, bobbing my head with a full-tooth smile and singing "Hit the Road Jack" as my little fingers tickled the plastic ivories.

That had been good enough when I was performing for my parents in our Madrid apartment. But not anymore. When I turned five, I asked my parents if I could start piano lessons—imagine that, a little kid actually *requesting* work. My father may have been distant about his own musical life, but he was happy to support mine financially. My mom was the nurturer, the one who would encourage me and connect with me artistically, but my dad was the provider. I didn't quite understand it at the time, but buying me things was his love language. It's how he showed he cared. So he gladly agreed to foot the bill for piano lessons, and I started classes with Mrs. Rude at her little house right by the high school.

It turned out that I have a good ear. I can hear music, sounds, and mimic them easily. I caught on quick to the basics of notes, structuring bars, and reading music. Take a listen, if you please:

When I started lessons, my dad even got me a piano of my own, set it right by the window in our living room. Now I could play whenever I wanted, in my own personal fortress of solitude.

I didn't spend all my time practicing or mastering musical theory. I never worked hard at it like a child Mozart. Instead I liked to experiment, try new things, create new sonic worlds with my music, new realities. And simply be ridiculous.

My life would have a soundtrack, and it would eventually be filled with some of my favorite artists, but I also wanted to compose my *own* score. I wanted to have my *own* voice. And to me, that's what music was—a new language to learn, a new sound to fill my universe.

. . . . .

I suddenly freeze in my tracks. Not moving a single muscle. At all.

It starts to get a little awkward.

"Um, Reg-Darr?" a kid asks as he hangs off my back. "What's up?"

It's recess, it's winter in Montana, and the playground at Chief Joseph Elementary School is covered in a thick layer of snow. Winters here are crazy. The sky is so broad I can see an eternity of snowflakes twisting around me. Blizzards leave snowdrifts so high I can open my bedroom window and roll right out onto my very own frozen mountain. No such thing as a snow day here, though—they almost never cancel school for any reason. Not that it bothers me, because I love extreme weather. The air is crisp and thin, almost hard to breathe, and I'm currently dressed in my favorite winter warrior's garb, a fully padded snowsuit along with moon boots. I really am uncommonly strong for a nine-year-old—a bit pudgy, perhaps, but strong—so I could stand here carrying these kids all day. It's pretty cold, though, so I can't really blame my friends for wanting to know what happens next.

But as much as I might want to tell them—and I do, I really do—I can't. I can't say a word. Can't even open my mouth. Because I'm not Reg-Darr the Barbarian anymore.

I just became something else, and that something else does.

Not.

Move.

· · · · ·

Then there were the darkest of the dark arts. The pursuits that all responsible, professional adults warned us innocent, pliable children away from.

By which of course I mean video games, toys, and TV.

Gasp! The horror!

Look, I get it. Sitting at home by themselves, other kids might've become couch potatoes with glazed-over eyes and drooling mouths. Staring at the TV. Watching the little white dot in Pong go back and forth across the screen. Back and forth. Back and forth. But I didn't only devour pop culture, I actively engaged with it. I used it to flex the muscles of my imagination, building my internal universe brick by brick.

My dad was always buying us the latest computers, marvels of '80s technology like the Texas Instruments TI-99 and the Commodore 64, which I mostly used for the games. None of these games were what you'd call elaborate. I mean, *Labyrinth* featured a long-haired, pixelated David Bowie, so that was pretty sick. But *Zork* didn't even have any graphics. It was text based, like reading an electronic Choose Your Own Adventure. And the "rooms" in *Mystery House* were literally boxes, a few lines that utilized forced-perspective design to give the illusion of depth. But they blew my preadolescent mind! Each game opened my eyes to the possibilities of new artificial realities, or simulations.

Rooms?? It's like I've got an *entire house* on this tiny screen right inside our own *real house*!

Little Suzy died of dysentery? My aching heart! How will we possibly traverse the Oregon Trail?!

My toys added texture. A lot of kids I knew got toys, played with them once, then forgot about them. Not me. I was the first kid on my block with a *Star Wars* AT-AT, the walking battleship from *The Empire Strikes Back*, but almost as soon as I got it, I was painting it different colors, transforming it into something new. My friend Didier's dad owned a hobby shop, and I would get model planes and the most perfect tiny shrubs, and I'd combine those with cardboard boxes or wire and string and build entire universes, acting out battles and storylines, doing all the characters' voices. When I was done with one universe, I'd tear it apart and build something else.

But nothing shaped the growing world inside my mind more than our TV.

Of course I dug the children's programming. But I didn't watch the stuff that talked down to kids. I was interested in *Sesame Street* and *3-2-1 Contact*. When it came to cartoons, I was attracted to fantasy, to science fiction, to narratives that didn't just feature strong characters but also strong, strange world-building. *Space Ghost* and all the journeys through the galaxy. *Thundarr the Barbarian* set on a magical earth torn apart by magic after the moon literally splits in two. And *Scooby-Doo* with its . . . well, I guess those guys pretty much just went town to town solving mysteries, but it was still an incredible show.

That is, until Scrappy-Doo showed up. Then they tried to modernize it, and it was more like Crappy-Doo, and I freaking hated it.

Honestly, though, the kids' stuff was only part of my TV experience. *Battlestar Galactica* was my first real introduction to sci-fi. But comedy was my true forte. *Three's Company, Mork & Mindy, The Carol Burnett Show.* I'd get hooked on the physical gags, but the humor served as a gateway into something even more transformational—the style. The more I immersed myself in my shows, the more I realized that the best of them created worlds that were just as detailed, just as compelling and explorative, as anything in science fiction.

Take *Three's Company.* You got Jack Tripper's butterfly collars, his blue jean jackets, and loud plaid patterns. Chrissy's gleaming blond hair and short shorts. Janet's short, black boss of a haircut. And the apartment with its bamboo furniture and fake wood paneling. That wasn't just funny, that was a vision of America, of an entire lifestyle that was bright, vivid, and carefree. The wardrobe and set decoration didn't just inhabit the world—they crafted it. For a kid like me who hadn't been born into this country—or into any country for that matter—the shows weren't just entertainment, they were an education. Style could *be* substance.

But when I started searching for true style, when I wanted to find smooth, suave sophistication, I looked beyond the shores of America. I looked to Britain. By the time I was eleven, I'd become a hard-core Anglophile.

Other kids might skip by PBS—most adults too—but for me it was a dream. I'd feast on period pieces set in the time of Jane Austen, lose myself in *Masterpiece Theatre.* I'd drink in Sherlock Holmes and Hercule Poirot on the series *Mystery!*, with its macabre animated opening and bloodcurdling screams. I'd even enjoy the interstitials PBS would play between shows. No silly commercials, just images of a peaceful brook babbling away over the sound of classical music.

There was something about how proper the British were, how

controlled, how civilized. If someone got pissed off, they'd arch an eyebrow. If there was a murder, they'd simply arch two. They seemed to have that same self-awareness I possessed, except it was cultural, not personal. I savored the intricacy of the mysteries, the cleverness it took to figure everything out. And the actors looked like normal, frumpy men and women—real people—instead of the supermodels who somehow decided to become gritty blue-collar cops in all the American shows.

I loved the way everyone talked. It wasn't a different language, not technically, but they made it *feel* different, just by the way they spoke it. I endlessly practiced the sounds—those soft *r*'s and drawn-out *a*'s and *beans*-not-*beens*—until I could zap in and out of a Cockney or a Scottish or the most pompous Queen's English you could imagine.

The visual aesthetics were stunning. The sumptuous costumes, the magnificent ball gowns, the waistcoats and the powdered wigs. The elaborate architecture, all the stately manors and the drafty castles, the cottages in the countryside. And the table settings. Oh, the table settings! I would sit in our den after school, studying the etiquette, mastering exactly where to place each plate, each bowl and soup spoon. I'd practice folding napkins—*how did they make this piece of cloth look like a swan? How??*—then crumple them up in frustration and start all over again.

"No, no!" I would chastise my parents at dinnertime. "You hold the knife in the right hand while the fork stays in the left! *The left!*"

Strangely, my French mother—who herself was very stylish—didn't quite get it.

But my one true English king was Bond. James Bond. Whether *Dr. No* or *Goldfinger* or, hell, even *Moonraker*, I gorged myself on all his films. If Mr. Darcy was cool, James Bond was a dry martini—shaken, not stirred. If Captain Wentworth was debonair, James Bond was devastating. If Mr. Knightley was British, James Bond was perfection.

He helped me cultivate not only my sense of style, but of adventure, of romance and chivalry. This was a man who didn't just know the correct spoon to use, he also drove an Aston Martin that fired rockets from its headlights. I dreamed of rescuing Pussy Galore from the deadly bowler hat of Oddjob. I imagined escaping with Honey Rider to the far-off beaches of Jamaica. I fantasized about hurtling to Venice by train with Tatiana Romanova.

Over time, something happened. Something strange.

The more I daydreamed, the more my fantasy world seeped into the real world. I may not have felt entirely at home in Montana yet, but I could create my own imaginary kingdom wherever I went, somewhere I always fit in, somewhere I always belonged.

I'd look at the squat structure of my grade school and see the elegant outlines of a castle in the Highlands. My favorite people on TV—Bond and Thundarr and Jack Tripper—became not just fictional characters but real friends who populated my life. I kept practicing my British dialects, and to those I added a German accent from *Hogan's Heroes* and a Southern accent from *The Dukes of Hazzard*, and suddenly I didn't have only accents, I had whole new identities I could turn on or off whenever I felt lonely or uncomfortable or shy. Instead of "Nice to meet you, I'm Reggie Watts," I could hit someone with "The pleasure is mine, good chap! Sir Reginald Wattsbury IV, at your service!" or a grunted "Me Reg-Darr, the Mighty Barbarian, here to save you from evil warlock magic!" And the silly songs I played on my piano became the score that underpinned all my daily adventures.

Until eventually my entire life became a swirl of sounds and sights and memories that I used not just to entertain myself but to engage with others as well, old friends and new. Carving out my own strange place in the reality of Great Falls.

· · · · ·

After a couple minutes of watching me stand there, silent, doing literally nothing, my friends finally give up and walk away. Except for a single girl who stays. A girl I may or may not have been really wanting to stay. She looks at me with a funny smile on her face.

"Why aren't you moving?"

Until that very moment, I actually didn't know. But as soon as she asks, I feel the wires sprouting in my body. Feel the old-fashioned transistor tubes growing in my brain. Feel my skin turn into a hard shell of wood and metal and plastic, feel my mouth open and suddenly transform into a single hi-fi speaker.

"I am Reggie, the Human Radio Robot," I announce in my best human-radio-robot voice. **"Change my station, and I'll play you a song."**

Hesitating just a tiny bit, she reaches out and presses one of the clasps of my snowsuit. Music explodes from some random radio station somewhere in the world.

> Let's get physical!
> Physical!
> I wanna get physicalllll,
> Let's get—

Giggling, she pushes the clasp again, and Édith Piaf pours out of my speaker.

33

Quand il me prend dans ses bras,
Il me parle tout bas,
Je vois la vie en rose——

She presses again, and suddenly my fingers are playing the air piano and "Chopsticks" is in the air.

DUM-DUM-DUM-DUN-DUN-DUN-DUM-DUM-DUM—

One more push, and an old favorite from someplace far away.

I'm a girl watcher.
I'm a girl watcher.
Watching girls go by.
My, my, myyyyy . . .

She laughs and I can see her breath like steam in the cold.

"Is that what you're doing, Reggie Watts?" she says. "Watching girls like me go by?"

"No, that's just something I used to sing with my dad. Long time ago."

She smiles, presses my clasp one last time, and runs off to join the others. I feel the clasp with my fingers. It's still warm from her touch.

Not too bad, I think. Not too bad at all.

chapter five
WAISTCOATS

Waistcoats.

Waistcoats?

Waistcoats.

Did you notice me use that word back there? It was pretty quick. May have just slipped by you. I was talking about stunning British visual aesthetics and such, and that was one of the examples I tossed in. You know, waistcoats. Kind of like a fitted vest that goes underneath a jacket. It can look pretty posh if you do it right.

Yeah, so I was listening to an audiobook the other day, and the voice artist—who was really very good, by the way—said the word *waistcoats.* Except he pronounced it "whest-cowts."

This wasn't a period piece. It wasn't set in a foreign country. No special accents or anything. He was just going along, reading the book out loud, and then all of a sudden here he comes with this "whest-cowts." And that *h* I put in there isn't incidental. He really laid into that sound. Almost like a whistle after the *w.*

And it made me wonder. Have I just been saying *waistcoats* wrong in my mind all these years? I mean, I've seen the word in print, on occasion. And I've certainly seen waistcoats themselves on all those TV shows. But how often do you say a word like *waistcoats* out loud? What if this voice actor is right, and I'm wrong? What if it really *is* "whest-cowts"?

What if everything you've read in your entire life, *every single word* you've read in this very book, is merely a subjective construct of your own mind, and the *true, objective reality* of those words exists only in the vocal cords of a moderately successful but talented audiobook voice artist whose name escapes me *right now*???

Anyhoo! Food for thought.

chapter six

LOVER BOY

I was really very practical about it all.

My friend Whitney was in the fourth grade, just like me. I found out her parents were about to go out of town. So I devised an entire plan. Logistics, timing, wardrobe changes. Snacks. It would be perfect. Nothing could go wrong.

"Hey," I whispered to a few of my best girlfriends during class. "Meet me at recess! By the fence at the edge of the schoolyard! *Top secret!*"

An hour later, we all gathered near the big white fence at the back of the playground. It felt like a very private location, perfect for what I had to say. Nothing but marshland and trees on one side, and on the other side . . . us. And all the other kids a solid thirty feet away, playing their children's games of tetherball and four square and jumping over ropes.

I cleared my throat dramatically, and the girls stared as I solemnly pitched my idea.

"I think," I said, "we can meet at Whitney's house . . . and have an orgy."

They looked at each other. Then burst out giggling.

"Um, probably not."

"Okay!" I said. "Sounds good!"

And so I began to explore the most compelling, most mysterious part of my universe yet. More vibrant than paisley-print butterfly collars. More remote than crumbling planets in outer space. More intricate than the most elaborate table setting. Girls.

Ever since I'd moved to Great Falls, my best friends had all been girls. I had always been a maman's boy at heart, and she and I had grown even closer as my dad pulled further and further away. I felt more comfortable around her feminine energy, more secure, more whole. Something about women just drew me to them. I found girls more interesting than boys. Not in a sexual way, at least not initially. They simply fascinated me. The way they talked, the way they laughed, the way they moved. The things that interested them.

My ideal was Pippi Longstocking. I liked girls who were strong, who were bold, who had a little unexpected magic about them. And yeah, it didn't hurt if her dad was a pirate and she owned a pet monkey. I felt a bond with them that I never felt with boys my age, and the girls reciprocated. First grade, second grade, third grade—I was always the favorite of the girls in my class.

But as I got older, I grew curious about . . . other things. Sex, yes. Though to be honest, despite the diabolical details of my plan, I was only vaguely aware of what an orgy actually was. I knew a lot of nakedness was involved, and that sounded pretty stimulating, for sure. Don't get me wrong, Pippi was still my main squeeze. But I figured if she just happened to look like the Samantha Fox and Tawny Kitaen posters I soon pinned to my wall, that didn't seem like such a bad thing. But sex was only part of my new fascination. Just a jumping-off point, really.

I wanted more. I wanted to fall in love.

Love ran through my veins—almost literally. The French, of course, are the greatest lovers the world has ever known, or at least that's what my French relatives like to tell me. My mom had that possessive streak in her. A natural redhead. From the moment she met my dad years earlier at the Charlie Bar, she knew he belonged to her. And he did. I'm cooler, more mellow, and you know I'm not a natural fighter. But that just means I got more energy for loving.

My dad's family wasn't French, but they were from Cleveland. You know how I said my grandfather died violently? I left out a small detail. The truth is my grandfather loved women so much they were the death of him. For real. Apparently, he was married to my grandmother and having affairs with two other women at the same time when *one* other-woman discovered him in bed with the *other* other-woman. The two of them teamed up and stabbed my grandpa to death.

Now, my father wasn't a womanizer like my grandfather, but he was a deeply sexual, passionate man. My mom liked to say he'd been a real lover boy before they met, dated a few women around the continent before she finally claimed him. Years later, long after we moved to Montana, I was down in our basement when I found a cardboard box full of *Playboys* and porn movies. The old-school type. We're talking 8 mm film. I checked to make sure my parents weren't home, then threaded our little projector and screened a movie against the basement wall. It was pure '70s stuff, *Deep Throat*, Dirk Diggler. More twangy disco music, permed hair, and corduroy slacks than sex. Style, yet again.

And yes, there was some fucking too.

As I watched, I kept one eye on the basement's window wells. As soon as I saw the headlights flash in the driveway, I scrambled to pack it all up. I'd never moved faster in my life.

Even one of my most cherished memories of my dad revolved around women, appreciating them, admiring them. All those times in Madrid when he and I would sit together at the bar, sipping our drinks, singing our favorite song, and girl-watching. Dark women, light women. Slender women, curvy women. All speaking different languages. Even then, at that early age, I had sensed that there was something special about girls. Something unique, something magical.

Of course, I understood now that *real* love, *real* relationships like my mom and dad's, were a lot more complicated than meet-cutes at French restaurants and catchy songs by the O'Kaysions. For all the love in their genes, my parents weren't exactly a model couple. So much had changed since we'd moved to Great Falls. So much of that free, fun-loving, adventurous spirit of Europe was gone. My parents still supported each other, yes. Provided for each other's basic needs. They were still in love, in their own way. But now my dad seemed just as quiet with my mom as he was with me. Emotionally he'd put up a wall. He didn't want to talk about what had happened to him in Vietnam. He didn't want to talk about a lot of things. Maybe he simply lacked the right words to express himself.

"Go to ze basement if you must," she would tell him. "Just scream, Charles! Shout and yell as long and hard as you want! Please, let your feelings out!"

He never did.

The love I dreamed of wasn't messy like theirs. I saw just how hard that was, and I rejected it. What I wanted was more fantasyland. I became obsessed with the trappings of relationships, the style, the sensuality, the *idea* of love. I fell in love with falling in love. Healthy communication? Emotional availability? The hard work any authentic relationship requires? Never even crossed my mind. I'd never witnessed them at home, so I had no interest.

Instead, I wanted to be like my hero, James Bond—but better. In fact, I started noticing that as cool and suave as Bond seemed, he didn't always treat women incredibly well. He didn't appreciate them in all their fullness and facets, the way I knew someone like my mom, who I adored, deserved to be treated. And it wasn't just Bond. I started to realize that most shows portrayed women as nothing more than props, one-dimensional objects.

Like *Matlock*. That one always annoyed me. Matlock's assistant was gorgeous, but they never gave her any good lines. Just great blond hair and a soft focus on her close-ups. But there was a human being under there! Who knows? Maybe she dreamed of being a lawyer too—a lawyer ten times better than her boss. Or maybe she didn't care about the law at all, maybe she was obsessed with crossword puzzles or particle physics. Maybe underneath that perfect, lacquered hair there was a pigtailed Pippi Longstocking just waiting to bust out. My fantasies may have idealized love and women, but they never minimized them.

So I decided to be the *sensitive* James Bond, the *funny* James Bond, the James Bond who *respected* women. I would be James Bond with a heart of gold. I fantasized about just how well I would treat my woman, just how chivalrous I would be. I would take her out to dinner at a romantic restaurant, pulling the chair out for her before she sat down. We'd select a delicious wine together and spend the night laughing about ridiculous things. We would explore the world together, having adventures and traveling to one exotic locale after another, the French Riviera, the Swiss Alps, the Carnevale in Rome. And if she happened to be Andy Griffith's hot assistant, all the better. We'd travel far away from the tedium of the courtroom, and we'd connect on levels the writers of *Matlock* couldn't even comprehend. We'd fall deeply, madly in love.

And I tried to fall in love, I tried so damn hard!

Foiled plans for orgies. The father of one of my best girlfriends discovering us in the basement, her lying on the couch, right as we were about to play doctor for the very first time. I'd even found a book of magic at the library—the cover was dark blue and had stars and crescent moons and witches all over—and I'd gone home and actually cast spells to help me with the ladies. A summoning spell that required me to bury a piece of paper with a girl's name on it in my yard at midnight, and the next day Autumn Clark—*the Autumn Clark*, the most beautiful girl in school!—came up and *talked to me* when I was locking up my bike. Sure, she never spoke to me again, but it was enough to make me try a love potion for Kristen Gunderson, who I had a crush on. That was a little trickier, because I needed a lock of her hair. But I asked her if I could look at her comb one day, and I snuck off a couple blond strands, and, well, she may have asked me to hang out at some point. But yeah, nothing really came of that either.

Then, finally, a chance I thought was true.

In fifth grade, my best friend—of course she was a girl—invited me to her house. Just like all my other best-friends-who-are-girls, our relationship had started innocently enough. I liked hanging out with her, getting to know her. I found her to be an intriguing, compelling, fifth-grade human being. That's it.

But just like all my other best-friends-who-are-girls, that purely platonic interest had started to evolve. For both of us.

Her house was big, twice the size of my own. Two stories, brick, white picket fence, American flag waving from the porch, the whole deal. It was like the *Brady Bunch* house. It looked like the ideal household, the very picture of domestic bliss. Like I'd round a corner and see Carol on her fifth cup of coffee that day or Jan crying because Marcia got all the attention. My friend kinda looked like a young Marcia, which was obviously hot, but with more of that Cindy joie de vivre. Exactly my type.

Her parents were home, and she told them we were going up to her room to play. Something we had done many times before, except for some reason this time felt . . . different.

I suddenly noticed just how elaborate, just how *stylish* her bed was. This thing had four posters, it had a full canopy, it had fluffy pink pillows piled on top of fluffy pink pillows. It was like a show-piece from *Pride and Prejudice*. And the next thing I know, I'm lying on it like a prepubescent Wickham and my best-friend-who-is-a-girl is at the foot of the bed doing a striptease and the only thing I can think is *Wow, this is crazy!*

That and *I gotta get these suspenders off!* Because my suspenders-and-sweaters phase really did last a pretty long time.

Now, you may believe this, you may not, but what you have to understand is that what was amazing about this experience for me wasn't simply the sexual element—and let's be clear, there was no actual sex, we had no idea what we were doing—it was how per-fectly, fantastically romantic every detail was. The gorgeous house, the decadent canopy bed, the slow but fumbling way each of our articles of clothing came off, one after the other. I was transported to another place, another time, to a scene out of *Masterpiece Theatre*. *This* was what it must mean to be truly, passionately in love.

And then we heard her mom shouting to come down for dinner. Oh. Boy.

My friend and I snatched up all the clothes strewn around the room and struggled to put it all back on. Zippers were zipped, but-tons were buttoned, suspenders were suspended. We pulled ourselves together and we rushed down those stairs, our faces flushed and our hearts slamming against our chests—"We look fine, right?" "For sure! No one will ever know!"—and we sat down at that Very Brady kitchen table for a nice, totally innocent casserole dinner.

"Oh! My favorite! Smells delicious! Ha-ha-ha!"

And you know what? I think we would've gotten away with it too.

But then my suspenders popped off.

Pop! Pop!

I chuckled nervously. My fork—the correct fork, obviously—clattered against my plate. Her parents looked at me. I looked at them. They didn't say anything, of course. But I *knew* they knew. I don't know how, I don't know why, but I did. Maybe they could sense my fear. Maybe they could smell my pheromones. Maybe it was all in my head, and they were simply thinking, "That's strange—maybe Reggie should start wearing a belt instead."

But whatever it was, I was never invited back again.

So yeah. Maybe sometimes I got a little *too* carried away with my fantasyland. A little too disconnected from the reality that was all around me in Great Falls. A reality that was every bit as textured and fascinating as the life of make-believe I'd created for myself. A reality just waiting to be explored.

The person who would finally help me discover that world—who would expand my universe, even challenge it—wasn't a girl but a boy my own age. He became my first true partner in crime, my first soulmate. His name was Jon Thomas.

chapter seven

ODE TO A GROWN-UP
PIPPI LONGSTOCKING

Pippi Longstocking,
O Pippi Longstocking,
Wherefore art thou, Pippi Longstocking?

Now that you're, what, about eighty-six years old
based on my calculations.

Art thou busy sailing the seven seas with your pirate dad?
Or lifting horses over your head with a single hand?
Or living comfortably off your suitcase full of gold?

Whatever it is, I hope you've aged well
or this could get kind of awkward.

Is there room in your grown-up heart for me,
    Pippi Longstocking?
Making mischief together with your monkey, Mr. Nilsson.
Lost among your freckles like fiery stars.
Tangled in your red, red hair.

REGGIE WATTS

Dost thou still wear those magical pigtails?
Or hast thou moved on to something more sensible,
Like a bun or a bob?

Does Villa Villekulla have a respect
                              able
                                   Zest
                                        i
                                          mate?

FWIW
I think the pigtails could be pretty hot
If we're in the right mood.

Shit, I hope that's not
too weird.

chapter eight

THE KID WHO WOULDN'T GIVE UP

Class had ended five minutes earlier, but I was blissfully unaware. I was lost in the circuits of my cyborg.

Sitting at my desk, drawing detailed schematics of how my creation would work. Cutaways showing the high-powered lenses in his bionic eye, the spring-loaded shock absorbers in his robotic leg, the hypersensitive olfactory filtration system in his nostrils so he could smell a rose from ten miles away. And, you know, all the various organic muscle fibers and brain tissue that connected it all, because obviously he was a cyborg and not a full robot, and if my creation didn't have authentic biological components that would just be silly.

Then I looked up, and I realized I wasn't alone. On the other side of the classroom sat a boy with short blond hair and high cheekbones who was just as lost in his drawing as I was in mine.

"Hey," I said.

He looked up. "Hey."

"What are you drawing?" I asked.

"Spaceship," he said, holding it up. I was impressed by the smooth, streamlined design. This wasn't kid stuff. This was a serious spacecraft. "How about you?"

"Cyborg," I said, holding up my picture. "Which obviously has both biological and robotic components in its anatomy, because it's a cyborg."

"Totally," he said.

That was how I met Jon Thomas. We were both in the same class in junior high. It was 1985, and the school year was almost over. I'm not sure how we hadn't noticed each other before, but now that we had we shared an instant chemistry. We walked out of the classroom together, excitedly sharing theories about wormholes, artificial intelligence, the space-time continuum, and all the underpinnings of our mutual obsession with science fiction. Jon had a driving, frenetic energy about him. He'd be in the middle of one topic, then he'd jump to another, switch gears and go back, then bounce to something new.

"I think we'll all have cyber implants in at least five years, okay maybe ten. Hey, what's your last name? And the first thing I'm going to get is a bionic ear. Do you live with your dad? I don't. I live with my mom and my brother. Cuz I think supercharged hearing is a totally, like, underrated power to have, don't you?"

He pinged and ponged, darted from one idea to the next, and I got more and more swept up in his buzz, his momentum, the sheer glory of all his incredible strangeness. And then he asked it. The one question I really wasn't into.

"Hey, you wanna hang out sometime?"

"Um, cool talking to you, man!" I said. "See you around!"

And I promptly got the hell out of there.

As much as I felt a quick connection with Jon Thomas, I also valued control. I had grown comfortable with the fantasy world I'd constructed for myself at home, the TV shows, the toys, my piano. Girls for me were a fantasy unto themselves. I found them fascinating—I'd dream of going on romantic adventures with them, but I hadn't figured out how to translate any of that into reality. It was easier, safer for me to regulate every aspect of my life, internal and external. The same way I distanced myself from my own emotions, I tended to distance myself from other people as well.

But every now and then, someone would drift into my life who'd try to shake me out of my comfort zone. A charismatic disruptor who'd try to put me in new, uncomfortable, challenging situations. Who'd mess with my perspective, just because he could. Jon Thomas wasn't the first.

The summer before junior high I hung out with a kid named Kris Steichen. I knew Kris from class, but he lived just ten blocks away from my house. The first afternoon we met up, we were doing the usual—watching TV, playing G.I. Joe in my basement—when he suddenly got this sly, conspiratorial look on his face.

"You ever sneak out before?" he asked.

My eyes grew wide and I lowered my voice to a whisper. "Like at night? But what if my parents find out?"

"Don't worry," he said, "they won't."

His logic seemed unassailable. But I resisted. Playing in my basement was so much fun! Did I really need more than that? "I don't know . . ."

"Trust me. When we meet up, I'll show you something even cooler than all this kid stuff."

Later that night, hours after my parents had gone to sleep, I carefully slid open my window, popped out the screen, and stole out into the dark. It was so easy, but it felt so crazy, so dangerous. My heart was pounding, my adrenaline was flowing, I felt so alive. What if we got caught? What if someone saw us? And why oh why had I never tried this before?

Kris and I met on a corner halfway between our two houses. His eyes gleamed in the moonlight as he revealed the illicit treasure he'd promised to bring. A pair of real-life, stainless-steel throwing stars.

"Oh, fuck!"

Kris and I spent the rest of the summer meeting up as much at night as we did during the day. We became consumed by martial arts. He'd bring throwing stars he ordered from the backs of Sears catalogs. I found a utility belt from my dad's days in the air force, and I bought a Rambo-style survival knife from an infomercial. This thing was huge! It had a serrated edge, a compass at the end of the handle, and inside the handle there were even waterproof matches and a fishing line. Like if you were starving and alone in the middle of the wilderness you'd go, "Thank God I've got my knife—are the trout biting today?"

Now, me being me, of course I had no interest in any actual fighting. Instead, we would have adventures. Practice tossing the razor-sharp stars at trees. Venturing outside our neighborhood to the local twenty-four-hour convenience store and buying beef jerky just because we could. And of course TP-ing houses, and other ridiculous, silly pranks. *Hey, let's put this bag of lawn clippings on top of that car! Oh man, the neighbors won't know* what *happened!!*

That summer, my fantasy world finally met reality on the streets of Great Falls. At night, we owned that town. We could go wherever we wanted to go, be whatever we wanted to be, play with toys that weren't even really toys—they were legitimately dangerous. We could break all the rules and not give a crap about consequences. The same way my dad found his power on the streets of Madrid and Stuttgart, I started to find mine on the streets of Great Falls that summer. I started—just barely—to grow up.

Then Kris and I simply drifted apart, like so many friends do at that age. There was no disagreement, no hand-to-hand combat with nunchucks and throwing stars. The summer—and our friendship—just kind of dissolved.

Maybe that's part of what made me so reluctant to start a new friendship with Jon Thomas the following year. As much fun as all my ninja adventures with Kris had been, maybe it was easier to go back to playing it safe. Spending time alone watching TV, unrealized fantasies with girls. Maybe I needed time before I could open myself up to a new, risky friendship. Maybe I just wanted space.

Whatever it was, those first few weeks after I met Jon Thomas, I did everything I could to avoid him. He didn't make it easy. Whenever he saw me at school, he'd bring up hanging out, and I'd awkwardly change the subject, or suddenly spot a teacher I really needed to talk to, or just hit him with my patented "Cool talking to you, man, see you around!" line and make a break for it.

None of that stopped him. He figured out where I lived (not too far from his own place) and he started showing up at my house at all times, on all days. I'd hear a *knock-knock-knock* at our door, and my mom would yell, "Reggie! It is zat boy! Zat Jon Thomas!" And I'd run and hide in the basement, shouting, "Don't let him in! Don't let him in!" and I wouldn't come out till he left.

Finally one day he decided he was done with doors altogether.

I was walking into my bedroom when suddenly I heard a tapping at the window. I turned, and Jon Thomas was peering in right at me.

"AHHHH!" I screamed.

He tapped harder, motioning me toward him.

My eyes darted around frantically, searching for a way out. I could dive under my bed! No, too obvious! I could lock myself in the bathroom! No, too stinky! Wait! I could sprint for the—

He tapped again. Now he looked genuinely angry. Or was it confused?

I sighed. I slid open my window, just as I had on all those summer nights sneaking out to meet Kris.

"What??" I said. "What could you possibly want from me?!?"

He shrugged.

"Ever play Dungeons & Dragons?"

· · · · ·

I walked into the dim and dusty room, my eyes slowly growing accustomed to the low lighting. It was the middle of

· · · · ·

[Dramatically clears throat.]

To be clear, I have moved to a new topic and am no longer talking about Jon Thomas or Dungeons & Dragons.

I know. It's a potentially jarring transition, because there could theoretically be a dim and dusty room in the game Dungeons & Dragons or, proverbially, in Jon Thomas's soul. But I assure you that this is a different sort of dim and dusty room, which will ultimately have a subtle thematic relevance to the current chapter, "The Kid Who Wouldn't Give Up."

Thank you. Carry on.

[Coughs, looks askance.]

· · · · ·

Anyway, so I'm in this dim and dusty room.

It was the middle of the school day, and time for everyone in our class to choose an instrument to learn for orchestra. I didn't think much of it. This wasn't like the piano, where I had imagined being Ray Charles tickling the ivories long before I ever started lessons. I had never dreamed of playing a mean tuba or thrilling any crowds with my rendition of "I Got a Woman" on the bassoon. This was something I had to do to be in orchestra, and now I was going to do it.

I looked around the instrument room, took a moment to take it all in. It felt like a giant cave. I've always loved caves—there's something about that closed-in feeling, it's somehow both cozy and mysterious, sheltered and surreal, all at the same time. This room had exactly that vibe, and piled everywhere, like the riches of Aladdin's lamp, were all the old instruments. The trumpet, the sax, the cymbals, the bass drum. Passed from one generation of schoolkids to the next, all lying about in a clutter, barely organized, waiting for their next temporary owner to lug them home on the bus.

Then I saw it. The violin.

I knew, of course, what a violin was. Knew what it sounded like. But not much beyond that. I'd never really considered making it my instrument before. But now, as I picked it up in that magical, public-school cave, it just felt right.

This'll sound weird, but my instinct didn't have anything to do with music per se. Simply holding the violin in my hands had a visceral, almost overwhelming impact on me. The curve of the wood against my skin. The smell of the rosin, the texture of the horsehair on the bow. Even the smoothness of the velvet cloth that covered the violin while it was in the case. That old, slightly damaged instrument engaged every one of my senses.

My love affair only continued when my mom took me to a small music store outside Great Falls to buy my very own violin, one I wouldn't have to share with other students. The shop was run by a Scandinavian luthier—that's fancy talk for "talented guy who makes violins and guitars." I marveled at his craftsmanship, the scrolls carved to look like dragons' heads at the ends of the violins' necks, the special strings he had added under the fingerboards that resonated with sympathetic vibrations as you played different notes. The violin we bought was refurbished and much shabbier, of course, but still—maybe one day one of these special, fantastical instruments would be mine.

I knew I was meant for the violin. Now I just had to learn to play it.

Easy, right? After all, the piano had come so naturally to me. I had a good ear, and the technique was easy to master. My piano teacher, Mrs. Rude, marveled at how quickly I had picked it up. She never pressured me, never yelled. If I missed a lesson she shrugged it off. The whole experience had been so fun, so simple, so light. Playing the piano had become a safe, reliable part of my comfort zone. Why should violin be any different?

Spoiler alert: it was very, very different. Playing the violin would challenge me musically, make me question my creative boundaries, much like Jon Thomas did as my new best friend.

· · · · ·

[Clears throat.]
I am now transitioning back to Jon Thomas.
[Clears throat again. Coughs.]

· · · · ·

Jon Thomas paused dramatically as his younger brother, JJ, and I awaited his proclamation.

"And the final weapon will be . . . the Klipsch sword."

"Klipsch?" JJ said. "Like the speaker system? You can't just make a Klipsch sword!"

"I can if I want!" Jon said indignantly. "I'm the Dungeon Master!"

"But what does that even mean?" I said, laughing. "Like, it's a sword made of speakers?"

"I don't know! But Klipsch makes the most premium audio equipment in the galaxy, and if I say there's a Klipsch sword, then there's a Klipsch sword! A *totally powerful one*!"

And thus, our epic game of Dungeons & Dragons paused momentarily as we all rolled around on the floor laughing our asses off.

If Kris Steichen had opened me up to a life of adventure outside the confines of my home, then Jon Thomas opened me up to a new way of looking at life itself. D&D was what started it. If you've never played the game before—I hadn't myself before I met Jon—it's a little hard to understand what makes it so compelling. It basically consists of your imagination, a set of rules and parameters, and a lot of dice rolling. And I mean *a lot* of dice rolling. You want to generate a character, you roll the dice. You want to battle, you roll the dice. You want to talk to a shopkeeper, you roll the dice. You want some Charisma—and you *definitely* want Charisma—you roll the dice.

But the magic of D&D comes from the people you play it with, your friends, your community. You weave your own stories, you create your own worlds—not as a solitary individual, but *together*. You can be serious or you can be goofy. You can go from intense focus one minute to arguing about a ridiculous Klipsch sword the next. The community you form playing D&D expands your mind in ways you've never dreamed of. And it's a shit ton of fun.

Especially if you're high. Though that part didn't come till years later.

But Dungeons & Dragons was just the start of how Jon Thomas changed my perception of the world. My family and I had never been rich, but we'd also never been poor. Our house was small, but it was comfortable. If I asked for a toy, I got it. If I wanted music lessons, they were mine. I was an only child with two caring, hardworking parents, and I enjoyed all the benefits that came with that.

Jon Thomas lived in a small apartment, crammed in with his mom and JJ. He told me his dad was out of the picture, but he wouldn't say why. It's not like they were destitute, but his mom had to support the family on a schoolteacher's salary. There was a tension in their household that I didn't experience in mine. They argued, they fought, there was always a fire that needed to be put out somewhere, somehow. Like that old nursery rhyme "Bickery Bickery Dock." You know, kind of. It was what I now understand is a very normal single-parent-with-multiple-kids dynamic. But for me it was all new. True, my relationship with my dad was becoming increasingly strained, but he was still present. He still provided for us. I had always taken that for granted. Jon didn't have that luxury.

Maybe that's partly why Jon could also be so emotionally volatile. Impulsive. Hit by sudden bouts of depression and anger. We'd be in the middle of one thing and he'd want to do another. We'd have plans and he'd cancel them, or he'd show up at my window out of the blue, tapping away with some new adventure in mind. It could be intimidating at times, but I could also see how there was a certain power to it.

He was independent, unrestrained in a way I'd never known. He thought and acted however he wanted, and he didn't give a fuck what other people thought. While I tended to tailor my weirdness to others—always trying to put on a show, always wanting everyone to like me—he was weird on his own terms. Just because.

Nowhere was that more true than in the music he loved.

Although I'd grown up initially with a strong international musical influence thanks to my parents, once we moved to America my tastes had run decidedly Top 40. Night Ranger. Whitesnake. Foreigner. Big rock, bigger hair. That was all I listened to the summer I hung out with Kris Steichen. I tape-recorded *American Top 40* with Casey Kasem off the radio each week just to make sure I kept up with all the hits. Sometimes I'd even listen to Rick Dees's competing *Weekly Top 40* show too, even though it featured the exact same songs. I couldn't get enough of the stuff! And the music is legitimately great. I still love rocking out to "Sister Christian" today.

But it's also limited. It's fun and . . . it's fun. It's like living on icing without any cake.

Of course, in junior high I had no problem being on a constant sonic sugar high. Butt rock forever! I wanted no part of what Jon Thomas wanted to force-feed me.

"Come on, man," I said the first time he busted out his radio. "Are you kidding me?"

He had one of those classic '80s boomboxes. Two big speakers, tape deck in the middle, a clunky graphic equalizer, powered by a dozen fat D batteries. He donned a trench coat, perched the box on his shoulder, and struck a defiant pose—and this was years before *Say Anything* made it cool.

"Listen!" he said. "Just listen."

He pushed play—of course he'd made a mixtape—and the next thing I knew I was swimming in a stream of songs by Art of Noise and the Smiths, two bands on the forefront of alternative weirdo music in Britain years before it became mainstream in America. Instead of big, blaring guitars and power chords, this was a decadent blend of basslines and harmonicas and synthesizers. There were ten-minute instrumentals and lyrics about loss and love and gloves and Lesley-Anne with your pretty white beads and a bunch of esoteric shit that went completely over my head. This wasn't frosting; it wasn't even food! It was haunting and spiritual as hell.

Jon Thomas carried that boombox everywhere, listened to that music everywhere. It was a part of his ether, his atmosphere, his being. Other kids around school would make fun of him: "Here comes that Jon music!" "What the fuck is that crap—Big Audio Dynamite?"

But Jon didn't care. It was his, and that was all that mattered.

The more I listened to it, the more I liked it. And the more I liked it, the more I understood that music wasn't just a soundtrack. It wasn't just a mood. It was a statement. It was your identity. It was a new world to explore. Music wasn't one language, it was many. It was a way to declare your independence, or to stake your claim as a member of a very exclusive group.

And that wasn't only true for the music you chose to listen to. It was also true for the music you chose to play.

· · · · ·

[Clears throat ridiculously loudly.]
Never mind.

· · · · ·

Remember that spoiler? Well, if you didn't read it, here comes the big reveal: learning to play the violin was very, very different from learning to play the piano.

Shocker, right?

The technique required for the violin was intense in ways I hadn't appreciated when I was caught up in the romance of it all, the smell, the feel, the look of the instrument. With a piano, I could hit a key, and it would sound like the given note. I could create variety in the sound—by hitting the key harder or softer, for example—but it was relatively straightforward. Producing the right tone on a violin, however, required multiple skills all at the same time. Knowing where to find the note on the fingerboard. Good bowing technique. Hand position. Relaxing your fingers just the right way to create the perfect vibrato.

Even taking care of my violin was painstaking. When I finished playing my piano, I simply stopped. Next time I wanted to play it, I played it. Every now and then it might need tuning. Whatever, no big deal. But my violin? When I was done, I had to loosen my bow so tension wouldn't stretch out the horsehair. Every time I played, I needed to fine-tune it all over again. Cleaning it required an ultrasonic cleaner. Even the rosin—rosin, one of my favorite smells in the world—had to be the right kind, applied correctly, or it could interfere with the violin's sound.

Now, don't get me wrong. I didn't mind the extra challenge. At least not initially. I'm the king of that first steep bend in the learning curve. I really do have a knack for catching on to the basics. When I'm into something new, it's almost like I fall in love. Like an infatuation. I romanticize it, I give myself over to it—the look, the feel, the style, the sound—and I become good at it very quickly. Miss Lidiard, my instructor in orchestra, was just as impressed with my blossoming violin skills as Mrs. Rude had been with my piano playing. At first.

But then reality set in. If I wanted to be truly great at the violin, if I wanted to master all its intricacies, all its subtleties, I'd have to work. Hard. I don't just mean practice five times a week. Itzhak Perlman didn't become a virtuoso by putting in a half hour after school. I mean hours and hours every single day.

And I was only a kid! Was this really something I wanted to devote my life to?

Miss Lidiard knew the answer. Without a doubt.

"Reggie, you have so much talent! Apply yourself! Focus! Discipline! That's what this takes! You can do it!"

But I wasn't so sure. I loved the way the violin felt in my hands. I even loved the way it sounded. But did I need to be a prodigy? Did I care that much?

Most of what I loved about being in orchestra wasn't even the music. It was the social component. New friends to joke around with, new girls to try to impress with my goofball strangeness. And here I was being told that if I wanted to truly be great at the violin, I'd have to sacrifice all the other parts of my life I loved—my TV shows, my toys, Dungeons & Dragons—to *practice*? No thanks.

I started acting out in class. Showing up late. Talking back to the teacher. Making obnoxious jokes that got the girls giggling but completely disrupted the lesson. I was a natural at being class clown, and it didn't take nearly as much devotion as the violin.

Any other kid probably would've been kicked out, but Miss Lidiard saw so much potential in me, so much promise, that she always let it go.

Until one day she finally snapped.

I had shown up late for the thousandth time. Miss Lidiard made me stay after class. I was not in the mood.

"Reggie, listen to me—"

"I'm tired of listening!"

"We've discussed your behavior over and over again."

"So stop discussing it!"

"I just want you to think about—"

"No!"

I turned and made for the door. In a flash she reached out her hand and grabbed the collar of my shirt, tugging me back.

"*Ow!*" I shouted. "You cut me!"

"What?" she said.

"My neck! You scratched my neck! I'm bleeding!"

Her face turned a deathly white. "Oh my God! Reggie! I'm so, so sorry. I just got so angry, and . . ."

She trailed off, tears welling in her eyes.

It's funny. These days, given current trends in education and, I guess, society in general, that would've been it for Miss Lidiard. She would've lost her job. She hadn't been trying to scratch me, of course. One of her fingernails simply happened to catch my skin as she was trying to stop me from walking away. But it had happened. I really was bleeding. And if it had been the twenty-first century, she would've been fired. Immediately. Never would've taught again. All in the name of protecting my welfare.

But you know what? As intense as that moment was, it made me think.

I stood there looking at my teacher, this lady who was on the verge of tears because she'd lost her cool for a single instant. She'd given me so many chances. She'd believed in me and my talent. And how had I rewarded her? With attitude.

Part of me wanted to quit orchestra, to give up on the violin—and on Miss Lidiard—right then and there. But I don't know. Maybe a little tough love, a little discipline, was good for me. Maybe it was time to venture outside my comfort zone. To put myself out there and actually commit myself to honing my craft. To not take the easy way out. For now, anyway.

"Don't worry about it," I told Miss Lidiard. "I'm sorry too. I'll be better. I promise."

I left out the "for now" part.

· · · · ·

The summer of 1985, a few months after I met Jon Thomas, he invited me to spend the week at his grandma's cabin on Lake Five, a small lake surrounded by miles of pine trees and cradled in the mountains south of Glacier National Park, about three hours' drive from Great Falls.

I'd been away from home without my parents before, not too far from the wilds of Jon's grandma's home—computer camp on the shores of Salmon Lake. Camp, of course, had been inherently social. We'd spend mornings doing all the typical camp stuff, like hiking and swimming and canoeing. But the afternoons were saved for coding. Hours in front of TI-99 computers with tape drives, locked in a world that consisted entirely of "How do I make this group of green dots move five spaces to the right?" Like my toys and TV, coding was good for my brain, good for my imagination, but more internal. Hidden inside the life of my mind.

My new adventure, on the other hand, involved spending ten days with a boy who until relatively recently had been knocking on my bedroom window, bugging me to hang out. I'd be stuck with a whole new family with its own dynamic, a single-parent vibe that could feel both vibrant and a bit unstable. I had no idea what to expect.

The morning of our trip, we loaded up Jon's mom's green Ford LTD, a massive tank of a car with a metal grille like a battering ram. The back seat was a mess of papers and blankets and clothes and errant bags of potato chips—not supplies for the drive, just the accumulated detritus of a chaotic existence. I burrowed my way inside like a caterpillar snug inside his cocoon as Jon and his mom and his little brother rushed around doing last-second packing.

"Boys! Did you remember your swim trunks?"

"How should I know?"

"Because presumably you're capable of keeping track of your own swim trunks, Jonathan."

"Hey, watch it, butthead!"

"*Mo-om*, Jon just called me a butthead!"

"The last thing I need right now is more arguing from you two! Reggie, I bet you don't act like this with your mother, do you? *Where are the toothbrushes?*"

"I just called him a butthead because he's a butthead. It's just a fact. I'm just reporting facts."

"*Mo-ooooooom!*"

"Jonathan and JJ, I am going into the apartment right now to find toothbrushes and swim trunks, and when I get back I want you to stop acting like knuckleheads! *Do you understand?*"

They glared at their mom as she stomped off. JJ rummaged through the trunk as Jon got in the front seat. He stared straight ahead.

"I hate my dad."

"Yeah?" I said.

"He drinks a lot."

"Oh. Wow. I'm sorry, man."

"I hate his fucking guts."

Moments later, his mom got into the car without saying a word. She started the engine and we pulled onto the road. What the hell had I gotten myself into?

"Hey," Jon said. "You ever listened to the Smithereens?"

"No," I said. "Is that more Jon music?"

He smiled. "Just listen."

Jon had installed some speakers right behind the back seat, a DIY job with these cabinets he had made himself and everything. He popped a cassette into the radio and hit play. Suddenly the entire car was flooded by the most incredible sound. It was part indie, part punk, part retro '60s rock with this funky beatnik aura. It was fresh, original, like nothing I'd ever heard before, with angsty, heartrending songs about lingering perfume and hearts and houses falling apart, and devastating girls named Elaine.

And just like that, all the bickering, all the brattiness, all the drama that had marred the beginning of the day was washed away. We all got caught up in the music, it carried us to another place even as that old green LTD was carrying us to a small house on a lake in Montana. Sharing that music connected us, bound us together. It created a force field that inspired and infused every element of our trip for the following ten days.

Even then, even on the drive there, I could sense that something was happening. Something new. I guess some of that might've been the incredible Smithereens song "Something New," but it was more than that too. There was something about that drive that felt like growing up. Like independence. It was a little bittersweet leaving my home, even for a few days, but it was also glorious. My entire time-line, my entire sense of reality, was shifting, evolving, changing. It felt like a re-beginning. Like a new era.

And that's what it was.

We arrived and it was perfection. It was a place I'd never been to, but which somehow felt familiar, like maybe I'd traveled there in a dream. The lake was pristine, glittering, the weather flawless. The surrounding forest was thick with pines, and the Rocky Mountains loomed in the distance. An old railroad line passed somewhere nearby, and you could hear the train whistle as it chugged along.

Jon's grandma lived in a quirky log cabin that she had built decades earlier, adding new sections onto it bit by bit. His grandpa loved Studebakers, and a bunch of them were strewn about the property and he would spend afternoons tinkering on their old engines. Jon's uncle lived nearby with Jon's two older cousins. One of them was blond and one of them was brunette, and they were both gorgeous. The blonde's name was Schjanna—a fantastically exotic spelling of "Shauna"—and she owned an old-school Volkswagen Microbus, and she'd spray-painted a giant *DK* on it for the punk band the Dead Kennedys. I was in love. With her and with the entire experience. We all spent the week swimming and hanging out around the bonfire and playing D&D and listening to the Smithereens over and over. It was the Mountain Dew existence I had always dreamed of.

I finally understood that life itself could be a simulation. The best of simulations. It didn't have to be fantasy. It could all be real. And if real life didn't feel like this, then something was wrong.

My friendships with people like Jon Thomas, even teachers like Miss Lidiard, forced me out of my shell. Helped me venture to places that didn't always feel safe but almost always ended up being rewarding. In the process, they made me a stronger individual, less solitary but also more independent. Less constrained by the protective walls I'd built for myself at home.

It was enthralling to taste so much freedom. But soon I realized that it came with a price—any chance of a relationship with my dad.

I was about to learn firsthand what it was like to be raised by a single parent.

chapter nine

BEN'S FAST FOOD!

You ever get those cravings late at night for something to munch on? Like you're sitting there, bingeing *Star Trek: The Next Generation* or composing your latest aria, and suddenly you get that rumbling in your tummy.

Mmmm. Time to eat!

Well, that happened to me just last night. I was feeling hungry, and I was like, "Oh, let's grab a burger like usual!" Then I thought, *Nope, Reggie, that's not what you want at night.* So instead I tried Ben's Fast Food for the very first time.

And boy, was I glad I made that decision.

I ordered a bowl filled with slow-roasted chicken with greens and millet rice and some veggies, plus sauces you can choose for yourself. The packaging is all biodegradable. It was fast, it was delicious, the food was super high quality. I was just blown away. Like, "I got a really tasty meal, but I don't feel like an asshole!"

So next time you get those late-night munchies, consider ordering from Ben's Fast Food. You won't be disappointed. And if you see Ben there, say hi from Reggie. He and I go way back. Very, very good friends.

chapter ten

THE WAY OF THE BELT

It started the same way all our fights seemed to start these days. Over something incredibly stupid.

I was just getting home from Jon Thomas's place and a marathon session of D&D, about to walk through our front door, when I heard my dad's voice behind me.

"Hey, Reg, where you been all day?"

He was standing in the driveway, his arms crossed. He had a look on his face that dads can get. Angry, self-righteous. You know the look.

"I don't know," I said with a shrug. "Around."

It was late in the afternoon. I was twelve years old, and I had important things to do like watch TV. And then more TV. I opened the door.

"You're not going anywhere until you mow that lawn like I told you."

I stared at the lawn. Maybe it was a little long. Maybe. But so what if it was? It was grass. Who cared about grass? I mean, okay, I guess my dad obviously cared about the grass. My mom definitely cared about the grass. Everyone in this *whole neighborhood* cared about the grass, about keeping their lawns neat and tidy and perfect all the time. But on, like, a metaphysical level, did grass really matter? I could mow it now, or I could mow it tomorrow. Or I could never mow it again. Whatever I did, it would always grow back. Always get longer. Who cared? *It was grass.*

"Fuck the lawn," I said.

Poetry.

"What?" he said. "You wanna come over here and say that to my face?"

I looked at him. I stepped outside myself, processed the situation. This was one of those moments that exists in the multiverse. I had a choice to make, and that choice would have consequences. I could either ignore my dad and go inside, pretend nothing had happened, and hope this all went away. Or I could walk over to where he was standing in our driveway and say those words directly to his face. There would be a before and an after, a branching in the cosmos. And who knows? Maybe in another universe I chose differently and went on to become a respectful son and a humble fishmonger or something.

But in this universe, I chose to say it to his face.

I slowly approached until I was standing inches away from my dad. He wasn't tall, maybe five foot eight, and by this point I was almost his height. I didn't even really have to look up anymore. My mouth went dry as I spoke, just above a whisper.

"Fuck the lawn."

His hands moved so fast I didn't see them. One instant I was standing there looking into his deep brown eyes, the next instant he was behind me and I was looking at the ground, and the instant after that I heard my mother's voice from somewhere above it all.

"Charles," she called. "Come inside. Let me make you something to eat."

There was a pause. And then I felt my dad's hands release their grip on my arms. My mom was standing in the doorway. Only a small crinkle in her brow betrayed any anxiety. She was my protector. She always had been and always would be. My dad turned around and walked indoors as if nothing had happened.

I sat down hard on the pavement. The older I got, the worse our confrontations became. It felt like they happened all the time now, like my dad couldn't tolerate my newfound independence. Or maybe I was the one who couldn't tolerate him.

Either way, I didn't know how much more of it I could take.

・・・・・

Okay, I have to admit that I don't know if there really is a Ben behind Ben's Fast Food. These guys didn't solicit my endorsement; I honestly know nothing about this company beyond my meal last night. The dude who made my delicious slow-roasted chicken bowl actually looked more like a Carl. Possibly a Steve.

But hey. Ben, Carl, Steve—if any of you are out there and you want to toss me a free beverage sometime, you know. I wouldn't be opposed.

・・・・・

Both of my parents had always believed in old-school discipline. My dad had grown up with it. His stepdad had never held back from bringing out the belt. Even my mom, my protector, thought there was nothing wrong with old-fashioned corporal punishment if I got out of line. She was raised in small-town, postwar France. Went to Catholic school, was taught by a bunch of nuns who ardently believed "spare the rod, spoil the child." That's just how it was done.

And I have to admit. I was never much for following certain rules. Specifically, the bad ones.

I do appreciate order. Structure. Society wouldn't exist without it. Even playing a piece of music on the piano, there's an order, a sense to it all, a sequence and structure for the notes. That's what gives you a song, and it's beautiful.

In the same way, I really appreciate rules as long as they make sense, as long as they have purpose. Intention. Take my orchestra instructor, Miss Lidiard. She'd get after me for showing up late or mouthing off. And that was annoying, because I wanted to do what I wanted to do. But still, at least I *understood* the rationale behind it all. She wanted me to get better at the violin. The only way that was going to happen was if I focused in class. So it was entirely logical for Miss Lidiard to get mad at me for disrupting class. She cared about me, and she was genuinely looking out for my best interest. And eventually, I always did what she said.

But sometimes the best thing about order and structure is knowing how to push against it, how to hack it. Once I've got that original piece of music down on my piano, that's when I can start to improvise. That's when I can take my music to another level. Same thing with society's rules. If I want to explore new experiences, try new things—be different—why would I automatically conform to the same rules that both confine and define people? I have to push against them to make progress, to find new ideas. Not in a mean-spirited sort of way, necessarily—I consider myself a benevolent hacker—but I have to be willing to challenge authority.

Especially authority for the sheer sake of authority. Power for the sake of power. Rules for the sake of rules. Those are the bad kind. Those drive me nuts. Even as a young kid in grade school, if one of the aides at recess told me to do something, I'd always ask why. Partly to challenge them, but partly because I was simply curious.

You want me to get back in line? Why? You want me to stop talking to my friend? Why? You want me to report to the principal? Why? I'm not against you, not necessarily, please just give me a reason.

If your answer is "Because I said so," then I'm gonna do my best to do the exact opposite.

That was how I got sent to the principal's office for the first time at Chief Joseph Elementary School, back in the third grade. I was in the middle of a very dramatic game of TV tag—if you get tagged, you're frozen until someone else tags you and you shout out a TV show, so this was definitely in my wheelhouse—when a recess aide told us it was time to go inside.

"Why?"

"Because I said so."

No way was I gonna budge. She put her hands on my shoulders to get me moving.

"Get your damn hands off me!" I screamed.

Honestly, she barely touched me, but I've always had a penchant for the dramatic. All this time later, my greatest point of pride is that my battle cry predated almost the exact same line from *Back to the Future*—when George McFly rescues Lorraine from that goon Biff he shouts, "Get your damn hands off her!"—by at least four years.

It was straight to the principal's office for me. The school called my mom, and true to her roots, she actually requested that they paddle me for my offense. This was long enough ago that a grade school in Montana would still agree to paddle a wayward child, but recent enough that they requested that the parent be present for said paddling in order to insulate them from any liability.

So that was how I ended up in my principal's office that afternoon, bent over a chair, as my mom watched a meek, middle-aged man give me ten whacks to the behind with a wooden paddle.

I actually felt kind of bad for the guy. He was clearly embarrassed to be paddling the butt of an eight-year-old boy. He'd make a big show of winding up for a big swing, but then moments before impact he'd hold back and barely give me a tap. I couldn't have felt *that* bad for him, though, because my penchant for the dramatic still won out.

"Oh, dear God, no!" I sobbed. "Oh, the pain! THE PAIN!"

Perhaps not coincidentally, that was the last time the school agreed to paddle me.

As I grew older, I started to truly test the limits of my independence. Sneaking out at night with Kris Steichen. Spending weeks away from home with Jon Thomas. Expanding my boundaries—and lashing out at any teacher, any adult, any authority figure in my way. By the time I was in junior high, I wasn't just racking up detentions and getting sent to the principal's office, I was serving in-school suspensions on a regular basis. Not so much because I was doing anything incredibly bad—I never hurt anyone, I was never violent, I still wasn't a fighter by nature—but because I would just take things too far. I could never take no for an answer. I always had to get the last word in. Or, in the case of my dad, instead of simply ignoring him and going inside, I'd come back with a gem like "Fuck the lawn."

My dad was increasingly consumed by his own issues as well. The same problems that had begun to plague him when we moved to Montana—feeling trapped by his identity in a mostly white society, his lingering PTSD from the Vietnam War—seemed to be backing up on him more than ever. Professionally, he was going nowhere. Once, he had been a soldier. Now he was stuck working jobs processing meat or behind the cash register at convenience stores. Personally, he felt stifled. As a young man he had always dated, always flirted, always been in demand. Now he was married to a woman who was incredibly strong and independent, who earned her own money, who loved him but didn't seem to depend on him for anything. He felt like he wasn't in control of his own narrative anymore. He was trapped.

To have a son with so many options, with his whole life spread out in front of him, may have felt satisfying to my dad on one level. After all, he worked his ass off to give me everything I ever wanted— toys, computers, music lessons, anything. I was a mark of his success. But it may have also been difficult. I represented all the freedom he had lost.

We still had our good moments. TV wasn't something I only enjoyed by myself. He and I watched episode after episode of *Star Trek* together. I remember watching *The Pink Panther Strikes Again* with him, Inspector Clouseau flipping off some parallel bars and down a flight of stairs, and my dad laughing so long and hard that tears were actually rolling down his cheeks. My dad could still be charismatic, full of life.

But those moments were increasingly offset by conflict.

Just as his stepdad had with him, my dad used a belt on me. Now, don't get me wrong. This wouldn't be me dropping my pants, my bare skin exposed to the biting leather. I kept my pants on, and I'm sure my father never used the full force he was capable of. There were no welts, my skin was never broken. Physically, the pain wasn't that much more intense than getting snapped hard by a wet towel in a locker room.

But still. The sheer psychological impact was about as bad as you'd expect. I'd have to stand there, bent over the bed in my parents' room, waiting as my dad undid his belt, curled it in his right hand, reached back, took a swing. Over and over again. It hurt. It was humiliating, diminishing. A betrayal. In ways that went beyond physical pain, it hurt.

I tried to make light of it. Once, as he got ready to use his belt,

I stuffed a big thick book in my pants to take the impact. He was about to hit me when he realized that my butt looked like a perfect rectangle. We both started cracking up. No punishment that day.

But over time it got too severe to ignore. Again, not necessarily in a physical sense. But emotionally. It's one thing to get spanked or hit by your dad when you're eight or nine or even ten. He's bigger than you, he's older than you. He's the adult, you're the kid. You accept your punishment, you learn from your mistake—or you don't—and you move on. But once you get to junior high? Eleven, twelve? Thirteen years old? That's when I started thinking of myself as a man. Or at least something close to one. I was capable of making rational decisions. I was big enough to fight back. I felt like I had earned some level of respect as a human being. Some kind of dignity. That's when getting whupped by my dad's belt started to feel not just like discipline—but personal. Like an attack.

I do something to piss you off—break a rule, say something stupid, whatever—and your response as a grown man is to hit me? Seriously??

Even my mom, a big believer in discipline in her own right, sensed that something had changed. Something was broken in the dynamic between me and my dad. We had reached a dangerous threshold in our relationship, and if we crossed it we might not be able to find our way back.

Shortly after my dad and I almost came to blows in our driveway, she called up my father's own mom, who was still living in Cleveland, seventeen hundred miles away.

"I'm a Catholic woman," she told my grandmother. "I will always stand by my husband; I will never get a divorce. But Charles is being too harsh with Reggie. He is getting very difficult to live with. I try to talk to him, but he doesn't listen. Please, talk to your son. Ask him to change."

I don't know if my grandma ever did have that talk with my dad. But if she did, it didn't work.

· · · · ·

Okay, okay, okay. So apparently in my current reality Ben's Fast Food exists only in California. In a total of four locations. So I guess if you don't live near any of those locations, and you try to go by next time you get the late-night munchies, you may, in fact, be disappointed.

But I don't know. Maybe they deliver? By jet plane?

· · · · ·

It was our first night going out to eat in a long time.

Of course, these days eating in a restaurant is no big deal. Everyone eats out all the time, at least a few times a week. You're in the mood for a snack? Don't have enough time to cook something for your family? You go out or order something in, no problem. It's just a part of our culture.

But back in the '80s? Going out to eat was an *event*. It meant something. Even grabbing fast food was considered a special treat. And for the first time in a long time, my dad decided to treat the family to dinner at a nice restaurant. And we weren't going to some McDonald's or Burger King. No, he was taking us someplace fancy. A real steakhouse. The local Black Angus.

Maybe that's part of why I decided to act up, you know?

Deep down, understanding that this night meant something to my dad, a chance to live it up with his wife and kid on his 7-Eleven pay—a chance to provide for us, to really be the man of the family— maybe deep down I knew that this was the perfect opportunity to stake my *own* claim to manhood. To show my dad that I was going to do whatever I wanted, be whoever I wanted, no matter what it meant to him.

Or who knows. Maybe I was just in the mood to goof off.

Whatever it was, that's exactly what I did from the moment we took our seats. Slurping my drink through my straw. *SLURRRRRRRRRRRP!* Complaining about the table settings. *James Bond would never tolerate this pedestrian salad fork!* Speaking French to our befuddled waiter and exploding in indignation when he didn't understand—also in French, of course. *Mon Dieu, ce restaurant est horrible!*

Nothing big, nothing crazy. Kid stuff. Funny way to assert my independence, I guess. But it pushed my dad's buttons, exactly how I knew it would.

"Enough!" he finally said, his voice harsh but low enough to not attract attention. "You are gonna get it when we get home, all right? *You are gonna get it!"*

I opened my mouth to say something smart, when—

"Hot dog!" my mom exclaimed as the waiter arrived with our food. "Hot dog" had become one of my mom's go-to Americanisms. She said it whenever she got excited. Thought it made her sound like a real local. "Would you two look at zis steak? So delicious, right? *Hot dog!"*

The irony of repeatedly proclaiming "hot dog" over a deluxe meal of sirloin and ribeye seemed completely lost on my mom. Or maybe it wasn't lost at all. Maybe she knew exactly what she was doing. Because my dad and I couldn't help but share a knowing look and bust out laughing.

"Okay," she said, now smiling herself. "Let's enjoy! Bon appétit!"

And we did enjoy ourselves, a lot, for the rest of the dinner. I saw a light in my father's eyes I hadn't seen for months. My mom was warm, happy, full. And I felt like I could *be* myself without constantly needing to *prove* myself. It felt like a return to a normal I barely remembered anymore. Who knows? If we could have a night like tonight, maybe everything would be okay.

And then we got home, and the first thing my dad did was take off his belt.

"All right, Reg," he said. "Go to your room."

I couldn't believe it.

"No, Dad. Come on."

It had ended up being such a perfect night. Why did he have to ruin it? Why couldn't he let it go?

"You heard what I said. To your room. Now."

I started to walk. I thought maybe if I forced some tears, he would relent. I was the king of fake crying for sympathy—that penchant for the dramatic—but somehow, this time around, I found that once I started, I couldn't stop. Before I knew it, I was sobbing uncontrollably.

"Charles, please!" my mom said as she followed my dad into my room. "He's sorry!"

"I never heard an apology," he said, coiling the belt in his fist.

"Leave the boy alone!"

"I told him he's gonna get it, and now he's gonna get it."

I was crying and crying and crying. It was the humiliation of it all. Just the humiliation.

"No!" my mom said. "It's too much!"

"Bend over, Reg! Let's go!"

The next moments came like flashes. Broken, fragmented. As I experienced and detached and observed and

My dad pushed

                   me
                  down.

     My mom shouted

                     My dad   raised his

        "Enough of this!"

hand to strike.

                I'm crying now—this is what it feels like—
                to cry.

     My mom jumped between

                I couldn't believe   how

                       strong

           My dad froze—hitting

us.

my mom   was a line

         She pushed him.

                          he'd never cross.

    she is.

"Reggie, stay here!" she shouted.

She forced my dad out of my room and into theirs, shut the door behind them. I heard muffled shouting, his voice, her voice. Mostly her voice. I had no idea how much time passed. Suddenly the door opened. My dad walked past me, didn't make eye contact. My mom walked into my room. Her eyes were rimmed with red.

"I told your dad he must go," she said.

I heard our front door open and close. My dad was gone.

·····

Okay, okay, okay. All right. Okay.

So I just remembered that last night, after I binge-watched *Next Gen*, while I was composing my next aria, and before I ordered that delicious bowl of slow-roasted chicken from Ben's Fast Food, I smoked a little peyote. And it may have been a lot of peyote.

And I may not have actually ordered anything to eat from Ben's Fast Food.

Especially given that I'm actually in Santa Fe, New Mexico, right now. And I highly doubt that Ben's really does deliver by jet plane from their four California locations.

But hey. Next time I'm near one of those locations and I get the late-night munchies, I one hundred percent am going to order one of those slow-roasted chicken bowls. And I one hundred percent bet it will both be incredibly delicious and also not make me feel like an asshole.

So, Ben, Carl, Steve? Still expecting that free drink. Thanks, fellas.

·····

Do I really have to keep talking about this?

·····

Shortly after that final blowup, my father moved out. Found a place in Arizona and left.

Did he move out entirely because of my increasingly volatile relationship with him? Or was he also looking for a fresh start in the midst of a broader crisis? New job, new city, new life, that kind of thing. Maybe all of the above. I don't know.

But at the time, I didn't really care. You might think I'd have been broken up, devastated that my father was gone. After all, he was still my dad. The same guy who used to take me to air shows when I was little, who took me to buy my first model plane and helped me put it together, who sat with me on all those afternoons in Madrid watching the girls go by.

But I wasn't devastated. Not at all. The man I had once been so close to had become a hurtful presence in my life. He and I were barely communicating anymore, and when we did it was usually to argue. In Jon Thomas's family, not having a dad around lent itself to a lack of order, to stress and uncertainty. But in the weeks and months that followed, my world didn't descend into chaos. If anything, I'd never felt more in control. I was used to being alone. I loved and respected my mom, and now I had her all to myself. If I did have any feelings of loss after my dad left, I buried them deep down.

Once he moved to Arizona, my dad started reclaiming some of the power he'd lost living with us in Great Falls. Some of his autonomy. He went back to school to study business management, hoping he could move beyond gigs in retail and food services. He also began to have an affair, moved into a place with another woman.

I'm still not sure how my mom found out about it. My dad had always been a bit of a ladies' man, especially when he was younger, and my mom knew that. But he'd never strayed before. To her mind, even though he had left, even though she *told him* to leave, the two of them were still husband and wife. It was just like she told my dad's mom—she didn't believe in divorce, and she had no intention of divorcing my dad. Ever. Him living apart from us was just a necessary evil, something she had to endure for the safety of her son.

My mom confronted my dad about his new live-in girlfriend, and he backed down. He got a place of his own, and within a few months he'd moved to Cleveland to be close to his extended family. He'd stay faithful to my mom, but he was also staying far, far away.

I found her in our kitchen one afternoon, crying by herself.

"What's wrong?" I asked.

"Nothing," she said, dabbing at her eyes. "Nothing."

She didn't want to trouble me. My mom never wanted to trouble me. But she also didn't cry. I sensed, somehow, that this was because of my dad. That she was in pain because she missed him. I should've empathized with her. Here was the woman who always stood up for me, no matter what, and she was hurting. But instead I got angry.

"Why are you crying?" I said, my voice full of contempt. "Dad is out of here. It's done. Who cares."

I went straight to my room and slammed the door behind me like the petulant teenager I was. Even then, even in the haze of my selfish rage, I knew in my gut I'd just done something awful. What was my problem? Why had I belittled my mom like that? She was my favorite person in the world, and I hadn't offered her an ounce of understanding.

But I also had an adolescent's knack for rationalization. The more I thought about it, the more I felt justified, even wronged. So what if my dad was gone? I should be enough for my mom! I had felt fine after he left, I told myself. My mom should feel the same way. So what if she wanted to cry a little? Go ahead, let her. In the grand scheme of things, we were happier now, right? We were all better off. Weren't we?

I pushed my shame at the way I'd treated my mother out of my mind. Buried it where I kept all the other emotions about my dad I had no interest in dealing with.

I didn't have time for this crap. I was thirteen years old now, on the cusp of what I knew would be one of the greatest chapters of my life. Here was my chance to finally carve out my own unique identity outside of my dad's shadow. My chance to truly become the strange, odd person I wanted to be—whoever that was, I didn't even know yet!

I was completely free. To try everything, to be everything, to break every boundary. And it all happened just in time for the most iconic, most quintessentially American phase of every kid's life. The ultimate crucible of sex and music and hormones and rebellion.

High school was right around the corner.

chapter eleven

PROPS TO THE ORIGINAL

Hey, you out there. My treasured reader. My good friend on this shared journey of literature. I just wanted to take a quick moment to give a shout-out to Ferris Bueller, the guy who really invented this whole "breaking the fourth wall" thing.

I remember seeing his movie in the theater, and of course I loved the way he pushed back against society's conventions, and I really wanted him to foil his nemesis, Principal Rooney, and obviously Sloane was gorgeous in her white fringe leather coat.

But what really blew my mind, what really shifted the entire paradigm of my reality, was when Ferris got in that shower with his soapy faux-hawk, turned to the camera, and sang "Danke Schoen" directly to *me*. When he told me that life moved pretty fast and I had to be careful not to miss it, I was like, "Yes! Ferris! You *get me*!"

Sure, he was technically talking to everyone else in the theater too. But I knew by the way he looked me right in the eyes that the connection he and I shared was special. That message about life and European socialism and Wayne Newton songs was for me and me alone. I wasn't just watching, I wasn't simply being entertained—I was a part of Ferris's world.

So, Ferris, thanks for being the first. A pioneer. A true innovator. Me and Shakespeare and all the great Greek tragedies would be lost without you.

chapter twelve

R. WATTS, NUMBER 69

I walked into Great Falls High on the morning of my very first day, and my jaw dropped.

Sure, I had been in the building a couple times before to see plays at the theater and that kind of thing. And I'd always enjoyed its literally old-school aura—its red-brick facade, its central tower with a pavilion roof, even the classic analog wall clocks protected by metal mesh. I'd always been impressed at the size of the place, which was ten times bigger than my junior high and one of only two public high schools in the city. My freshman class alone would have more than three hundred kids!

But this was my first time seeing it so alive. All three massive floors of classrooms, lockers, labs, auditoriums, and gymnasiums all jam-packed with over thirteen hundred students—jocks, preppies, nerds, popular kids, and nobodies—laughing, shouting, bumping into each other and flowing through the halls, some of them racing to get to class, some of them taking their sweet time, but all of them simply, purely, magnificently *alive* in this giant hormonal petri dish called high school.

It was even bigger, even better than I had dreamed it to be. And I had dreamed of it a lot. I'd gone to see *Sixteen Candles* two years earlier, in 1984. A matinee show at the Cine 4, its bright green sign glowing in the strip mall on Ninth Street South, its floors covered in popcorn and crazy psychedelic carpeting. I'd found a coupon for a free ticket on the back of a Burger King ad, and I went by myself, one of only four people in the theater. But I didn't need a crowd to make the experience memorable. I sat there with my eyes locked on the screen, soaking in everything about Sam and Jake and Farmer Ted, studying the movie the way I had once studied *Goldfinger* and *Three's Company* and PBS's *Mystery!* Of course, some parts of *Sixteen Candles*, like its portrayal of the foreign exchange student, Long Duk Dong, haven't exactly aged well, but that wasn't the lens I was watching it through at the time. I was focused on the glories, the high jinks, the unlimited juvenile potential. Were the parties in high school really this epic? Were the women in high school really this beautiful? Was the drama and the comedy and the romance in high school really this . . . *real*?

From that moment on, angsty high school films became my religion, Molly Ringwald became my high priestess, and John Hughes became my god. *The Breakfast Club, Weird Science, Pretty in Pink*—I practically memorized them all. And I didn't stop with the John Hughes classics. *Fast Times at Ridgemont High, Grease, The Lost Boys, Three O'Clock High*. Sean Penn as a surfer dude? Sign me up. John Travolta and poodle skirts? Hell yeah. Teenage vampires? Why not. In high school, it seemed, everything and anything was possible.

My summers at Jon Thomas's grandma's cabin on the lake only added to my obsession. Jon's older cousins were all in high school, and weren't they just as gorgeous as Molly Ringwald's Claire? They swore and smoked and listened to industrial metal bands like Ministry, and wasn't that just as raw and rebellious as Judd Nelson's Bender? They drove a graffiti-covered Microbus and wore stylish, funky hats, and wasn't that just as quirky and cool as Jon Cryer's

Duckie? So the unlimited magic of high school was not only possible—it really was real.

Now I was finally free to grab some of that magic for myself. My dad was gone, hundreds of miles away in Cleveland, and so were all his rules and discipline. I'd taken a new bedroom for myself down in our finished basement. It was bigger, with more room for my posters—Night Ranger, the Cure, and of course a breakdancing Snoopy. The wallpaper was white with an elegant floral print. I had a bathroom of my own, with a big enough window well that I could still sneak out if I stood on my dresser. It had a cave-like vibe that was cozy and mysterious, just like the instrument room where I first chose my violin all those years before. But most of all it was *mine*, my own turf, my secret lair, a place where I could be myself, find myself, in every facet and mode of expression.

Since grade school, I had developed this entire Toolbox of Weird to draw upon—my imagination, my languages, my characters, my music—but now, as far as everyone at high school was concerned, I was an unknown quantity. A nothing. A nobody. I was also one of nine Black kids in the entire school, so even as a nothing I stood out, almost like when I first moved to Montana all those years ago.

Except for one big difference. Now I had true agency. Now I was in control.

Who would I choose to be? Would I be a charismatic outsider like Duckie? Would I be a Brian the Brain? Would I be a disturbed rebel like Bender or a popular athlete like Andrew? Maybe I would be some crazy blend that nobody, not even John Hughes himself, had ever thought of before. For the first time in my life, I had the power to embrace—to craft—whatever identity I wanted. If my goal was still to be the biggest oddball in the history of Great Falls, I would be on exactly the right road.

So I came to a decision. I would conduct my very own experiment of social engineering. What if a kid started high school determined to try out every single group? To infiltrate every single clique? Cool kids, smart kids, jocks, dweebs, squares, you name it. Picking and choosing, coming and going as he pleased. Like a spy. Like a chameleon. Like a walking, talking *Breakfast Club* all rolled into one.

Would that kid be accepted? Would he be happy? Would his identity get so scrambled that he'd finally go stark raving mad? Or would he just have a shitload of fun? Maybe even find a home, a family of friends, along the way?

I had no idea. But as I walked into Great Falls High on my very first day, I couldn't wait to be the guinea pig.

· · · · ·

"What number you wanna be?" the equipment manager demanded.

"Um," I said, barely able to hide my smile, "I love 69."

"Fine. We'll give you 69. What's so funny?"

"Nothing!" I snickered. "I just really, really love 69."

I was now the proud owner of a brand-new football jersey in royal blue and white, the colors of the mighty Great Falls Bison, emblazoned with *R. Watts, 69* on the back.

In a way, it might seem surprising that the first social group I chose to infiltrate my freshman year was jock. After all, I was a notorious dreamer, a musician, I loved the arts. The nature of sports is competition, and I was a lover, not a fighter. Or I at least dreamed of being a lover.

But something about athletics had always intrigued me. I always got the sense that my dad—a former solider, a brown belt in judo who'd competed in Japan—had been disappointed that I wasn't more into sports. I'd struggled with my weight most of my life. Never getting outright obese, but always a bit on the chubby side, or at least that's how I felt about my body. The main reason was because my diet was garbage. I ate so much chocolate, absolutely vacuumed the stuff up. Especially Reese's peanut butter cups. I was addicted to that chocolate–peanut butter combo. But my dad would come up with excuses for my pudginess, crack open medical books and say, "Here, take a look at this. I think you've got a bowel condition."

And, yeah, my bowels were doing crazy shit; I had bad constipation issues—but you try eating peanut butter cups morning, noon, and night and see how well your intestines respond.

In junior high, in an attempt to get into shape, to sculpt my chubster body into a chiseled, muscular physique, I'd even tried weightlifting. Under all that flab, I knew there was sheer power waiting to come out. I'd always been stronger than the average kid, even back during my Reg-Darr the Barbarian days, when I would carry kids across the snowy playground at recess. If I was a guy in the circus, I'd be the strongman. Why not go to a real-life gym and pump some iron? If it was good enough for Conan the Barbarian, it was good enough for me.

So my mom actually took me on a weekend to a bodybuilding gym. This wasn't some easygoing Planet Fitness–style deal where an alarm went off if someone exerted themselves too hard and had the nerve to grunt. This was an honest-to-God "Pumping Up with Hans and Franz" heavy metal gym, with huge, sweaty, muscly dudes in shorts and sweats. Grunting—very loud, vocal grunting—wasn't discouraged, it was required.

And you know what? I actually liked it! The physical part, anyway. I realized that weightlifting wasn't just picking up heavy objects; there was a technique to it, it was regimented, controlled, nuanced—almost like playing the violin. There was a science, an art to extreme exercise. If I squatted fifty pounds, I could feel the strain and the strength in my arms and legs and back. The payoff was tangible, it was immediate. *I am lifting this weight. Right. Now.* When I finished, my muscles were sore, but it was a good sore, a sore that told me I had put in work, that I had accomplished something. I was getting stronger, and I could feel it.

But if I'm being honest, the grunting part was a turnoff. I mean, there I was, this little twelve-year-old chunky Black kid surrounded by these big, beefy red-faced white men with veins popping out of their necks. It wasn't the most comfortable situation.

Flash forward to my freshman year of high school. I was a little older, a little stronger, the other kids on the freshman team were my same age instead of forty-something weekend warriors, so maybe it was time to try again. Maybe it was time for redemption.

I signed up for the team with my wingman, Jon Thomas, who, like me, was entering high school as a blank slate and trying to figure out who he was. Football, of course, was America's sport. A training ground for warriors. A crucible of toughness, manliness, and honor. Instilling ironclad values into the proud, muscular, masculine youth of an entire nation.

I promptly put a very Reggie twist on the entire experience.

For my jersey, I chose number 69—I still don't know if our wrinkled old equipment manager ever figured out what was going on with that. For my position, I decided to play right guard. I had no idea what the right guard did in football, what he stood for, what he believed in, what skills he required. I simply knew that Right Guard was the name of my deodorant, and I thought the commercials were kinda funny.

I went to all the practices, but I didn't memorize a single play. Just sort of did what everyone else did. On the bus rides to the first few games, I'd sit next to Jon Thomas—who took it all as seriously as I did—and give the rest of the team my best impression of gruff Coach Nickerson from *All the Right Moves*.

"What colors are these guys we're playing? Baby blue and white? Shit, who do they think they are, playing us with colors like that? A bunch of Smurfs, that's who they are! And we're a team of Gargamels, and we're gonna go out there and tackle those Smurfs! And eat those Smurfs! And grind those Smurfs into gold! Now, are you with me, mighty fighting Bison Gargamels? *I SAID, ARE YOU WITH ME??*"

The coach wasn't putting me in, but that didn't bother me. I disengaged as always. Loved to stand on the sidelines and take it all in, the pomp, the pageantry, the festivities. This was better than TV! Better than the movies! I'd let it all wash over me . . .

The crispness of the fall Montana nights.

The cheer of the crowds, the brassy notes of the marching bands.

The smell of freshly cut turf, the steaming hot dogs in the concession stand.

The cheerleaders dancing and prancing and

"HEY, WATTS!"

"What? Me?"

"YEAH YOU, WATTS! YOU'RE IN!"

I jogged hesitantly onto the field. This was very different from standing on the sidelines. Suddenly I wasn't an observer watching everything from the outside. I was in the game, part of the action, living in the moment. I was the one being watched. And I had no idea what to do.

"*Omaha!*" our quarterback shouted. Wait, "Omaha"? Wasn't Omaha in Nebraska or something? We were in Montana! They had the totally wrong state!

"*Blue forty-two! Blue forty-two!*" Well, we were the color blue. But so were they, just a different shade. Huh.

"*HIKE!*" Even I knew that one.

Helmets cracked, pads crunched. Bodies went in motion, bodies stayed in motion. Sweat dripped down my face. I could taste it. A ball flew over my head.

"What do I do??" I shouted at the dude next to me.

"RUN TO THE RIGHT!" he screamed.

So I ran to the right.

It felt good. My muscles flexing, my lungs on fire, my breath like smoke in the cold air. I spotted the guy on our team who was carrying the ball, so I decided to run behind him. A couple guys from the other team ran up behind me, so I pushed them. First one, then the other. They both fell to the ground. Cool!

My teammate and I jogged into the endzone. This was a touchdown? This was a touchdown!

Everyone from our team piled around us, hugging, high-fiving, headbutting. Laughing and celebrating. The payoff was tangible, immediate. Kind of like weightlifting. Also, there was grunting. Always the grunting. But there was a social aspect too. I really was part of a team. We really were all in this together.

Shit! Wow. So this was sports. Sure!

After that, the coach started playing me in more games. Not a ton, but pretty consistently. Turns out that being a little big, even a little chubby, is actually a good thing at right guard. Who knew?

I also started getting invited to the football parties. Everyone knew that all the popular people went to the football parties, so that was perfect—one of the next groups I wanted to try in my experiment of social engineering.

Jon Thomas and I went to our very first football party on a Friday night after one of our games. It was in a broad, open, grassy field. Guys parked their pickup trucks, turned on their headlights, blasted their radios, and propped up kegs in the beds. The scale of it all was kind of neat, I guess. These parties would pull in dozens of people from the freshman, JV, and varsity squads, plus cheerleaders, popular hanger-on-ers, wannabes, the whole range. All underneath the big, wide starry sky that helped Montana make its name.

But beyond that, it was mostly a bunch of kids getting sloppy drunk and puking all over the place. There was nothing interesting about it. They weren't pushing themselves or having intriguing discussions or being creative in any way. They were just sitting around having great hair. It was all kind of boring. Oh well, at least I could cross "popular crowd" off my list.

After the season ended, I was in class when I got called down to the coach's office. I had no idea what was going on. What did this guy want with me? Was I in trouble? What did I do?

Football for me had been a fascinating experience, but that was all. I did enjoy the team aspect, but ultimately I couldn't connect to the cause that theoretically united us. We were supposed to care about taking this oblong scrap of inflated leather from one side of a field to another? That was somehow important? Why? I had nothing against these other teams. I had no idea who any of them even were. And I was supposed to get excited about beating them? Why did any of this even matter? So far no one had given me a decent reason beyond "Because we say so."

The coach motioned me into his office and had me take a seat by his desk. Next to him was a wheeled metal stand with a classic '80s tube TV and VHS VCR chained on tight.

"I wanted you to get a look at this, Reg," he said as he pushed play.

I watched, mystified, as he queued up a montage of football plays. Football plays that all featured me. Running, pushing guys, pushing guys some more. You know, doing football stuff. He pressed stop and looked me in the eye.

"You got size, you got speed, you got real potential. You should really think about joining JV next year. We could really use a 69 on our team."

"Yeah, okay," I said, barely stifling a laugh. "I'll think about it."

But I decided to change the world instead. Or at least our school cafeteria.

. . . . .

"But the crux of the matter," the president intoned, thumping his fist on the table, "is how many pizzas can we buy for the annual Sophomore Pizza Party *if* we only manage to raise a paltry three hundred dollars at the car wash."

I sat at the table in the school library listening intently, or at least pretending to.

"Indeed," I said, stroking the pencil-thin mustache I had grown because I was sure it made me look like a serious person. "Indeed."

The president turned and looked at me.

"Reggie," he said, "what do you think?"

"Well," I blustered, hoping that my snazzy red suspenders and waist-length sports coat would distract from the fact I had no idea what we were talking about. "As you said, that is the, uh, crux. Or whatever."

"Yes, but you're the class treasurer. It's your job to figure this stuff out."

"Figure out . . ."

"The price of pizza!"

"Ah," I said, stroking my mustache again. "Indeed."

In my sophomore year, I decided to embrace an entire mélange of identities, all of them marked by something that really was the biggest departure for me. I became the ultimate rule follower. An institutionalist, a member of the Establishment. A real light-side-of-the-Force guy. I would be a polished prepster. An over-achieving nerd. And yes, even a student government goody-goody.

"Whatever." The president sighed, rolling his eyes. "I'll figure it out."

The vice president and secretary, who weren't quite as pompous, chuckled. Honestly, I have no idea how I won that election for class treasurer. It may have helped that I ran virtually unopposed.

· · · · ·

I sat at our kitchen table surrounded by textbooks and notes, papers and pens. The small TV we had in the kitchen was just feet away, beckoning me with the siren song of *Mork & Mindy, The Love Boat, Battlestar Galactica,* and who knows what other televised rerun delights that awaited me if I could only *turn on my precious TV.*

Shit, how did the nerds do it?

I had always gotten decent grades, but I was determined to truly, authentically earn my way into the exclusive club of overachieving academic super-geeks. But all it felt like was test after test, quiz after quiz, homework assignment after homework assignment. Geometry, history, bio, civics. Essays, fill in the blank, multiple choice.

It just went on and on and on and

. . . . .

"Reggie, are you ready to go out there?"

I peeked through the curtains to see the scattered crowd—emphasis on the *scattered*—that awaited my very first stroll down the catwalk. I'd always had a bit of preppy flair—how many grade school kids do you see walking around in suspenders every day?—but now I was taking it to the next level, appearing in a real-life fashion show.

Granted, this was a fashion show at Herberger's, our local department store. Not exactly Paris Fashion Week, more like the kind of thing where an old-man shopping outlet says, "Look, all you kids, you can buy cool stuff at our place too! What do you call them? 'Blue jeans'?" But still, it was a fashion show. Our high school yearbook had sent a photographer to cover it, and I was ready for my star turn.

I'd just gotten into *Miami Vice*, so I decided to embrace the Rico Tubbs–Philip Michael Thomas look, heart, body, and soul. Over the last few months, I'd been running like crazy in gym class, and I'd slimmed down so much I was practically svelte. I'd teased out my hair in a perfect, glossy '80s helmet. I'd grown a mustache and trimmed it pencil thin. I was wearing one of the short, stylish, double-breasted blazers that were all the rage. I was a super-prepster. I could've been Molly Ringwald's adopted Black brother in *The Breakfast Club*. Except no way would I ever land in detention.

The next thing I knew, someone pushed me through the curtains and onto the catwalk.

"And next on the runway we have young Reggie Watts, showing off the latest styles from Lacoste!"

The flash of the camera blinded me as I strutted my stuff. I got my picture in the yearbook, but that was the beginning and end of my modeling career. Never mastered my left turn.

· · · · ·

I finally got my report card from the first semester of my sophomore year in the mail. My heart was pounding, my palms sweaty as I tore it open. And there it was.

A 3.8 GPA.

I was officially on my way to being valedictorian. Or salutatorian. One of those -torians.

Then it hit me. I really didn't give a shit.

I'd rather be watching TV.

· · · · ·

"Reggie," Miss Lidiard said, looking into my eyes as she squeezed my arm. "I knew you could do it. It's like I always said, you just have to *apply* yourself."

I had just earned the spot of first chair, second violin in the school orchestra, finally becoming Miss Lidiard's dream violinist. And I hadn't just devoted myself to my craft, I had also completely immersed myself in the culture of our group.

I became a full-fledged orc dork.

Going on group tours to Billings and Chicago, playing in high school competitions across the nation. Orchestra wasn't my entire life—but at times, it was pretty close. But even then I felt something tugging at me. A rebelliousness. A mischievousness. A sly taste for making trouble.

My first "professional" recording had nothing to do with playing classical music on my violin. It was a love song I co-composed with my buddy Mike the Viola Player for a girl we both had a crush on— the prettiest girl in orchestra, Colette with the Striking Blue Eyes, who happened to be first chair, first violin, a higher position than mine.

Mike and I recorded our ballad in a studio his cousin had set up in a storage space, and gave Colette a cassette. She was nice, she humored us, but she was unmoved, which was fine. Mike and I both knew she was completely out of our league, untouchable.

That went so well, Mike and I decided to record a second song—this one to share with the entire world, or at least the esteemed judges at *Star Search*, which was like the '80s version of *America's Got Talent*, starring Ed McMahon instead of Simon Cowell. So a lot cooler. The song is called "Long Ago and Far Away," and honestly I'd completely forgotten it existed until I asked Mike to search his house for some of our old stuff to include in this book, and he dug up "Long Ago" in an old cardboard box. Mike says I composed the lyrics, and when I hear us singing about a land of beautiful men with flowing hair I'm inclined to believe him, because I'd definitely sing about that. I'm playing piano and the two of us are on vocals and it's a pretty catchy tune for a couple high school kids. But the best part is that we recorded it at Jon Thomas's house, and you can hear all fifty-two minutes of the session, including Jon Thomas bickering with his brother, JJ; little bits and pieces of our adolescent creative process; me freestyle rapping but not necessarily well; and Jon's ever-patient mom asking us what exactly we're doing, to which we reply that mostly we just want to impress our friends in orc, because isn't that what life is really all about?

Please, enjoy:

We obviously never got around to sending it in to *Star Search*. But ideally one of the judges will hear it here and invite us back for the show's eagerly anticipated reboot.

· · · · ·

My whole sophomore year I went from one thing to another. I *became* one thing, then another. Switching back and forth, scrambling my identities, sometimes barely able to keep track of who I was supposed to be at any given moment.

Each day in the cafeteria, I would always look for the one or two kids sitting by themselves on the outskirts—the Weirdos in the Lunchroom—and I'd go up and join them. Let's see what they have to offer; maybe I can bring them along for the ride. Or if not, maybe I can learn something new in the time it takes me to finish my ham sandwich.

I did it all, but something was missing. There was something I couldn't find in any of the groups I experimented with. Something I definitely wasn't finding as part of the Establishment. For all the time I was spending with the jocks and the nerds and the preppies and the orc dorks, I wasn't fully connecting. I still felt like an outsider, like someone who didn't exactly belong, who didn't fit in. I didn't know why.

When I finally figured out what I was missing, what I needed to make myself whole, it didn't happen at high school, or even in Great Falls.

I found the answer in the summer. In Cleveland, Ohio.

chapter thirteen

I ALMOST FORGOT

I also tried my hand with the whole visual-artist, teen-Picasso set. Which resulted in masterpieces like this:

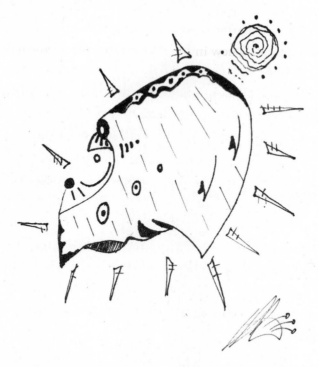

I know. Somehow it's both avant-garde and after-garde, incredibly stunning and completely somnambulant all at the same time, right?

chapter fourteen

EMBRACING THE DARKNESS

I hesitantly approached the group of kids on the porch next door.

"Hey, guys," I said, my voice tense in a way I hadn't felt in years. "What are you up to? You want to hang out?"

I was staying at my grandma's house in Cleveland, where my dad had moved after his stint in Arizona. I was only visiting for a couple of weeks, but the culture shock was intense. I hadn't felt this foreign since I first moved to the States.

"Man, listen to how this dude be talkin'," one of the kids said, laughing. "He be like, 'Hey, guys!' Like, 'Hello, fellows!'"

"Yeah, like, 'How do you do, my neighbors?'" his buddy chimed in, doing his best—and whitest—Mister Rogers.

"'Howdy, good friends!'"

"'Would you youngsters like to spend time with me?'"

"'Would you gentlemen like to shoot the proverbial shit?'"

By this point they were all literally rolling on the ground laughing, tears rolling down their cheeks. I tried to laugh along, but somehow it didn't seem so funny.

For the past decade in Montana, I had always been the odd man out because I was Black—or at least that's how all the white people thought of me. And I responded with what had become dozens of social hacks, tools to make sure everyone liked me. A quick wit, a vivid imagination, an ear for music, and so many foreign accents I'd lost count, all blending together in my own unique cocktail of weird.

But all those accents had been European. All my funny characters had been English or French or Spanish or German. I'd even consciously modeled my day-to-day American dialect on local newscasters, all of whom were white. I had a multifaceted, multidimensional identity, but it was built for a distinctly white world.

My grandma's neighborhood in Cleveland was not that. It wasn't poor or dangerous or any of the stereotypes that white America likes to apply to Black urban areas. It was simply . . . different, in a way that was deeply uncomfortable to me at the time. Here, there weren't miles of blue sky and prairie and pine trees. Here, there was more concrete than green, the yards were small, the aluminum awnings were drooping, and the streets were cracked and crumbling. Here, all of a sudden, all the control I thought I'd gained, all the armor I thought I'd constructed, was stripped from me in a flash. Here, I was the odd man out because I wasn't Black enough.

"Awww," one of the kids said. "Don't be lookin' all sad like that, Pinocchio. We just playin'."

"Aw, man, you right—look at that long, pointy, white-dude nose! He *do* look like Pinocchio!"

"Hey, Pinocchio, where you from?"

"Montana," I said.

"*Montana?* You mean like cowboys and shit?"

"Cowboys and puppets like Pinocchio!"

"It's all good, Pinocchio from Montana," one of the kids said, putting his arm around me. "You can '*spend time with us youngster fellows*' all you want."

They busted out laughing again. I observed myself feeling sad, feeling alienated and other. I went back into my grandma's house. I wasn't in the mood to hang out anymore—or any of that other stuff either.

· · · · ·

Visiting my dad wasn't my first time outside of Montana since coming to America, of course. In fact, I'd traveled to France a ton of times during the summer—sometimes for a month or more—to see my relatives from my mom's side of the family.

I'd stay with my uncle Andre in his old stone country home in the village of Onville in northeastern France, spend time with my aunt Carmen in Montceau-les-Mines, in the center of the country, sometimes even visit Paris with my mom. It was a very mellow, welcoming environment. I'd roam around the village, lounge near the fountains, and wander home when it was time for meals. I'd practice my French with my cousins and help them practice their English. And when it rained, I would sit by the window and listen to Michael Jackson's "Human Nature."

My trips to France played into all my most lavish, romantic ideals. This was where style and fashion and sophistication were born. This was where I could imagine myself solving cozy mysteries with Hercule Poirot. This was where I would adventure someday with my one true love—whenever I happened to find her.

This was very, very far from Cleveland.

Now, don't get me wrong. Cleveland is actually a very cool city, and I had a lot of amazing adventures there over the years. I'd go and visit my cousin, who lived in this fantastic house that seemed straight out of *Sanford and Son*, nothing but gadgets and gizmos and car parts piled everywhere, waiting to be explored. And my dad would take me all over, to the museum, to the mall. We'd go fishing together, go to concerts, including Faith No More—great music, but again, pretty white—and go out to movies at night.

Seeing *Ghostbusters II* at a packed theater with an all-Black audience was an absolute phenomenon. I felt like I had always actively engaged with the movies and TV shows I watched. Putting myself in the action, practicing new accents and characters, never simply passively consuming content. But I was *nothing* compared to that crowd. They were talking back to Dan Aykroyd in the middle of the show, heckling the screen, laughing like crazy at the jokes, shrieking in faux terror at the few "scary" parts, and booing their heads off at anything they didn't like. This audience wasn't just engaged with this movie—they were *living* it. They didn't wait for it to entertain them, they *made it* entertaining. Decades later, I remember them a hell of a lot more than I remember any of the plot twists.

But no matter what I did, no matter how much time I spent there, I couldn't shake the feeling that I was "other." That I was a tourist, a vaguely welcome guest in a land that was not at all my own. Ironically, Montana—which had started out feeling completely foreign to me—now felt like my truest home, with its libertarian attitude, its openness to experimentation, its "you don't mess with me, I don't mess with you" vibe. That made sense to me.

My relationship with my dad didn't help matters. It was around this time that his health really started to deteriorate. He had endured several heart surgeries shortly after we moved to Great Falls, but somehow he had always found a way to recover. To hold on to a piece of himself, the charm and big broad smile that made him Charlie Watts. But that was changing. He'd been a heavy smoker for most of his life, going through a couple packs a day. He was getting more tired more quickly, starting to lose that spark, and in Cleveland he was finally diagnosed with emphysema. He kept smoking anyway, and it only got worse.

My dad and I had had our issues, of course. Before he left Great Falls, we could barely be in the same room with each other. All the arguing, the fighting, the beatings with his belt. He'd wanted to impose a kind of aggressive discipline I just couldn't tolerate anymore. The tension got so bad that my mom had finally kicked him out of our house. So, yeah. "Issues" really doesn't cover it.

But for all that past trauma, you might have thought that his brush with mortality would've brought us closer together. That maybe some of the walls between us would finally start falling down, maybe he'd finally start opening up about his past, his trauma from the war, all the emotions he'd kept inside for so long.

It didn't happen. When I visited, we weren't fighting anymore, not like we used to, so that was good. It was like we reached some kind of unspoken truce to simply let what had happened between us in Montana lie. And he'd take me out to do father-son things sometimes—the fishing, the concerts, the movies.

But if anything, the emotional wall he put up was even stronger now that he had emphysema. Before emphysema, even when he'd been distant, he was still charismatic. He liked to laugh, liked to tell jokes, liked to meet new people. In his own way, he could still be his charming old self, in public anyway.

Now he was grim, serious, even depressed, all the time. Even when we were out trying to have fun. He seemed weighted down with regrets. His dreams of getting a degree in business were over; instead, he worked at a tollbooth at the turnpike. I think he missed my mom. I think he even missed Great Falls. But I couldn't really tell. No matter how often I tried to talk to him, he still lacked the vocabulary to talk about how he felt. Though, to be honest, even if he had told me he wanted to come back home, I'm not sure I would've wanted him to. It's hard for me to admit that now, but it's true.

I liked having my mom all to myself. I was happier not having to deal with my dad's anger constantly lurking around our house like a shadow that never lifted. I was savoring my freedom, both as a kid trying on every identity he could find in high school—and as a son, who no longer had to worry about what kind of mood his father would be in when he woke up that day.

So far in my life, I'd always been able to develop hacks to deal with all my problems. Clever ways to game the system, to short-circuit the simulation I was stuck in to make sure the odds were constantly in my favor. It turned me into what I liked to call a "practical optimist." Life would always serve up obstacles, of course—that was the nature of existence. But if you tried hard enough, if you acted smart enough, I believed you could always find a solution. Real life really could be one long summer at a friend's house on the shores of a Montana lake. You simply had to make it happen.

But my worsening situation with my dad, the alienation I experienced in Cleveland, it all made me start to question that faith. What if some problems were too big to solve, too intractable?

What if some barriers were so high you didn't even want to overcome them?

· · · · ·

My dad and I were coming back to my grandma's from fishing—another silent, serious expedition—when we spotted the neighborhood kids hanging out on their porch.

"What up, Pinocchio!" they shouted.

I sighed. My dad smiled at me. It was the first time I'd seen him smile in a while.

"Aw, that's just their way of having fun," he said. "Go on over. They won't bite."

I was about to shake my head no when I heard something coming from their boombox. It wasn't the Smiths, and it wasn't the Smithereens. It definitely wasn't Faith No More.

It was the Fat Boys.

I can bust riff rafs back to
back!
And I'll devour any MC as if he
were a snack!

The beat was sick. Of course I'd listened to the Fat Boys before—who hadn't? They were all over the radio and MTV. But Jon Thomas and my other Montana friends weren't exactly rap fanatics. My Great Falls soundtrack focused on angst and melodies and guitar riffs and electronica. The Fat Boys were all basslines and ridiculous rhymes. They just wanted to have a good time.

I made my way to the porch.

"Hello there, good fellows!" I said cheerily. It was one of my go-to moves—disarming my antagonists by using their own energy against them. But now I had an extra twist:

"Do any of you chums like to . . . beatbox?"

They took one look at me with my lighter skin and pointier nose and busted out laughing.

"Man, get the fuck out of here!"

"That fool can't beatbox!"

"He don't even know what it is!"

They kind of had me there. I had never actually tried beatboxing before. What was I going to do? Add a bassline to alternative Jon Thomas music like the Smiths? But I knew from all my music lessons that I had a great ear. I knew I could hear something and imitate it quickly on my piano and violin. Why not my mouth? I was great with accents and dialects. Wasn't beatboxing just a dialect of song?

So, as the neighborhood kids watched wide-eyed, I broke it down.

"Bah-bft bah-tshh! Bah-bft bah-tshh! Bah-bft bah-bft, bah-bft bah-tshhh!"

I started improvising, adding random laser blasts and other sounds I could've easily heard in *Star Wars*, all to the beat.

"Tah-puh-tuh bwoop! Tah-puh-tuh bwop! Buh-chigga-chigga-chigga-beeew-beeew-beeew!"

And it was like a bomb went off.

"OHHHHHHHH!"

"Motherfuckin' Pinocchio can beatbox!"

"That motherfucker be GOOD!"

"SHIIIIIIIIIIIIT!"

It was the same kind of energy I'd experienced at *Ghostbusters II*, except now I was the show. I was the phenomenon all the other kids wanted to be a part of. Suddenly they didn't just want to listen to me beatbox—they wanted to rap over my beatboxing. They all started freestyling, sometimes taking turns, sometimes all trying to rap at the same time. I was a human drum machine for a completely improvised band.

I had found my purpose—and my hack—in the group.

But even as I had fun with my new crew, I didn't forget the barrier that had seemed so insurmountable just a short while earlier. I knew that even though I'd made a connection, I'd never be a real part of this world. I knew my dad's health problems would continue, maybe worsen, as would his depression. None of these problems would magically go away.

But I understood something else too. From here on out, I wouldn't run from the darkness in life. I would embrace it. Reality wasn't all summers by the lake. It wasn't all smiles and positivity. Sometimes there was no good solution. But that was okay.

In fact, it was that darkness that made life more interesting, more compelling. More textured than anything I'd find on a rah-rah football team. More nuanced than any student government meeting about the price of pizza. Darkness, sadness, disillusionment—there was a power to it. A strength that came from simply embracing the role of the outsider.

I had never shied away from being different. If anything, the opposite. But I had typically tried to be the goofball, the entertainer, no matter which clique I was embracing. My new understanding of what it meant to be odd had a depth to it, a thoughtfulness, an openness to discord and disharmony. And a growing confidence in myself.

Perhaps in my excitement to try all those different groups at school, I had forgotten just how much I savored being the other—in all its shades, light and dark. But now I was ready to finally find my true home in Great Falls High. A real family of friends.

A bunch of weirdos like me.

chapter fifteen

AEROGEL

Have you ever experienced this amazing stuff called aerogel? Here, let me put some of it in your hand.

See how light it is? It's this high-tech aerospace material they use for insulation in space vehicles and things like that. It's made of carbon on this atomic scale, with all these air pockets so it's almost nothing but air. It's kind of brittle, but it's thin and translucent and weighs less than a human hair and all you need is a few layers and it protects you from heat and cosmic dust and pretty much all the negative energy in the universe.

Anyway, I'm thinking of having a few gallons of it applied directly to my skin. Or maybe just turned into a comfortable hoodie. Should be fucking awesome.

Oh, and you can keep the sample I gave you. No worries.

chapter sixteen

A FAMILY OF WEIRDOS

"There are these dudes from CMR I want you to meet," Jon Thomas told me. "They're coming by after school."

"Cool."

I'd be lying if I told you I gave what he said much thought.

It was our junior year at Great Falls High, and Jon Thomas was still my best friend. He'd always be my best friend, no matter what, I knew that. He'd started out in high school as a nobody, a nothing, just like me. And even though he hadn't joined me for all of my social experiments—there was no way that guy would've ever joined student council—he was my one constant through everything important. We'd played—and quit—the football team together. We still hung out constantly. Still listened to the Smiths, still played Dungeons & Dragons, still visited his grandma's cabin on Lake Five in the summer.

His mom had saved enough to buy them a small house practically right next to our school. His room was in the basement, like mine, but he was cool enough to have a waterbed and this cylindrical shower that looked like something out of a spaceship. I'd go to his place during open lunch and steal snacks, peanuts and Chex Mix and whatever else I could find, and that's where we were when he first told me about these guys he knew from CMR.

CMR, or Charles M. Russell High—named after the Great Falls artist famous for his paintings of the Old West—was located on the other side of the Missouri River, the only other public high school in town. It was kind of like the alternate-universe version of my own high school. Where Great Falls High looked straight out of a classic John Hughes movie with its old clocks and pavilion tower, CMR was newer and more futuristic, built in 1965 with modular sections and narrow vertical windows, almost like a colony on the moon. I dug the vibe, but our high school's style was the epitome of my perfect *Sixteen Candles* fantasy.

I still have no idea how Jon Thomas met these guys from our rival school. Why he thought we'd hit it off, I have no clue. Like I said, I didn't give it much thought at first. Maybe he sensed that I was restless, searching for a group—a family of Weirdos in the Lunchroom—that I could really call my own. Maybe he understood that I was ready for a darker, more experimental force in my life. Maybe he was just amused by men who wore mascara.

Whatever it was, that afternoon in the fall of my junior year, I stepped out of our school and saw two dudes who matched their school, looking like alternate-universe versions of anyone I'd ever known. They were in the senior parking lot—the *cool* parking lot, the *exclusive* parking lot—leaning against a lime-green '78 Monte Carlo, a massive boat of a car that was parked at this weird angle, as if bad driving could be its own form of rebellion against the Man. One of them had spiky blond hair, an acid-washed jean jacket, and a Marlboro Red dangling from his lips. The other had intense blue eyes, crazy curly hair, and perfect androgynous features, prettier than most girls our age. He was wearing a black trench coat, and he looked like a reject from a Duran Duran video. They had style, they had swagger, they were anything but safe. And all I could think was, *Who the hell are these guys?*

"Hey," the one smoking the cigarette said, nodding at me. "I'm Mike Benton. People call me Beave." He motioned to the pretty one next to him. "This is Fish."

"Hey," I said with a nod I hoped looked equally cool. "Reggie."

Mike Benton, aka Beave, grinned and took a drag. "So," he said, exhaling a long stream of smoke. "What's next?"

And just like that, everything changed.

· · · · ·

We were hanging out in my living room—me, Jon Thomas, Fish looking pretty, Beave in his acid-washed jean jacket, and Beave's sister, Mel—when Beave zeroed in on the piano my dad had got for me all those years ago.

"Hey, Reg, you any good at that?"

"Hell yeah," Jon Thomas said. "He's a natural."

It was a weekday afternoon, and coming over to my place after school had become a kind of ritual for the gang. My mom was in her bingo phase, so she'd be out at this bingo hall called the Sailboat, smoking with all her friends, leaving us with time and space to chill, to talk, to explore.

But up until now, never to listen to my music.

"Play something for us, man," Beave said. "Come on—everyone get down on the carpet around the piano. Like, flat on your back. Just stare up at the ceiling. Just, like, experience the reality that Reg creates for us."

I sat on the bench and almost like magic the vision Beave had articulated simply materialized. Four bodies lying in a semicircle at my feet, waiting for me to transport them . . . somewhere.

This was the way Beave operated. He had an ability to enter any situation and take control with this compulsive energy that constantly pushed things forward. First there had been Kris Steichen pushing me out of my comfort zone. Then Jon Thomas. Now Beave, maybe the most charismatic of them all. If Jon zigged and zagged, Beave barreled straight ahead. Once he got a head of steam, nothing would stop him. Not that I needed much encouragement in this case. Moments like this were why I learned to play the piano, really. Not simply because I loved the music, which I did, but because it served as a tool. To help me connect with others. To be everyone's favorite weirdo. To put on a show.

My fingers reached for the keys and I started with something familiar to me, something fun. A classical Beethoven minuet that I could speed up, slow down, build on, and improvise with, guaranteed to entertain. Easy.

DUN-DO-DO-DO-DO-DUN-DUN-DUN-DUN-DO-DO-D—

"Hold up, hold up, hold up," Beave interrupted.

"What?" I said. I could tell this was about to get strange.

"All due respect and all that, Reg, but you gotta open your mind a little bit."

"Mike," Mel said, calling her brother by his real name. "You barely let Reggie play! Reggie, it was beautiful."

Fish cracked up. "Don't get in the way of the she-wolf protecting her piano baby, Beave!"

Laughing, Mel chucked a pillow at Fish's head. Beave held his hands up for quiet.

"I know, I know, I know. It was awesome, it was. Reg, you're perfect. I just want you to hear some other stuff first, all right? It'll totally change your life. Prepare yourself for . . . Bauhaus."

"Bau-*what*?"

Before I knew what was happening, he'd popped a tape into our stereo and out poured the creepiest, most bizarre, most haunting music I'd ever heard. It was all deep rumbling basslines and dark screeching guitars summoning demons and apparitions and creatures of the night. And of course . . .

Bela Lugosi's dead . . .
Undead, undead, undead . . .

"Vampires?" I said.

"Vampires," Beave said.

I had been exposed to dark, edgy music before—Jon Thomas had introduced me to Ministry, and his cousin Schjanna turned me on to Front 242. But those were more industrial, aggressive sounds, especially Ministry, with a vibe that pretty much screamed "Break things! Jackhammer! Commit acts of violence!"

But Bauhaus was different. It was goth. It was brooding, introspective, contemplative. All about pondering evil whilst lingering on a throne in an oozing dungeon. I could imagine my dad listening to Bauhaus as he sat in our kitchen alone, staring off into the night. If Lord Byron, Mary Shelley, and a group of thin Englishmen made a pact with a lesser-known demon and his vampire bride, Bauhaus is the band they would form.

Now, when I decided to embrace the darker side of life, I never meant it quite as literally as Bauhaus took it. I was more of a new wave guy, less a dark wave ghoul. I loved music with a current of darkness running through it, yes, but I never wanted to lose the celebratory, soulful, future-forward energy of bands like ABC and the Human League and New Order.

But as we lay there listening to twisted crooning about blood and death and, yes, vampires, the music created a powerful field of reality around us, fusing us together as a group with a single identity, a single purpose, much as the Smithereens defined my experience years earlier when Jon and I drove to his grandmother's cabin on the lake. Except the bond that defined my new group wasn't pure fun, it wasn't the joy of summer—it was subversiveness, it was darkness, it was the counterculture.

None of us had ever really fit in before, but now we fit in with each other. I'd spent two years trying on different groups for size, and I'd had fun, but nothing truly felt like a match. Jon Thomas was my best friend, but his impulsiveness could turn people off, and he was more mocked for his obsessive alternative music tastes than he was respected for them. As for Beave, for as cocky and confident as he came off now, he'd been a loner back in grade school and junior high. He had been a dork with big buckteeth, which is how he'd earned his nickname. Then he hit puberty, and his teeth had all evened out, but he'd kept the name, and he'd kept a chip on his shoulder against all the jocks and popular kids who'd excluded him. Fish was pretty and androgynous now, but he'd been great at sports, an amazing swimmer whose natural athleticism was undercut by a subtle social awkwardness and a slight lisp when he spoke.

Whether by coincidence or not, none of us had great relationships with our fathers either. I'm not saying our dads were necessarily horrible people. But they were human. They had failings. Our lives were complicated. My dad was a fantastic provider who also lived a thousand miles away because we fought all the time. Jon's dad was a heavy drinker who had walked out on his family; he'd started drinking around the age of twelve to cope with the death of his own mom. Beave's dad could be emotionally distant and he'd beat Beave up once, and I'd heard that Fish's family had a history of struggling with alcohol. And none of us ever really talked about it, we never really opened up about our personal pain and trauma. But we felt it. We knew it was there. So to cope with our hurt, to mask the insecurities we felt in each other, we became our *own* family of post-punk oddballs.

Our family even had its own mom—Mel, Beave's sister. The first time I saw her at Beave's house, I almost couldn't believe I was looking at a real person, that's how beautifully transcendent she was. Her long silky hair was so blond, so platinum, it was almost white. Her skin practically glowed. She had a knack for devising cutting-edge fashion out of clothes she bought at the Salvation Army. She had bright blue eyes and a pointy chin and a mischievous smile and may have actually been an elf. But she also had a strength about her, a centeredness, a thoughtfulness that the rest of us boys lacked. She was our compass, our moon.

As part of my new family, I completely overhauled my style. The suspenders were finally gone for good. So was the Rico Tubbs–Philip Michael Thomas pencil-thin mustache and perfectly coiffed helmet head. Instead I donned a trench coat and started experimenting with my hair—mohawks, faux-hawks, stylish mullets—whatever the mood called for. My grades went to shit, and I was back to serving multiple in-house suspensions.

We were the bad kids, the troublemakers, the kids you were supposed to avoid. A cool, laid-back Spanish foreign exchange student named Alex hung out with us a couple times, until he was literally warned by his advisor to stop hanging out with us.

Stay away from those kids—they're not going anywhere.

So he did. He stayed away, started hanging out with the popular crowd. Then one night, driving back from a concert with one of his new friends, the car flipped. The driver was okay, but Alex died. The school announced it over the loudspeakers to the entire student body, and all I could think was, *Yeah, great thing he stopped hanging out with us.*

Beave went to Alex's funeral, but I couldn't bring myself to go.

So yeah, it was true. Me and my family of oddballs weren't going anywhere. But that was exactly the way we wanted it. We didn't want to be cool. We didn't want to be popular. We didn't particularly care about being successful in the traditional sense of the word. We just wanted to stay right here in Great Falls, to live life with each other.

"Okay, okay, Reg," Beave said in my living room. "Now here's what I absolutely, one hundred percent need you right now at this very moment to play on your piano, okay?"

He pressed play on his Bauhaus tape, and the melancholy chords from the opening piano solo in "Who Killed Mr. Moonlight?" seeped into the atmosphere around us. I slowly accompanied them on my own piano—

And our little family drifted and churned into the darkness of

· · · · ·

We're lying in the grass in a graveyard on the outskirts of town, staring up at a sea of stars spilling over us like a giant fuzzy blanket. And yes, that jumbled metaphor is absolutely the best way to describe the Montana sky right now.

A buddy of ours actually lives here, a younger kid named Robert Rummel; he and his family are caretakers, like something out of a movie. This isn't one of your posh, country club–style cemeteries with neatly trimmed hedges and polished marble tombstones. This cemetery is decidedly low-tech, almost like something you'd see in an old Western. It's just off a dirt road, with small, worn gravestones and sparse landscaping surrounded by an old fence. Whenever I'd watch *Scooby-Doo* and they'd show these mysterious, misty, totally spooksville cemeteries, I'd wonder if the reality was really that mysterious, really that misty, really that spooksville. And now I know—it is.

"Do you guys actually think there's a god in charge of everything in the universe?" I ask. Believe it or not, none of us is high. I still haven't even tried weed. It doesn't seem to matter at this point. Being sixteen is its own drug.

"I heard there are, like, lots of universes," Fish says. "So I don't know. Maybe there's a god for each one?"

"And each culture in our own universe," I say, "or even on our own planet! Not just cultures now, but from all history. Mayans, Vikings, Romans, whatever. What if they didn't just worship their own gods, what if those gods actually existed? What if the worshipping of those gods, like the collective human experience of the act of worshipping, what if it *created* those gods?"

"Yeah, yeah, yeah!" Beave says. "What if there's a god for each culture, and that means that even on this earth we all experience, like, multiple realities?"

Mel starts to laugh. "Yeah, whatever it is we're totally gonna figure it out in this graveyard in Great Falls, Montana."

Beave jumps to his feet. There's a smile on his face, but his eyes are blazing. "But we will! Even if the truth just comes out in grunts. We're only people, right? But that's enough! Even if we can't walk, we can't talk, we can't see—man, we can expand our minds."

Okay, so maybe Beave is high.

But we all know that whatever the hell he just said—he's absolutely right.

· · · · ·

A few of us are out camping near Simms, this tiny town of a few hundred people, the kind of place that has one road, one gas station, one bar, and that's pretty much it. And a girl we're with has all this makeup with her, foundation and eyeliner and mascara, so we all decide we're going to be vampires.

Not dress up like vampires. Be. Vampires.

We smear foundation all over our faces to give our skin the pale, otherworldly glow of the undead. Though as the only Black dude it's more like I'm in whiteface, a Bizarro World Al Jolson bloodsucker. I tease out my long hair to give it a wild, unhinged vibe, and we drape ourselves in long black trench coats and paint our eyes with mascara and eyeshadow to make our lids feel heavy and haunted.

And then we race out into the night to do . . . what, exactly? Because no matter how strange we are, no matter how goth or how vamp, we're definitely not up for drinking any blood. So mostly it's just howling and hissing and leaping off tree stumps and shouting *"Bluh! Bluh! Bluhhh!"* as we careen about what passes for a main street in Simms.

Until Fish and I realize that even vampires have to pee.

So we walk into the single local bar, packed with townies chugging beers, and it's like one of those movies where the protagonist walks through the door and suddenly there's this really loud record scratch as the jukebox shuts off and everything goes silent. Dead. Silent.

Because they're all staring at us.

Fish heads for the bathroom and I have to wait because it's just a one-person bathroom and this really is a very small, crowded bar and I'm very, very aware of just how white everyone is around me, just how drunk, and just how close they seem to be getting. And one of the townies looks at me and my fake white skin and my hair sticking up in spikes, and he says:

"Who are you supposed to be? *Alfalfa?*"

It's one of those jokes that aren't really jokes. His smile is a sneer, and his laugh is mocking and aggressive. There's definitely something racist going on here, and I'm definitely lucky I watch so much TV because otherwise I wouldn't know who Alfalfa from *Little Rascals* was.

I step outside myself, process the situation. This is one of those moments that exist in the multiverse. I have a choice to make, and that choice will have consequences. I can choose to respond in kind, to say something aggressive, to insult this man and all his friends, and who knows what will happen next. Or I can laugh it off. I can pretend to be in on the joke. And I can walk away.

If I listened to the advice my parents gave me when I was younger, perhaps I'd choose option A. If I were my mom, maybe I'd curse him out and call him a redneck. If I were my dad, maybe I'd take him out with a judo move. I'd respond from a place of anger and insecurity.

But I'm older now. Now, at this moment, I know exactly who I am. I'm part of a new family. A family of freaks. We're comfortable with who we are. We enjoy living on the margins. We revel in our makeup and our music and our oddness. And usually, the rest of Montana is fine with that. Usually, as long as we mind our business, the rest of Montana doesn't fuck with us. The rest of Montana is cool.

And in this reality, in this simulation, in this universe under my own private god, I decide that Montana can be cool this time too. I decide I don't need anyone's approval to be confident in myself. I choose option B.

I laugh along, like it's no big deal. The tension dissipates. I use the bathroom, and Fish and I walk back into the night, into the darkness, where we both become vampires again, together.

. . . . .

We called them coffin caves because each one felt like a tomb. They were caves—nothing more than mine shafts, really—that dotted the granite mines outside of town. We'd drive down a long dirt road and see a giant cliff rising on the left-hand side, the craggy, broken end of a massive plateau. And we'd turn up a small, steep hill, and there they were—the entrances to the coffin caves.

A bunch of us would go. Not just our smaller family of me, Jon Thomas, Beave, Fish, and Mel, but ten or fifteen of us. They were part of our crew, but more on the periphery. Extended family, cousins if you will. Or won't.

Joe Bates was a punk rock anarchist with a mohawk that was two feet tall. He wore an army trench coat and tall, laced-up Doc Martens, and when you saw him you were like, "Yep, that's a punk rock anarchist." His buddy Tony was half-Asian and more of a skater punk. Michelle Hult had these striking wolf eyes and giant moussed-up hair, and I'm pretty sure her mom was a nun. Chelsea Malloy was Joe Bates's girlfriend. They were like the Sid and Nancy of the group, and she liked to wear this transparent plastic jacket with nothing but lingerie underneath. Chris was stupidly handsome and half-French, so we'd speak French sometimes, and he lived in a hobbit house by the river. Travis was tall and lanky and kind of awkward, and he drove a Datsun, and one time he left a .357 Magnum in a stranger's mailbox.

Tonight we've gathered in the biggest of the coffin caves. I've brought a portable keyboard and we're listening to music and philosophizing when we hear dogs barking from the other side of the cliff, and the next thing you know we hear "POLICE! WHO'S IN THERE??"

We're officially busted. So we scramble down the hill, and the police are there because someone complained about the noise, and they're checking our IDs, and Joe Bates turns to the lady sheriff and says, "Hey, didn't I use my truck to help pull your cop car out of a ditch earlier?"

We all crack up, because Joe Bates is a punk rock anarchist.

Then even the police lady laughs, because he's right, this kid with a two-foot mohawk did help tow her car out of a ditch. She doesn't look like she wants to be here right now, and I can tell we're on the verge of getting off with a warning.

"Y'all aren't really up to anything bad in those caves, are you?" she asks.

"Not at all, officer," I answer with my most winning smile. "We're part of the new generation of kids that *don't* do drugs."

· · · · ·

I was really, really tired of not doing drugs.

It was definitely true that being a teenager was its own kind of mind-expanding drug, for sure. Whether it was the hormones coursing through my veins or something they put in the water of the drinking fountains at Great Falls High, every feeling I felt, every idea I conceived, seemed like the most earth-shattering feeling *anyone had ever had*, the most revolutionary idea *in the history of the universe*. Life was fresh, life was new, and I was absolutely, positively certain I was discovering it for the very first time. I was sixteen—but I wanted more.

I'd tried drinking by this point, at the various football and popular-people parties I'd gone to out in fields or in Burger King parking lots. I'd even drunk enough to throw up once or twice. But there was nothing interesting about it. It just made me slow and slurred and sick. It was the lowest form of drug, a dumb tool, a sledgehammer to the brain.

I wanted something that would alter my consciousness, transform it, raise it to a different level. That something I wanted was weed. At least that's what Beave assured me.

"Don't worry, Reg," he said as he put a tiny amount onto a dented pop can that was serving as our makeshift pipe. "This stuff will blow your mind. *Guaranteed*."

It was late at night. Beave had parked his lime-green '78 Monte Carlo in front of my house, and I'd snuck out to join him. Beave had been embarrassed when his dad had given him this massive dinosaur of a car for work, but it was so huge he could load it up with, like, eight kids at a time. The Monte Carlo became the gang's official car, our own private Scooby-Doo Mystery Machine, always ready to take us all on our next kooky, spooky adventure.

In this case, getting me stoned. Or at least trying to.

"Is it supposed to look like that?" I said. "All brown with all those seeds?"

"Sure!" he said. "It's schwag weed."

"Schwag weed? Is that good?"

"Dude," he said, looking me in the eye. "I gave you my personal guarantee."

I huffed, I puffed, I held the sour schwag smoke in my lungs for as long as I could—and I didn't feel a thing. Forget about sledge-hammer to the brain; this wasn't even a light breeze.

So I was naturally a little skeptical when Beave took me on our next adventure to get high a few weeks later.

"Don't worry, Reg," he said. "The stuff here will blow your mind. *Guaranteed.*"

"Right. The personal Beave guarantee."

But as he parked the Monte Carlo at the motel where we were meeting our friends, I started to wonder if he might actually be right. We were at the exact same motel my family had lived in when we first moved to Great Falls. Not only that, but the small party was in the room directly above ours, directly above my very first home in America. The coincidence was insane.

"How is this possible?" I whispered to myself.

We got out of the car, and Beave and I walked into the small, dingy room of my ancestral motel. I heard the Cure singing from Jon Thomas's old boombox about heaven and faith and seeing in the dark. I saw all the extended members of my post-punk weirdo family talking and laughing and just kind of enjoying their existence, and I had a feeling this was all meant to be. My mind was on the verge of expanding. Forever.

"Ah, Reggie! *Alo!*"

"Oh! Um, Ilse. Hey!"

Things were already looking up. In addition to the usual suspects, someone had invited Ilse, an exchange student from Argentina who was studying at CMR High. She had thick, black, wavy hair and olive skin and a striking beauty that seemed straight out of one of my James Bond fantasy adventures.

I'd met her once or twice before, but I was always intimidated, always had a hard time letting down my guard. But this time I didn't even have a chance to put my foot in my mouth before Beave came and grabbed me.

"Reg! Lookie what I found over here!"

I shuffled my way into the small bathroom, ran my fingers through the tangles of my faux-hawk, and stared in awe. There in the sink was the biggest bong I'd ever seen. It was electric orange and at least four feet tall, and a clump of kids was huddled around it like supplicants worshipping at the altar of high.

You might think that I hesitated a little, maybe took some time to appreciate the gravity of the moment or at least ponder the wisdom of taking a hit off a virtual nuclear weapon of weed.

But nah. I stepped right in and took a huge frickin' rip.

Who knows how many rips later, I stumbled out of the bathroom and searched for someplace to savor the experience. The door connecting us to the adjoining room had been left unlocked by the motel, and I sat cross-legged on the king-sized bed as the rest of my friends trickled in, till we all formed a circle, Mel on one side of me, and Ilse on the other.

And as we sit there talking about the nature of the cosmos and consciousness and metaphysics and now the Sisters of Mercy are singing darkly about floods and a reflection named Lucretia, I begin to understand that when people talk about expanding your mind, they mean it almost literally. Because right now I'm on a space trip, like space as in spatial and space as in outer space as in outside the here and now. As in growing and expanding and traveling somewhere out there, out beyond, blowing into the universe like dandelions. And I'm losing my orientation and I don't want to move but I'm pretty sure I am moving anyway even though I definitely am not moving and does any of this make any sense and I yell

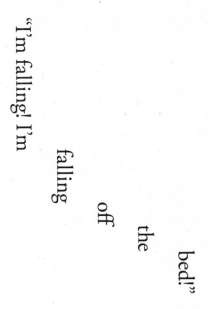

"I'm falling! I'm falling off the bed!"

The next thing I know or don't know, or maybe knowledge is all relative in this non-space space, Mel the Moon Mother and Ilse the Argentinian Dazzler are holding me and Ilse is saying, "It's okay, Reggie! It's okay! You're not falling! You're right here!"

And I realize that she's right. I'm right here. I'm right now. I'm simply being.

Somehow, I'm not sure how, Ilse and Mel and I move, we gravitate, we levitate, to the other room, and I need to lie down, so I lie down, and then I'm not sure how it starts, how it even happens, but suddenly they're each holding one of my hands, and they each have one of my fingers, an index finger, in their mouth. Mel with her long, almost gleaming, almost mythical blond hair, and Ilse is all waves and curves and sensuality, and now I'm starting to finally come out of my high, to finally awaken, but I see that none of this is actually a dream and all I can think is

What. The. Fuck. Is. Happening. Right. Now.

Suddenly it's time for Ilse to go home, and she asks me if I'd like to walk her to her car. I don't really understand the significance of this question, what it could lead to, what kind of cataclysmic awesomeness it could portend, but I understand enough to be like, "Oh, yeah. Sure."

We walk down the stairs of the motel and into the parking lot. We stop in front of her car, right by the door, but she doesn't open it, she just kind of stands there looking at me. And I'm thinking, *Why isn't she getting into her car? Am I supposed to do something?* If this were a James Bond movie, there would be explosions and a hail of bullets and a sunrise over the Alps, and I'd rescue her and we'd sail off together on a spectacular yacht. If this were a John Hughes movie, I'd say something witty and clever or full of pathos and thinly veiled significance, and I'd probably be wearing a quirky hat. But this is real life, so all I say is:

"So."

And finally she just grabs me and kisses me. Whoa, there's her tongue! That's a nice tongue, I like that tongue! I think I'll give her some tongue back. So I do, and she seems to enjoy it.

I'm not sure how long we're standing there kissing, but it feels both way too short and like forever.

"Good night, Reggie," Ilse says, pulling away. "See you soon?"

"Yeah," I say with a nervous giggle. "Definitely. Please!"

I wave as she drives away.

"All right!" I shout. "Good seeing you!"

Then I book it back upstairs to the party and immediately tell my friend.

"Beave, Beave, Beave!" I say. "It was amazing! It was insane! I was just like Duckie in *Pretty in Pink* or maybe Gary in *Weird Science* because Ilse does after all have that sexy accent—"

"What happened?" he says. "Spit it out!"

"Well . . . she kissed me! I mean, *a lot*!"

"DUDE!" he says. "YES!"

Beave gives me a hug. I collapse on the bed, lie back, and stare at the ceiling, which somehow seems to be a window into an entirely different galaxy. Is this love? Is it simply passion with a dash of romance and intrigue on the side? Is my life in Great Falls actually a teen comedy that someone somewhere is watching alone in a strip-mall matinee?

I have no idea. But I do know that I just discovered my two favorite drugs.

Weed and tongue.

· · · · ·

Two days later I was driving my car to school, when I stopped at a red light and sensed another car pull up next to me.

Driving had just started to become a thing for me. My mom had bought herself a new ride, and she gave me her old one. Appropriately, it was French, an old beige Renault 18i. Not exactly a muscle car, but I loved it. Jon Thomas helped me install a little sound system, and I'd practice different stunts and maneuvers whenever I got the chance. If construction crews left some cones on the street, I'd weave in and out as fast as I could. If I spotted a gravel road, I'd try what's called a "bootlegger's escape"—accelerating fast in reverse, slamming on the brakes, spinning 180 degrees, shifting into first, and taking off. I got good at it too! I was on my way to being a serious *Rebel Without a Cause* drag racer!

So that morning on my way to school, my blood still hot from my incredible night at the motel, I knew exactly what I was going to do. I'd glance over at whoever was next to me, and I'd make eye contact. *Is it on?* Then a subtle nod. *It's on.* And me and my beige Renault 18i would blow them out of the water.

I turn my head, and Ilse is staring right back at me. My jaw drops.

"You asshole!" she shouts. "You told *everyone*!"

"But—but—"

"I never want to see you again!"

RRRRrrrrrrrrrrrrrrrrrr!!!

She leaves me and my beige Renault 18i in the dust, idling at the green light.

My mind reels, my heart aches. The only person I had told was Beave! I mean, sure, he had told basically every other human in Great Falls, but still—was that my fault?

Women. After all these years, I still hadn't figured them out. As hard as I'd tried, I still hadn't fallen in love. But with Beave's expert guidance, that was finally about to change.

chapter seventeen

THE NATURE OF TIME

Hold up. When did I meet Beave and Fish again? Was it junior year or sophomore year? I'm having trouble remembering.

Let me text Beave real quick . . .

ME

> Do you remember what year
> we met? Junior, right?

BEAVE

> We met the summer after
> sophomore year, not junior
> year.

Huh. I guess that changes the timing of everything a little.

But really, what is time? At one point—in time, obviously and ironically—time did not exist, and someone had to create the concept that feels like what it feels like to conceive of the concept we conceptualize when we conceptualize time, and in the process of doing so, that someone—that someone being time itself—created time's self. Most people don't know that, but if you did know that, well, that's great.

And we all know that poverty is super easy to fix.

And using modular dynamicism, we can reshape, unfold, and understand the way we think about thought itself. By constantly monitoring thought itself, it will not only lead you nowhere in time—or out of it, and really that is the question at hand—it'll give you a headache. So try not to do that.

I'm going to take a nap.

chapter eighteen

SOPHISTICATED BRITISH LOVE

Beave parked his big old Monte Carlo and we both got out. This was a different kind of neighborhood than either of us was used to—on the outskirts of Great Falls, up in the hills, isolated and private. And the purpose of our mission was different too.

Beave was trying to set me up with a girl.

"So, Moneypenny," I said in my best James Bond, "you surmise that the situation upon which and thereof we are about to embark requires a level of sophistication, elegance, and sexual vibrancy unlike any before which I have yet achieved?"

"Reg," he said, "I got no idea what you just said. But you know what? I think for once she's got an even better English accent than you do."

"Shit. You're right."

"She" was Jo-ann, and she was British—like for-real British. She had just moved to town a year ago, at the tail end of 1987, because her mom had married a guy in the air force. Beave was dating Jo-ann's sister, Lucy, and I could tell he had one of his typical devious master plans—get me to go out with his girlfriend's sister, initiate them both into our little squad of post-punk oddballs, form some kind of weird couples' unit, and . . . Who knows how far he would take it, he was crazy.

Not that I needed any encouragement to go after Jo-ann. I'd already met her earlier in the day at Beave's house, this humble little abode that also happened to be right on the river. We'd spent the afternoon hanging out and swimming, and it was clear I was way outclassed.

Jo-ann was seventeen, a year older than me, and she was gorgeous. She had long brunette hair that she wore up in some kind of elaborate bun—I don't know, it must've been English—and she smoked cigarettes in this really elegant way, dangling them between her long, thin fingers. Her perfume of choice was Obsession for Men. For Men! How sophisticated is that? She was quiet, didn't talk much, but that just made her seem even cooler, more unknowable, like some unfathomable mystery of the cosmos.

And when she did talk? Holy crap. The way that real British accent dripped off her lips, it was like pure electric poetry.

Me? What did I have? By now I'd raised code-switching to an art form. I was still obsessively watching *Masterpiece Theatre* and James Bond movies. I constantly practiced those same sounds that Jo-ann made so effortlessly, and I was good at it, don't get me wrong.

Put me in a room of red-blooded, red-state Americans and I'd shift to my British accent, my French accent, my German accent, and right back to British. Even now, as a certified antiestablishment Rebel Without a Clue, it was my go-to icebreaker. I knew I looked different from everyone else, I knew they had no idea what to make of a Black dude with crazy hair, so it was my wacky way of defusing the situation. When it was all said and done, my Toolbox of Weird was one giant strategy of deflection. I'd talk and act like anyone except myself.

And it worked every time.

But Jo-ann? She didn't have to pretend to be someone else. She was the real deal. Authentic British. Sexy, beautiful, confident, pale. Hell, she was seventeen! A woman! Experienced in the ways of life and love!

Compared to her I was a pretender. A kid who, for all his bravado, for all his goofy charm, had never had a girlfriend in his life. Now here I was, venturing onto her turf, marching up to this big brick house in the middle of nowhere, thinking I could somehow, someway make this alabaster Anglo goddess like *me*?

"Hey, Reg," Beave said, eyeing me with concern. "You okay?"

I cleared my throat. "Yeah." And then in my best Irish brogue: *"Totally."*

The door to Jo-ann and Lucy's house was open, and we went in. It was '80s opulence like I'd never witnessed before. Sofas and love seats upholstered in creamy white leather. A giant TV with real wood paneling that sat on the floor like it was a real piece of furniture. And a brand-new Bose Acoustimass sound system, the kind with the perfect square speakers you could rotate independently. I'd only seen that in magazines. *These guys must be millionaires!*

We walked out to their backyard, and there was a big freestanding trampoline—because of course there was—and then we finally saw Jo-ann and Lucy lounging on the second-story deck. Jo-ann with a beer in one hand and her trademark cigarette hanging from the fingers of the other, gazing down upon us from on high like a beneficent queen.

"Aha!" I blurted out. *"Les dames du manoir se détendent avec quelques bières au-dessus de nous. Allons-nous nous joindre à vous et participer à une conversation animée?"*

Saying nothing, she smiled coyly and slowly exhaled a delicate stream of carcinogenic hotness.

Jesus. She was perfect.

But I was falling on my face. For the next hour, I tried all my best material up there on that balcony. I swirled together every accent I had, every language I knew. French, Spanish, German, and of course all the different flavors of English. I sprinkled in *sacrebleu*s and *bloody-well*s and *merde*s. I tossed in some Brooklynese *fuhgeddaboudit*s. I even beatboxed.

Nothing worked. I mean, I got a few laughs and smiles. I was being entertaining. But I wasn't *connecting*. I needed to break through that veneer, that English remove that I so admired I even emulated it myself. All those manners, all those accents, all that pomp and circumstance—it was great fun, but it never really let you in emotionally. It was delightful obfuscation, amusing distraction. Now it was working against me, and I had to find a way to push through.

Then it hit me. Something radical. Something I'd never tried before. I'd tell Jo-ann exactly how I was feeling. Just thinking of the prospect gave me goose bumps. To me there was nothing riskier, nothing more terrifying, than truly putting myself out there.

Thank God these rich people owned a trampoline.

I raced from the deck, down the stairs, and to the backyard. I climbed onto the padded metal edge of the tramp, took a deep breath, and leapt right into the center. I'd never been on a trampoline in my life, but I figured, how hard can it be, right? You jump, it's chill.

Wrong. Not chill at all. On that first big-ass bounce, I went flying into the air. But not a cool, controlled, Superman flying. This was more like *Greatest American Hero* flying. Remember that crazy show from the '80s? The blond guy got a suit that gave him superpowers, but he didn't know how to use it, so when he tried to fly he was a mess, twisting and tumbling in the air, completely out of control.

That was me on that trampoline—an incompetent superhero. Living in the moment, my mind clear of all rational thought. No longer self-aware, no longer in control. And absolutely unstoppable.

I soared higher and higher into the sky, past the first floor of the house, past the bottom of the deck, and finally so high that I could wave right at Jo-ann. She saw me flying through the air, waving around my hands and feet like crazy, turning around and around, and she lost it. Started laughing so hard she was practically crying. All that English reserve melted away.

And every time I bounced, I finally did it. I told her exactly what I felt.

"HEY!"

Bounce.

"JO-ANN!"

Bounce.

"I!"

Bounce.

"LOVE!"

Bounce.

"YOU!"

And with that, I flopped in the middle of the trampoline onto my butt, my momentum slowly dribbling to a halt. I lay back, my arms wide, and looked up at the blue Montana sky. Jo-ann peered down at me over the deck's edge, a smile on her gorgeous, pasty, British face.

"Would you like to go for a walk?" she asked.

I don't remember what the two of us talked about on that walk through the hills. But I do remember how it felt. It was easy, natural, not forced or contrived. When we came to the end of the trail, we sat on a large rock, holding hands.

"Um," I said, "wanna go out with me?"

She looked at me and kissed me. It was the most beautiful word anyone ever

. . . . .

BAH-BFT BAH-TSHH! BAH-BFT BAH-TSHH!

The bass was blasting as Jo-ann and I sauntered onto the dance floor. The Gold Rush was a real bar in the heart of downtown, with real booze and sweat dripping off the walls and a fancy dance floor with squares that lit up and everything, except tonight all the booze was locked up and the sweat reeked of hormones, and the fancy dance floor was packed with teenagers for the All-Ages Night, and now every one of them was staring at us as we made our way to the center, and who could blame them?

BAH-BFT! BAH-BFT!

I looked like, well, me—brown slacks and a short-sleeve, button-down old-man shirt I got for two bucks at a thrift store—but Jo-ann?

She had on a black rubber miniskirt that was practically painted on and this fashionable dark green English blouse that was unbuttoned as low as it could go without breaking local laws, like some kind of real-life Kelly LeBrock from *Weird Science* with the sexy accent and the style and the pouty lips. I had seen *Weird Science* like thirteen times in the theater. I loved *Weird Science*. I wanted to live *Weird Science*. And now here I was—me, Reggie Watts—with this paragon of sexiness straight out of *Weird Science*, and all the other kids were watching us dance on that floor, our bodies moving in perfect harmony, every single one of our molecules in sync, and they all had this look on their faces like *WOW*.

BAH-BFT BAH-TSHH!

What was happening was I was in love.

It seemed like I'd been dreaming of this moment forever. Back when my dad and I would sit and gaze at all the beautiful women as they strolled along *la avenida*, singing *"I'm a girl watcher."* Back when I'd watch TV alone, fantasizing about taking my beautiful beloved on adventures across the world, treating her to sumptuous dinners, and talking to her about sweet nothings until the break of dawn.

Back in grade school, when I fell in love with Pippi Longstocking. When I cast magical spells with locks of hair that never resulted in love. When all my best friends were girls, until things got a little too serious, until my curiosity got the better of me, and I'd suggest having silly orgies or blush when my suspenders mysteriously popped off at dinner. Back in junior high, when I'd recorded a song for the prettiest girl in orchestra, Colette with the Striking Blue Eyes, who I knew was way out of my league.

And all through high school too. Long before I'd ruined any

chance I had with Ilse by blabbing about my first French kiss to all my friends, I would go to parties and sit in the corner by myself as everyone made out around me and "Somebody" by Depeche Mode played in the background. Dave Gahan would croon longingly about finding a woman who knew his deepest, blackest, most perverted thoughts and loved him anyway. She'd argue with him, she'd try to convince him he was wrong, but every night she would still hold him tight in her arms.

Yes! I thought. *That's what I want! How does Dave Gahan know?!*

I'd once thought that maybe, just possibly, something might happen with Mel, the Moon Mother. We'd have moments, fleeting moments, when our fingers touched, or we exchanged a look, and I could feel an energy between us, and I think she felt it too. But we never acted on it, even that night when I first smoked weed, because even though we could feel a spark, we never wanted to risk our friendship for it. Never wanted to sacrifice that family bond for a fling or something potentially fleeting. That's how it had always seemed to go for me. Always the friend, always the nice guy, the fun guy, but never anything more.

I'd always loved to dance, all the way back to when I'd do silly little jigs to win over other preschoolers. That same freedom I felt when I was flying on that trampoline in Jo-ann's yard— freedom from thought, from worry, from consciousness itself— that's what I experienced when I was dancing. I was able to just let go and be me.

But I was always doing it alone. I would practice by myself in the basement at home, playing records by Prince and Chaka Khan and honing my footwork on our linoleum floors. In junior high, I would enter dance competitions at the air force base's Kiddie Disco Night. The music would blast, the floor would crowd with dancers, and the judges would tap out one contestant after another. I was always the last man dancing. The champion. But I never had a girl-friend to celebrate with.

There was no woman to treat to a fancy dinner. No woman to take on adventures around the world. No woman to love.

Until now.

Now, as Jo-ann and I move together on the Gold Rush floor, I understand in a way I can't yet articulate, in a kind of thought that transcends consciousness and conversation, that exists only in the sweat on our faces and the sway of our hips and the touches and brushes of our fingertips—I understand that as empty and desperate as all my years alone have been, this is happening now for a reason.

And that reason is that none of those other girls was Jo-ann.

Jo-ann is the only woman who can make me feel like this. Jo-ann is the only woman who gets me. Jo-ann is the only woman who appreciates my unique brand of weird, who doesn't just applaud me on the dance floor; she can match me step for step. She's my equal, the yin to my yang, the Isis to my Osiris, and when I'm with her I'm not simply myself, not simply Reggie, I'm a part of something bigger, something special, something *forever*.

And yeah I'm only sixteen but when you're sixteen years old every single second feels like

BAH-BFT BAH-TSHH!

· · · · ·

I reached into the piano and plucked the strings and pressed the sustain pedal, and a deep, rich rumble spilled through my living room and filled every silent space between me and Jo-ann. It was just the two of us now, none of the rest of the family for this home concert.

The lights were off, the curtains were closed, everything was black, and the sound seemed almost tangible. You could feel it, wet against your skin, shaking your atoms to their very core.

I tried other strings, other pedals, other keys. Never thinking or anticipating, simply feeling my way, taking us to a dark place, a melancholy place, a place where all of our emotions were exposed and raw. I felt like a magician. I could play a simple melody or a few chords at a certain tempo and dictate what we experienced, what we felt. It was like I had been invited into Jo-ann's mind, her heart, and I was exploring the most intimate, most personal fibers of her being, going deeper, further, into her past, her fears, her dreams.

I still considered myself an optimist. But I also remembered my loneliness at parties and how much dark wave bands like Depeche Mode had spoken to me. The aching, dystopian music that Beave had first exposed me to was everywhere now. Twisted teen-angst ballads like "Blasphemous Rumours" were *cool*. Being depressing was *sexy*.

As a musician who was just starting to find his creative voice, who still marveled at the power that song could have over others, I got sucked in. I'd sit in my basement bedroom and write songs about girls who had suicidal thoughts, racking my brain for the most disturbing imagery possible. Maybe her little brother could die in a tragic car accident but her dad just *couldn't understand*?? Yeah! The ladies would totally dig that!

Back in my living room, I looked up. I could see Jo-ann's eyes shining in the dark. She was crying. I stopped playing.

"Reggie," she said quietly. "Could you play something happy, please?"

. . . . .

"No, no, no, Reg," Beave said, shaking his head. "You don't just, like, 'hook up' with girls like Jo-ann and Lucy, okay? These are classy girls, okay? Classy. They got *morals*."

It was the middle of summer, and I was helping Beave work one of his jobs. We were on our hands and knees clearing a couple acres of dandelions near the river, covered in sweat and dirt. Beave got paid five bucks an hour and I got paid four. I knew I was getting ripped off by my best friend, but somehow Beave always talked me into it. The man just had a way with words.

"Morals," I said. "Right."

Jo-ann and I had been going out for over four months, which in teenager time is forever. I'd pick her up at night and we'd meet up with friends, go to parties out in the fields, or just chill and talk. We did everything together. Everything except . . . *that*. I mean, I fantasized about what we'd do together when we finally got the chance. Hell, I'd been fantasizing about this moment my whole life. And Jo-ann and I kissed all the time. So I felt like I'd be able to handle myself. But Beave wasn't going to leave anything to chance.

"You gotta be subtle, Reg. *Real* subtle. Like maybe you two are kissing, but as you're kissing you're also, like, dis-clothing her, okay? But with one hand only, all right? Popping those buttons. *Pop-pop-pop*. Taking that bra off."

"With one hand only."

"Absolutely. Practice that shit, man. Get it down. And then with the other hand you start rolling that nipple, right?"

"Rolling the nipple."

"Yeah," he said. "Like this."

He held up his grimy hand and kind of rubbed his thumb and index finger together. "They love that."

"Uh-huh."

Beave had started out slow back in grade school as the kid with the buckteeth. But then he hit high school. His teeth turned normal, his frame grew long and lean, and he started spiking his hair with Aqua Net hair spray every single day. And women adored him. He'd been going out with Lucy for a year now, but that was his longest relationship by far. Before he met her, the British girl with morals, all he did was bang.

"But the key, the key is the knee. You start rubbing your knee against her jeans, okay? Just rubbing, nice and slow. Oh man, that drives 'em crazy. And, you know, your other appendages are doing their magic as well. Everybody's got a job to do, understand?"

"Yeah."

Timing was of the essence here, because I was about to get my best chance at moving from kissing to whatever the hell Beave was talking about. That weekend, Jon Thomas was inviting a bunch of us up to camp at his grandma's house on Lake Five for two nights. I'd spent so many summer weeks there before, each perfect in its own way—but nothing like this.

First off, I'd finally have some real money to spend. Whenever I watch a movie, I'm always curious about the random little details they never tell you about. Yeah, James Bond action scenes are bad-ass, but when and where are all the bathroom breaks? Even when Sean Connery is dodging bullets or surviving explosions, there must be times when he just, like, has to go, right? Yet you never see that in any of the movies. It's as if bladders simply don't exist.

Same thing with money. Unless it's a major plot point—*The*

Goonies isn't *The Goonies* if they don't have to find treasure—characters kind of do stuff and you never really find out how they paid for it. Who's buying lunch? How could they afford those slacks? Or in this case, how could Reggie and his teenage buddies pay for a sick weekend camping trip?

Well, the answer is flat-out thievery. A couple months before the trip, I was at a house party when I decided to see if any of the cars parked nearby happened to be unlocked. You know, just something a few of us enjoyed doing at the time. Searching for spare change on dashboards, interesting little trinkets dangling from rearview mirrors, no big deal.

But this ended up being a very big deal. Turned out that not only was a pickup truck a few blocks away open, but it also contained a brick of weed hidden in a compartment under the bench seat. Plus an empty vial of cocaine and this cool Polynesian-style carved wooden box. But mostly . . . a brick of weed.

I raced back to the party—and, of course, showed Beave.

"Dude!" he said, his eyes opening wide. "You hit the *jackpot!*"

But he didn't want to smoke it. He wanted to sell it. I guess I could've felt guilty about all the money we made over the next few weeks. These were, after all, stolen goods. But Beave and I just spent most of our profits buying more drugs anyway. Drugs that all probably originated from the same pickup-truck drug dealer I originally robbed.

So, you know, the circle of life.

I did, however, keep the cool Polynesian-style box. And I used some of the proceeds from our drug sales to finance the camping trip on Lake Five. Which brings me to my second point.

On this camping trip, I'd finally be bringing a girlfriend.

Oh, the dreams I had. We'd all stay up late, smoking our illicit weed and philosophizing around the bonfire, then fall asleep on the beach underneath the stars. Jo-ann and I would share a sleeping bag. Free to do whatever we wanted. Go all the way. Hit a home run. Do the nasty. Get laid. Who knows? If I got real lucky, maybe all of the above.

Now, I don't want you to think I was just some horndog—I mean, I *was* a horndog, if only because the term *horndog* is absolutely ridiculous. And because at sixteen years old I had enough testosterone running through my body to kill a baby elephant.

But spending the night with Jo-ann was about more than just my fumbling desire for sex. It meant something deeper, something significant, something real. I wasn't quite sure what that something was yet, but I wanted to be prepared.

A few days before the trip, I went to talk to my mom. She had a favorite ring she always wore everywhere. It was simple, made of Black Hills gold with hints of green and pink and an elegant, twisting floral design. I wanted to give it to Jo-ann. After all, that's what boyfriends did, right? They gave their girlfriends rings. Why not the most beautiful ring I knew?

"Maman," I said with my most charming I'm-your-only-son smile. *"Je me demandais . . . tu penses que je pourrais avoir ta bague?"*

She was sitting in her red kitchen, still her favorite room of the house. *"Ma bague?"* she said, suspicion in her eyes. *"Pourquoi?"*

"Pour Jo-ann," I said, shifting on my feet. *"Mais juste pour un temps. Je vais le récupérer."* And then, when I saw her hesitate: *"Je jure!"*

She slowly pulled off her ring and handed it to me. *"D'accord. Mais si tu ne le ramènes pas, je te tuerai. Je jure."*

And for those of you who can't speak French redhead, that means: "If you don't bring this ring back, your ass is mine."

• • • • •

That Friday evening, the lake was as beautiful as it had ever been. The sun set over the mountains in a brilliant explosion of orange, pink, and purple. But let's be serious—I only had eyes for Jo-ann.

When my friends and I went on our weekend camping getaways, the vibe was always super casual. There was no dressing up, no putting on airs, barely even any basic hygiene. It was just guys and girls in baggy sweats and jeans. We'd spend the days with bedheads and *l'essence parfumée de* BO. The only person who wore any makeup was Fish, who had more mascara on his lashes than the entire Cure—and myself, if I'd decided to be a vampire that particular weekend. We all felt this camaraderie, this bond with each other. In nature, even more than in Great Falls, we could drop all pretensions, forget about conventions, and simply be whoever we wanted to be.

But even within our tight-knit family, what I had with Jo-ann felt special.

In her oversized sweatshirt and torn jeans, she still somehow seemed elegant, sophisticated. But there was nothing aloof about her anymore; the distance between us was gone. As everyone laughed and goofed off, we would share secret glances, whisper inside jokes that only the two of us knew. It was the inverse of being on the dance floor at the Gold Rush. That was performative; we had been showing off for the world. Here, tonight, on the shore of this tiny lake in the Montana wilderness, this was about us and only us. We formed our own private, protected space.

So later on, when we slipped into our sleeping bag as the fire crackled and the stars filled the sky, it didn't matter that other people were sleeping or talking or, yeah, even laughing at us just a few feet away. If anything, it accentuated our intimacy, because when it was the two of us, together, just me and Jo-ann—nothing else mattered.

As our bodies pressed together, everything Beave and all my buddies had ever told me—all the freaky wisdom, all the knees and rolling nipples—it all slipped away. I forgot everything else and just listened to her body, responded to her energy as I touched her.

We didn't have sex, but we didn't need to. I felt a clear conduit open up between us. Felt her tremble and release and sigh without a sound. And then . . .

Holy.

Shit.

Did she just have an orgasm?

I was in high school. I had no damn idea. But whatever it was, it was the greatest thing I'd ever experienced in my life.

The next day I gave her my mom's ring. I knew I would never ask for it back.

· · · · ·

My fingers play across the piano keys in my living room, improvising something happy, because Jo-ann likes happy.

"Reggie," she says from somewhere in the dark, "tell me a secret."

"A secret," I say, considering. "Okay. You know that amazing show *Battlestar Galactica*?"

"No."

"Well, all the Cylons in the show, those aren't *actually* robots. They're just *people* wearing *costumes*. Crazy, right?"

I can sense her smile. This is what I always do. Use humor, jokes, to distract, to avoid uncomfortable questions about myself. Questions I'm not even sure I know the answers to. But Jo-ann knows me too well to give up so easily.

"You know what I mean. Tell me a *real* secret. Something about yourself you've never shared with anyone else. Something you could only ever tell me."

My fingers keep playing. My mind spins as my music wraps itself around us, pulling us closer and closer together. Do I trust her? Am I really safe in this woman's hands?

• • • • •

BAH-BFT! BAH-BFT BAH-TSHH!

• • • • •

It was the Wednesday after the camping trip. Totally normal Wednesday.

That night, I had a few people over at my house. Our entire extended family of weirdos had crammed their cars in my driveway or on the front curb. We were hanging out in my backyard, gathering around the cast-iron patio table or smoking a little by the big pine tree. The only ones we were waiting on were Beave and the girls, who he'd pick up on his way over as usual.

"Hey, Reg."

I turned away from my conversation. It was Beave. I could sense something was off. He was usually larger and louder than life, squeezing a hundred words into every breath, brimming over with energy and action. But now he seemed quiet, even somber. He was avoiding eye contact.

"Hey, man," I said. I smiled at Lucy, who was standing next to him, but she looked away. "Where's Jo-ann?"

"Yeah," he said, hesitating. "Jo-ann wants to talk to you."

I didn't see the problem.

"Cool. I'm right here."

"Not here," he said. "In my car."

Suddenly the whole group was silent. It felt like they were all in on some crucial piece of information, and I was the only one who didn't know. Why would no one look at me?

"Oh," I said. "Really."

I put my hands in my pockets and slouched my way to the front of the house. Jo-ann was sitting in the back seat of Beave's car. I got in the other side. The thing was so damn wide that even though I was technically right next to her, it felt like we were miles apart.

"Hey," I said.

"Hello," she said in her sophisticated accent. She was staring out the other window. What was it with people and eye contact tonight?

"So, um, Beave said you wanted to talk."

"Yeah. I want to break with you."

Break with me? What the hell was that? Some kind of weird Britishism? Finally she looked me in the eye. And once she did, I understood why no one else had.

"Oh," I said. "You mean break up with me."

She kind of shrugged. "Yeah."

"Why?"

"I don't know, all right? I just do."

"I don't—I don't understand," I said. My mind was reeling. "Is this because of something at the camping trip? Something I did? Something I said? What happened? What changed?"

"Look," she said, "I'm just going to find my sister, all right?"

"What?"

"I just want to go home."

And that was it. It was over. She got out of the Monte Carlo and went to get Lucy. I got out of the Monte Carlo and started to cry.

Let's be perfectly clear about this, okay? When I say "cry," I don't mean some dignified, manly tear tracing a solitary path down my solemn cheek. No, I mean I straight-up fucking lost it.

We're talking fluids *pouring* from my face, tears from my eyes, snot from my nose—*crying, I'm crying right now, so this is what it feels like to*—gasping for breath, eyes red, body trembling, just "*gah-gah-gaaaaah!*" emo bawling. I didn't know where I was, I didn't know what I was doing, but somehow, someway I ended up in my backyard again. Everyone was staring at me, but did I care if all my buddies saw me as this quivering wreck of a human being? Hell no!

The only thing that mattered was that this entire reality I had built—we had built—over the last five months had just exploded in a matter of six simple words. *I want to break with you.* I still couldn't wrap my head around that bizarre phrase. Yeah, I wasn't English, but I watched English shows. All of them! Holmes never said *I want to break with you.* Marple never said *I want to break with you.* James Bond definitely never said *I want to break with you.*

If she was going to get it wrong, she could've at least just cut to the chase. *I want to break* **you**. Because that's what she did. She broke me.

I had opened myself up to Jo-ann in a way I never had with anyone ever before. I'd let down my guard, allowed myself to be vulnerable. I had given her every atom of my being, physically and emotionally. I had gone beyond the surface romance I had always craved, and I'd fully invested. For me, it had been real.

But here's what made it even more devastating. I thought it had been real for her too.

I thought it was the two of us against the world, yin and yang, holding nothing back, revealing all, together forever, in love forever—or apparently until a random Wednesday night in the back seat of a lime-green '78 Monte Carlo.

Maybe that closeness was the problem, I reasoned. Maybe she'd gotten scared because she'd made herself too vulnerable, too exposed. Maybe she simply couldn't handle the intensity of her feelings for me. The incredible intimacy we'd experienced that night in the sleeping bag. Maybe for her it had gotten *too real*.

Yes, that had to be it, I thought through my sobs. To believe anything else meant to believe that everything I'd experienced, everything I'd felt, was bullshit. And if that had been bullshit, then what was the point? If it was all meaningless, all simply a game, if love really was nothing more than surface fantasies of fancy meals and far-off adventures with impeccable manners, why should I truly be myself with any woman ever again?

I had to believe Jo-ann felt it too. Had to.

· · · · ·

A few days later Beave came by to see how I was doing. Lucy was with him.

In my haze of tears and grief, one thing had occurred to me shortly after Jo-ann had left my house for the last time. My mother's ring. Jo-ann still had it. Should I let her keep it? As a token of everything we had felt for each other, everything we'd experienced together? Or should I honor my mom's wish and ask for it back?

It was her favorite ring, after all. I had made a promise, and I knew the French redheaded fury that awaited me if I didn't get it back. Whatever emotions Jo-ann and I might attach to it, maybe getting it back was the right thing to do. Maybe.

"Hey, Lucy," I said, clearing my throat. "Um, before you go . . . I don't want to be insensitive or something, but you know that ring I gave Jo-ann? That belongs to my mom. Do you think she'd mind if I could get it back?"

Lucy looked at Beave. He sighed.

"Reggie," she said. "Jo-ann has an entire box full of rings that boys have given her. Honestly, I don't know if she could even find yours."

I opened my mouth, but for the first time in my life I had no words. Not English, not French, not a syllable. The ring that I thought meant so much . . . it was nothing more than a cheap trophy to her. I was just another conquest.

"Sorry, Reg," Beave said, patting me on the back. "Love hurts, right?"

"Yeah," I said as they walked to his car. "Right."

This time, I didn't shed a tear.

chapter nineteen

INTERMISSION

Wouldn't it be cool if movie theaters started doing intermissions again? Like, why did those stop? You've got the sick velvet curtains coming down, maybe some corny lounge music playing in the background. A chance for everyone to stretch their legs, buy some popcorn with extra butter, and exchange important viewpoints about the movie so far, plus hopes and expectations for the future.

"Andie *better not* end up with Duckie."

"I bet under all Allison's mascara there's a Claire just waiting to burst out!"

"I really think Principal Rooney is misunderstood."

Who knows? Maybe if theaters re-embraced the intermission—like, cut right in the middle of a super-suspenseful moment and said, "Sorry, suckers! Time for the bathroom!"—then going to see movies would become relevant again? I sure hope so.

Maybe we can start a movement, right here, right now, with my book. Just me and you. So go ahead, get up, stretch those legs, go number one—or number three—and enjoy this soothing intermission theme music I've created for you.

And if you hear the doorbell ring, that's me dropping off the bag of popcorn with butter in the middle and also on top. You're welcome.

No . . . um . . . that wasn't serious. I'm not actually at your door right now. I'm actually in a small yurt in the Himalayas, typing away on this manuscript, listening to the Eurythmics, and sipping a matcha latte. So if you do hear a knock or whatever, before you answer the door please be sure it's not a serial killer. Even if they happen to be holding popcorn.

Thank you. Carry on.

chapter twenty
ONE GUY DOING STUFF

I was standing in our high school's theater, scanning the list of performance categories I could try out.

"How about comedic solo?" I asked the instructor, Mrs. Thiel. She had bright red hair, a different shade from my mom's, but it struck me as being very bold and artistic.

"Absolutely!" she said. "Is there a reason you're interested in humor?"

"Well," I said. "I do love Monty Python."

"Fantastic. There are so many humorous monologues you could perform, including from Monty Python."

"Uh, yeah," I said sheepishly. "I'm terrible at memorizing. Is there something I could do where I just kind of show up and do my thing?"

Improv comedy would go on to be a foundation of my entire life—as a performer, as an artist, as a human being. Its quirky laissez-faire style even influences the way I interact with people socially. And it all started because I had zero interest in learning any lines.

I wasn't a genius; I was just lazy.

It was my junior year, and I had just decided to try the theater program for the very first time. I'd always loved performing, being in front of a crowd. I loved taking care of my audience, knowing they were having a good time, whether it was playing my piano in a recital or playing violin for the school orchestra. My goal was never to win people over, not exactly. It was more about achieving that synchronicity, about connecting. Back in the fourth grade, I even devised a scheme to act in front of the whole school at Chief Joseph Elementary.

I had set a meeting with our principal, the same man who had once paddled me for insubordination. Sat down across from him with a few of my friends as he peered at us curiously from behind his big desk, and I looked him right in the eye.

"Sir," I said, "we'd like to perform a sketch for the school. About the dangers of doing drugs."

I was ten years old. I didn't know about drugs, I didn't care about drugs. But it was the early '80s, the peak of "Just Say No." Nancy Reagan was sitting on Mr. T's lap, preaching against the evils of crack, and the entire nation was caught up in antidrug hysteria. What red-blooded principal could possibly turn down my brilliant ploy for propaganda?

A few days later, we went in front of the entire school in the gymnasium and performed our masterpiece. My buddies were the vile druggies and I, of course, was the hero—the cop. I'd created an elaborate costume for myself, very authentic, with navy pants and shirt and my dad's utility belt from his job with the military police, and I ran around chasing after the goons, jumping over chairs and breaking up the dastardly sale of two ziplock bags filled with parsley and flour. For our dramatic conclusion, we stood in a line facing our classmates and shouted in unison, *"And that's why you should never use drugs!"*

Seven years later, I smoked weed on a regular basis—and I

decided to finally explore my love of theater in Great Falls High's competitive drama program.

That's right. Not just drama—*competitive* drama. When I first learned about it, my mind was instantly blown. *Competitive drama?* What the fuck did that even mean? How the hell did it work? A bunch of actors going at each other with shivs as they recited "To be, or not to be"?

But Mrs. Thiel explained it all. There were a whole bunch of different categories you could enter—dramatic solo, dramatic duo, comedic solo, comedic duo, mime. Yes, you could actually be a competitive mime. Each week the team would travel to schools across the state to compete in different tournaments. The setups typically weren't elaborate, no theaters, not even stages. It wasn't glitzy or glamorous, more like nerdy, Harvard-style speech and debate except, you know, acting. You'd just perform in a mostly empty classroom in front of a handful of adult judges and maybe some competitors from the other teams—yeah, the same people you were trying to beat were also your audience. This sounded so bizarre I had to experience it.

When it was time for my first comedic solo contest, I walked into the random classroom in the random Montana school and looked around. There were no family members to support me, no friends, no fellow post-punk oddballs. It was just me in front of these . . . strangers. Judges trying to look all judgy and official, even though they were basically community volunteers. My fellow competitors trying to look cool and relaxed even though we were all tight as hell, wondering how we'd survive our ten-minute performances. A little bit of nervous, awkward chatter, but mostly just cold, dead silence.

"Mr. Watts," a judge said to me. "We're ready for you."

I nodded, walked up to the front of the classroom, and

"ROOOOOAAAAAAR!" I snarled.

Competition rules stated that comedic solo performers were supposed to pick an existing piece, learn it, and perform it. But Mrs. Thiel let me not only create my own show, but adapt it, evolve it. Plan a few beats, perhaps, but improvise the rest as I went along. She let me do me.

And right now, "me" was a four-hundred-foot-tall Godzilla, roaring and smashing and stomping on innocent villagers as they ran from my fury.

I sensed the judges sit up straighter, my rivals' eyes open wider, the energy of the entire room shifting in a moment. They had no idea what was going on. And I loved it.

The same way I had always drawn from the different elements of my life—my Toolbox of Weird—to build my fantasy world, to shape my identity and entertain my friends, now I was drawing on those same tools to entertain my audience. Voices, accents, characters, dancing, and physical humor. Inspiration from my favorite shows, *The Carol Burnett Show*, *Mystery!*, James Bond, *Battlestar Galactica*. And the wacky surrealism I had always loved in Monty Python. I used it all, riffing on it, making it my own, a Black kid with a faux-hawk inhabiting a dozen diverging identities in a big mushy mélange.

Suddenly my Godzilla morphed into—why not?—Bill Cosby. But not even an impersonation of the real Bill Cosby, but of Eddie Murphy doing *his own* impersonation of Bill Cosby. An impersonation twice removed.

"Oh, I could use a Jell-O Pudding Pop," I said, smacking my lips and spewing absolute gibberish. "But if a pudding pop pops in the middle of a forest of poppies and no one is there to enjoy its yummy pudding poppy goodness, does the pudding pop really pop at all?"

Scattered laughter now. People were warming up, opening themselves to the experience.

I loved how immediate improv was, how in the moment. It was just me in front of a live crowd, and *anything* could happen. We imagine there being a wall between performer and audience, but improv broke that wall down completely. I could say whatever I wanted, do whatever I wanted—and they responded instantaneously. I had always been so self-aware, but for those few minutes while I was up onstage I was completely engaged, completely present. I could forget myself, leave all my inner turmoil behind. The betrayal I felt after my breakup with Jo-ann. The conflicting emotions behind my relationship with my dad. When I was improvising, all that would disappear. It was just me and the crowd, connecting in the now.

But I also loved to use that immediacy to poke fun at my natural self-awareness, breaking the fourth wall with absurd non sequiturs and interstitials. It was the ultimate irony, a perfect contradiction. I'd lose myself in my performance while calling attention to the inherent absurdity of that very performance. *You, right now, are watching me as I talk to you about watching me, and we are both pretending that this reality—this stage, these props, this monologue—is actually real, and not simply a construct. A simulation of our own making. And isn't that just fucking silly?*

Suddenly, in the middle of riffing on pudding pops and whether I was really Bill Cosby or Eddie Murphy or Reggie Watts, I realized my tighty-whitie underwear was poking out the top of my khaki pants. Annoyed, I reached down and started tugging at the elastic band, harder and harder, stretching it, straining at it, gasping and gagging, until finally it tore away.

I held up my shredded Fruit of the Looms for the crowd,

stunned, humiliated, shocked—though I shouldn't have been, because I'd prepped and cut my drawers with scissors in advance.

The audience exploded with laughter. Nothing with me was what it seemed, all the way down to my tighty-whities. Honestly, I can't tell you if I won that day or placed dead last. But one thing was certain—I had a passion for being up onstage.

And I never wanted to leave.

· · · · ·

The band was all assembled in Beave's garage on the outskirts of town. Electric guitars, bass, drums, all the instruments we'd always seen on MTV were now in our own sweaty adolescent hands.

Our amps were plugged in, and I was sitting behind the electric keyboard, foot poised on the effects pedal. There were a bunch of tools hanging from the walls—handsaws, mallets, ratchets—and an old TV sat broken on a shelf. Girls from around the neighborhood were hanging out, watching us and smoking cigarettes, everyone trying to look both cool and disinterested all at the same time.

Doug Smith, our lead guitar player, put his foot up on a stool and called out authoritatively, "All right, let's take it from the bridge again!"

Hell yeah. I'd always wanted to "take it from the bridge again."

When I first began doing improv my junior year of high school, music was one element that was completely missing; I wouldn't try fusing beats and melodies and loop machines with comedy until years later. But music was always present in my life, always running parallel to everything I did creatively.

This was the late '80s, right on the cusp of the grunge era, and Great Falls was just a few hours from Seattle. Rock was evolving, everyone was experimenting, sound was changing. I'd always soaked up the different bands in my orbit—from hair bands like Whitesnake when I was a kid, to Jon Thomas music like the Smiths when I was in junior high, to post-punk like the Cure, and dark wave like Bauhaus when I hit high school. Different phases of rock had provided the soundtrack to my life and helped shape my identity.

Now I was actually going to play rock music myself. So of course I had to join a garage band. And of course we had to be called Autumn Asylum.

And by "of course" I mean I have no idea why we were called Autumn Asylum.

It had all started like so much in my life—serendipitously, as if I was fortunate enough to live in the ideal Reggie Watts Simulation. I was hanging out at Nicholls Music on Central Ave near Sixth Street North, checking out all the latest synthesizers in their basement showroom, and I began to play the bassline from the Cure's "Just Like Heaven." Then out of nowhere from the other side of the room I hear the guitar part join in with me, and there was Doug Smith with his long, crazy, beautiful brown hair playing his black Gibson Les Paul, and we hit it off and decided to start a band.

Doug played guitar; I was keyboard, bass, and vocals; a guy named Joel was drums and vocals; and another guy named Dave played guitar and knew a dude who knew a guy who had a studio downtown, and Beave let us rehearse in his garage. So, yeah. Autumn Asylum.

We didn't do that much when it was all said and done, but we did enough to get a taste of all the amazing experiences a new, totally clueless band can have. One time, a popular girl who wanted to sing with us kissed Doug even though she had a boyfriend. *Sex!*

A parent accused us of ripping off the Red Hot Chili Peppers, which we didn't, but even if we did, it's like, we're a garage band in Montana. *Drama!*

We recorded a self-titled EP, had a school photographer take our photo for the brooding album cover, and performed a few U2 covers for some old-timers at the local community center. *Fame!*

But I also used the experience to start truly developing my own voice. In one sense, I mean that literally. Doug didn't just have great hair, he was also an amazing musician, and the two of us spent hours upon hours listening to two of our favorite groups—Cocteau Twins, indirectly named after the French poet and surrealist Jean Cocteau, and the Sundays, directly named after a day of the week. Both groups had incredible, expansive, experimental vocals. In fact, Cocteau Twins didn't have lyrics so much as complex phonetic sounds. And the lead singer of the Sundays, Harriet Wheeler, had a voice that was borderline ethereal. Doug and I weren't only listening, we were learning, practicing, playing along. I listened to the Sundays' album *Reading, Writing and Arithmetic* so many times I practically learned the whole thing by heart. Both of those groups challenged my preconceived notions about vocals, taught me that the voice was more than just a conveyor of words and lyrics—it was an instrument unto itself.

I also started to become a more authentic, more original writer of both music and lyrics. Before Autumn Asylum, I had usually performed other people's compositions. If I was playing the violin, I was playing classical. When I played the piano for my friends, I would riff a little, add my own take to Beethoven or Mozart or—if Beave was around—Bauhaus, but it was still other people's music. Even when I wrote songs about depressed girls pondering suicide or whatever, they were entirely derivative, me doing my best Depeche Mode impression. And of course Autumn Asylum started out by playing covers—that's a good way for a band to learn how to play together, figure each other out, get into a groove. But I also started composing stuff of my own. Stuff that wasn't derivative. Stuff that felt like me.

One night we were all hanging out, my oddball family, band members, the whole gang. We were at the graveyard we liked to frequent, and Doug Smith and I were chilling in Jon Thomas's Oldsmobile Cutlass, taking tabs of acid as Doug strummed his acoustic guitar. And outside, like a vision, Mel just seemed to appear. Our Moon Mother, my friend who sometimes felt like more, her hair so blond it was almost white, almost glowing.

We were out in the country, but right there in the middle of it all was this solitary streetlight giving off an eerie glow. Mel stood under it, her eyes closed, dancing to her own private melody, and it started to rain. Not hard, almost like a mist, just enough to magically refract the light around her, like a gleaming, golden rainbow in the dark of night.

I started to compose verses, and Doug added his guitar and lyrics of his own, and the collaboration was so seamless, so organic, it was like we were discovering this song, discovering Mel, discovering each other, as we went along.

We called our song "She Stands." There was nothing ironic or clever about it. It wasn't derivative or taken from the Red Hot Chili Peppers or Depeche Mode. It was about us, about our experience, about everything that was real and authentic about growing up in Great Falls. No one could've composed that song but us.

And it was like, *Oh*. Art can be true. Art can be pure. Art can break through the artifice that seems to mark so much of existence.

Oh.

There was a power to finding my own voice—and to finding it as part of a band, part of a collective that shared a creative sensibility. And I was about to find that same kind of strength in my very first partnership in comedy.

· · · · ·

I sit there reading my book. It's not really an important book; I found it on a table just moments earlier, and in fact I'm realizing now that it's simply a phone book, but for some reason I'm finding this phone book deeply engrossing. Flipping through one page after another after another. Scanning through the *A*'s, the *B*'s, the *C*'s.

Suddenly I look up. Sitting right across from me is another person and he also seems to be reading a book, a cookbook perhaps, and he too is deeply engrossed, and then he looks up and sees me looking at him.

"Oh, hello!" he says, startled. "I didn't see you there."

"Intriguing," I say. "I didn't see you there either."

And then I turn my head and—*fascinating!*

"Oh my God!" I say to all the people watching us. "I'm so sorry! Have you been here this whole time?"

I turn back to the gentleman reading the cookbook.

"We seem to have an audience," he says to me gravely.

"I agree," I say, suddenly remembering that the gentleman reading the cookbook is not just any gentleman, but my improv partner, Wally. "Perhaps we should put on a show."

"Yes," he says, putting down his book. "I think we should."

And that's how Wally and I would begin our act for comedic duo in competitive drama. Well, not *exactly* how we'd begin it, because Wally, just like me, loved the immediacy, the spontaneity, the sheer thrill of improv. So we adapted, evolved, changed simply for the sake of change, every single time we performed it.

That's actually how we first got to know each other. Our teacher, Mrs. Thiel, had a feeling that we would hit it off, so she suggested performing a selection from Herb Gardner's play *I'm Not Rappaport* together.

What? You mean memorize lines? No thanks.

But we formed an instant bond over our mutual, but principled, laziness. My senior year I gave up my comedic solo act and started crafting an act with my new partner.

The whole competitive drama scene in Montana was full of exceptionally talented people. I loved the crackle of chemistry between rival performers, the chance to meet new fascinating people to add to my extended family of weirdos. At one of the competitions, a girl from a competing school got up onstage in a very staid business jacket decorated with a brooch shaped like a small lizard. She began to deliver a very serious, very powerful address—then noticed the lizard pin on her shoulder and absolutely freaked the fuck out. It blew my mind. Leslie wasn't even from Great Falls, she was from Helena, but soon after that she was coming over to Beave's and hanging out with us.

But Wally was on a different level. We didn't only share a love of improv; we had the same comic sensibility. A blend of highbrow and lowbrow humor that drew a lot of inspiration from Monty Python, using characters, physical gags, and straight-up silliness to both make our audience laugh and disrupt the way they perceived the world. Were they watching a comedy show? Or were they watching two guys read? Was there really any difference? Our audience might believe that there was a concrete line between them and us, between reality and artistry, fact and fiction. But maybe, just maybe, they were wrong. Wally and I both loved using our very odd, surreal humor to show them just how wrong they were.

I'd never met someone I could connect with in precisely that way, where I felt completely open, even encouraged, to indulge all my creative impulses—the weirder the better. We'd bounce ideas off each other, build on them, open our minds to even crazier, stranger things. It was incredibly liberating and empowering.

Although our act was largely improvised, we developed an over-arching framework we used to guide our performance. That framework consisted of pods, each of which was defined by a different theme or light premise. So once we reached a pod, Wally and I would know what the given theme or premise was—for example, two guys sitting in chairs reading books—but where we took it from there was completely up to us in the moment. We just . . . did stuff.

That, in fact, was the name of our act. Two Guys Doing Stuff. I mean, what the hell else were we going to call it? It was the most accurate description of our performance.

My solo act the year before had been strong—I'd placed third in the state finals—but our two-man act was on another level. Over the course of the season we even developed a bit of a following. Well, you know—in the Montana high school competitive drama scene, anyway. Parents, friends, people who were nerdy enough to go to competitive drama tournaments across the state for fun, they all enjoyed our act. We had a freshness, a chemistry that no one had experienced before. From a competitive vantage, improv allowed us to adjust our performance based on whoever came before us. If the teams ahead of us went with dry humor, we could go slapstick. If they went super silly, we could answer with a more subtle irony. We didn't just accept the uncertainty, we throve off it.

But we kept coming in second. All year long.

We had a blood rivalry with Billings West High School. Billings is Montana's biggest city by far; their population of 115,000 is almost double that of Great Falls. Billings West was bigger than us, slicker than us, better funded than us. They'd been the dominant team in the state for five years running. They were a juggernaut. And they kept beating us, over and over again.

I'd always thought this kind of stuff only happened in movies—but this was real, this was personal. One of their coaches even had it out for Wally, who admittedly could be a little arrogant, and would actually talk shit to us before competitions to try to get in our heads. Think of it! A grown-ass man, a teacher, actually talking smack to an eighteen-year-old kid. In a competitive drama tournament. This was like Daniel-san versus Johnny Lawrence in *The Karate Kid*. Rocky versus Drago in *Rocky IV*. Or Anthony Michael Hall versus Robert Downey Jr. in *Weird Science*. I loved every second.

It all came down to the state finals in the spring of my senior year. Which were held at none other than Billings West High. Enemy turf, two hundred miles from home.

A tournament of this scale could take over an entire school because competitive drama took place at the same time as speech and debate, and there were so many different categories and so many different contests and they'd all be happening at once. We're talking classrooms spilling over with classical plays, debate teams, extemporaneous orations, gangs of rabid mimes. We're talking cutthroat creative dweebs everywhere, roaming the halls, out for blood. I gotta admit I was a little nervous.

Wally and I showed up in our assigned classroom. Just two guys there to do stuff and win a state championship. Usually the audience was pretty sparse, just a few diehards, maybe some parents, the other competitors, and the judges. But this time it was packed. Beave and

Jon Thomas and Fish were there to cheer us on. Dozens of other students and parents. And presumably, somewhere in the crowd, our three judges. The air was thick with tension, every chair was filled, a bunch of people sitting on the floor, crowding the area designated as our stage. Which excited me, because so much of the absurdism of our act was about playing to the audience, making them both laugh and a little uncomfortable, a little uncertain about what might come next.

Wally and I started out sitting across from each other, each reading whatever books we happened to find as we entered the room. Reading, reading, reading. I could feel the crowd getting antsy, restless. *What the hell are these two doing?* Then suddenly:

"Oh, hello! I didn't see you there!"

A laugh as the audience released some of that pent-up nervous energy.

"I guess we should put on a show?"

And we did well. Maybe not our best performance, maybe not enough to dethrone the Billings West powerhouse on their home field, but our audience was engaged, they laughed at the right spots, Beave and the oddballs making sure to laugh loudest, and we fed off their energy. We gave ourselves a shot. At least that's what I thought.

Wally and I left the classroom and saw our teacher, Mrs. Thiel, standing there looking concerned, her arms folded. This is not the body language you want from your coach after the biggest performance of your career.

"Guys," she said, "there's a problem. One of the judges wasn't present when you did your performance. I don't know why, but he wasn't."

"But the other two judges were there, right?" Wally said.

"Yeah," she said, "but it doesn't matter. Rules are you gotta go

When they met in Europe, my dad and mom would dance late into the night and go for long drives during the day.

ABOVE: Classic grade school yearbook photos.
I really need to find that shirt I'm wearing on the left.

COURTESY OF MEGAN MCISAAC

Cleveland, to me, represented a chance to get more in touch with the African American side of my identity. From left, that's my grandma, me, my mom, my dad, and my aunt Rowena.

I was always a maman's boy growing up.
I also had amazing taste in cardigans.

*Unless otherwise stated,
all photos are courtesy of my self, Reggie Watts.*

Me and my dad.
He was never too open
about his feelings,
but he could still exude
an incredible charisma.

My parents a few years
before my dad passed.
You can sense their dynamic here—
my mom cheerful, my dad gruff.
They never fell out of love.

My dad had a fantastic dry
sense of humor.
He was a man who loved hats,
and France.

Crashing on a road trip to Helena. That's Jon Thomas and Michelle Hult to the right. The girl to the left is a mystery, but she has a cool Ally Sheedy–meets–Molly Ringwald vibe. I'm in Duckie mode.

COURTESY OF MICHAEL BENTON

Me and Fish hanging out with some Canadian girls we met at the county market. I can't remember anything about this moment, but it captures my high school experience perfectly.

COURTESY OF MICHAEL BENTON

ABOVE: This is like an introductory photo to my character in an '80s Great Falls coming-of-age movie: "Reggie when he's wide-eyed and just starting to explore life!"

RIGHT: This is the "after" pic: "Reggie in the hazy madness of teenage absurdity." Note the (probably empty) Robo in the background.

COURTESY OF MICHELLE HULT FINSETH

Our weirdo ringleader, the infamous Mike Benton, also known as Beave. This is Beave when I first met him. Spiky blond hair, electric blue eyes, cocky and clean.

COURTESY OF MICHELLE HULT FINSETH

This is Beave after you get to know him.
Edgy.
A little dangerous.
The kind of guy who wears sunglasses indoors . . .
and almost pulls it off.

COURTESY OF MICHELLE HULT FINSETH

Senior prom. From the left, that's Fish and his date, Jon Thomas and his date, Tony, Mel, me, Beave's date, Beave, and two human beings who are probably excellent people but whose names are lost to me.

COURTESY OF MICHAEL BENTON'S MOM

This is the night Doug and I wrote "She Stands" about Mel for the first album for my first band, Autumn Asylum. I'm pretty sure the two of us were already high on acid.

COURTESY OF MICHAEL BENTON

Mel the same night we wrote "She Stands." This doesn't capture how magical she looked standing under the streetlight in the rain. But somehow it still feels right. Somehow this photo feels just right.

COURTESY OF MICHAEL BENTON

Camping with a vampire. Or is that Fish? I can't tell– the makeup is just that convincing.

COURTESY OF MICHAEL BENTON

I don't actually know if this is of Michelle Hult right after she found out what I did to her car. But if it's not, it should be.

COURTESY OF MICHELLE HULT FINSETH

I went through a big Philip Michael Thomas-in-*Miami Vice* phase in high school.

COURTESY OF MICHELLE HULT FINSETH

oy **17**

Math exam Saturday **18**
~~Saturday~~ up to
12 noon

(usic) Didn't go

11:30

work 9—6 (2-3)

Fun!

Came home & Reggie came.
I fixed my room FAST &
went to meet them at
Burger King. Went to some beetel
(w/ Pete, Melanie, Tony, Dustin, etc.)
Kind of fun. Kissed Reggie. Home at 11 pm.

FEBRUARY
S M T W T F S S M T W T F S
1 2 3 4 5 6 7 8 9 10 11
12 13 14 15 16 17 18 19 20 21 22 23 24 25
26 27 28

MARCH
S M T W T F S S M T W T F S
1 2 3 4 5 6 7 8 9 10 11
12 13 14 15 16 17 18 19 20 21 22 23 24 25
26 27 28 29 30 31

APRIL
S M T W T F S S M T W T F S
1 2 3 4 5 6 7 8
9 10 11 12 13 14 15 16 17 18 19 20 21 22
23 24 25 26 27 28 29 30

I got in touch with Ilse, and at first she didn't remember the kiss we shared. But she checked her old calendar, and here it is! I'm proud to say she told me she couldn't even tell it was my first one.

COURTESY OF ILSE

From left, that's Mel, Lucy, Beave, me, and Jo-ann, my first real girlfriend, hanging in my basement. Check out Lucy's incredibly '80s shoulder pads, and the fact that almost everyone is smoking. I can't believe I let people smoke inside!

COURTESY OF JO-ANN

Hanging in the Big Cave. Look at me with my stupid pants. They're these jeans I got visiting family in France, and they're covered in patches of tourist attractions like the Eiffel Tower. My friend is drinking a Lucky Lager. Quintessential '80s Montana.

COURTESY OF JO-ANN

Lucy, me, Beave, and Mel at the piano my dad bought for me. The candelabras and the creepy doily curtains provided a perfect setting for Bauhaus interpretations.

COURTESY OF JO-ANN

Me and Beave in Jo-ann's bedroom. Looking at her wall, I'm pretty sure every one of her posters is of Bon Jovi.

COURTESY OF JO-ANN

Me holding Jo-ann.
She was very light.
Or perhaps I was very strong.

COURTESY OF JO-ANN

Me and Jo-ann
posing before junior prom.
Except why does my mom
still have the Christmas tree up?
Embrace life's mysteries.

COURTESY OF JO-ANN

Me and Lucy, Jo-ann's sister.
I actually hugged all my good friends
like this all the time. No joke.

COURTESY OF JO-ANN

Autumn Asylum was literally
a garage band.
That's me on keyboards,
Doug sitting looking very lyrical,
and Dave standing looking very rock 'n' roll.

COURTESY OF DOUG SMITH

Fish, Beave, and me
in classic '80s photo-booth shots.

COURTESY OF MICHAEL BENTON

Me with DJ Disguise
at a Seattle house party in 2001.

COURTESY OF BRANDY WESTMORE

A little dancing
with my friend Elizabeth
and my pager at
the Scarlett Tree in Seattle.

COURTESY OF BRANDY WESTMORE

SEATTLE WEEKLY FREE

AUGUST 20–26, 2003

TOP DOG

Reggie Watts and MAKTUB win big in the
**WEEKLY'S FIRST ANNUAL
MUSIC AWARDS**

For Seattle's other favorite bands, p.10

HITS HOME
...-year-old is buried
... County.
...son p. 14

DYSFUNCT...
Can the school board
...t? p. 11

FIRE AND ...E
Upper West Side
dining at the Market p. 31

BUMBERSHOOT
Official program
pullout inside

Daniel Spils was not only Maktub's
insanely tasteful keyboardist,
he also ended up being the band's
unofficial archivist, keeping a whole stack
of our old clippings,
including this copy of *Seattle Weekly*
from twenty years ago.

MAKTUB LEAD SINGER
REGGIE WATTS

This is an even earlier press clipping of ours from the iconic Seattle music magazine *The Rocket*— four years earlier, to be precise. The style I'm going for in this photo is to really look like a somebody. Like a real person.

The Northwest Music and Entertainment Magazine
August 11-25, 1999
No. 307

FREE

TheRocket

Solid Soul

MAKTUB

The Flatirons • Shellac • Leatherboy • Captain Beefheart • WOMAD in Review • Introducing Terminal Noise

I love this photo of Heather Duby, me, and Ryan Link standing against the wall in a promotional pic for our band, Clementine. It feels so perfectly '90s. Heather took a photo of this photo and you can kind of see the reflection of her phone in the bottom right, which just makes it cooler.

COURTESY OF HEATHER DUBY

It might be worth saying that this is me and Eugene Mirman at Rififi in New York City. Then again, it might not.

COURTESY OF EUGENE MIRMAN

Hi from 2005.

My good friend Megan McIsaac is an amazing photographer who helped capture some incredible images of my mom. This is the two of us together in our backyard.

COURTESY OF MEGAN McISAAC

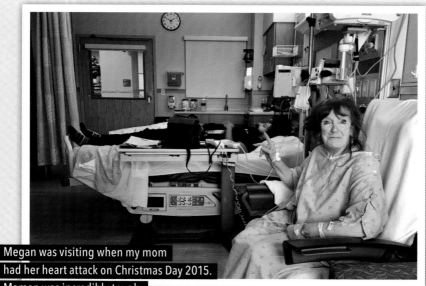

Megan was visiting when my mom had her heart attack on Christmas Day 2015. Maman was incredibly tough, and the hospital bed was pretty comfortable.

COURTESY OF MEGAN McISAAC

I'm not sure if I ever got this crucifix off my forehead.

COURTESY OF MEGAN MCISAAC

Maman and me.

COURTESY OF MEGAN MCISAAC

I also showed Megan around my old stomping grounds at Great Falls High. This is me in the choir class. Yeah, didn't last too long in this one.

COURTESY OF MEGAN McISAAC

I can't remember if Duckie made this precise pose in front of his locker in *Pretty in Pink*, but if he didn't, he should have.

COURTESY OF MEGAN McISAAC

Dear Reader,
I accept the fact that you see me as you want to see me. In the simplest terms, a brain, a failed athlete, a basket case, and a criminal. I hope I've answered some questions? Sincerely yours, the Brunch Bunch.

COURTESY OF MEGAN McISAAC

in front of three judges. You can either do your show all over again in front of all three—or you forfeit."

"This makes no sense!" I said. "Why are we being punished for the judge's mistake?"

"It's your choice," she said. "You can always forfeit."

Wally and I started to confer. The idea of performing again didn't bother me, not at all—it was the inherent unfairness of the situation. I was being told to follow a rule—a rule I didn't even break!—not for any good reason, but just because someone in charge said so. It was my biggest pet peeve. And part of me wanted to back out simply to prove I could.

Then the teacher from Billings West, Wally's nemesis, walked over with a smirk on his face.

"Might as well forfeit," he whispered. "You guys are laughing-stocks anyway."

An interesting choice of insult given that our competition was comedic duo. I turned to Wally and Mrs. Thiel.

"Okay," I said. "Let's do it."

Word of what happened spread fast. Imagine Daniel-san does his heroic one-legged crane kick, and the judges are like, "Sorry, we went out for a pop, can you run through that for us again?"

That's what this was, except real. And, well, minus any actual physical combat. But the tension was just as high. People had heard about the mistake and our second performance, and this time, the classroom was absolutely overflowing with spectators. The anticipation was crazy—people pressed against walls, kids peering through the ground-floor windows, their faces pressed against the glass. How would Wally and I respond? How would we top our initial performance? How would we get in the right headspace to do it all over again?

But in a weird way, this was the perfect scenario for Two Guys Doing Stuff. After all, we were improv. There was no such thing as "doing it all over again."

We started out, as always, sitting and reading—except this time, on a whim, Wally and I faced opposite directions. I could hear an appreciative murmur from the crowd. A lot of them had already witnessed our initial performance. They may have technically been aware that we were improvising earlier, but seeing us change and adapt in real time—that was something else.

"Wait," Wally said, looking around confused. "Where did you go?"

"Oh!" I said without turning around. "I'm over here. Looking the other way."

"But didn't we have a show to put on?"

"I thought we already did our show."

"We did, but . . . I think we're doing it again. Like, right now."

The audience lost their minds, exploded in laughter. We rocked it. Our second performance—not despite doing it over again, but *because of it*—was our greatest show of the year.

At the end of the day, the auditorium of Billings West High was electric with anticipation for the final state championship awards. Comedic duo was only one of many categories, but the earlier controversy gave it an added layer of suspense. People had dug our act, that was clear, but the Billings West team had been unstoppable for so many years, literally undefeated. The idea that they could actually lose in the biggest tournament of the season was unfathomable.

Wally and I sat there as the official stepped to the microphone to read out the winners. It almost felt like, somewhere in the ether, John Hughes himself was floating above, looking down and guiding our lives in one of his scripts.

"And the winners in the category comedic duo are . . . Wally and Reggie, Two Guys Doing Stuff, Great Falls High!"

The crowd erupted. Beave and Jon Thomas and the rest of our weirdo family jumped up and down in the stands, pumping their fists, hugging each other, howling with joy.

Wally and I walked up onstage with a swagger in our step as the whole world seemed to cheer us on. And guess who was presenting the trophy as representative of the host school? Our archrival, the coach from Billings West. Wally graciously accepted our award, grinned, and said loud enough for everyone to hear:

"Look who's laughing now."

John Hughes couldn't have written it any better.

· · · · ·

At the same time that I was exploring new parts of my creative life, another one came to a dramatic conclusion—horrific pun absolutely intended.

My junior year, I finally got kicked out of orchestra.

Orc had been one of the few constants in my life since grade school. I had once been Miss Lidiard's most promising student—well, at least in her mind. I had earned the prestigious position of first chair, second violin. And I still loved everything about the violin, the way it felt in my hands, the way it sounded. It was such a sensual instrument. I loved the friends I'd made in orc, the trips we went on, the concerts we performed in together.

But ultimately, I couldn't be the prodigy she wanted me to be. Hell, I could hardly even show up to practice on time. Although I'd worked hard enough to make first chair, second violin, I had no ambition beyond that. First chair, first violin was still held by my friend—and occasional crush—Colette, and that was fine by me.

Colette cared more than I did, she worked harder than I did, she was a flat-out better violin player than I was. I didn't get first chair, second violin because I was competing for it or because I was even really trying. It was just my natural talent, shining through again.

So I kept mouthing off, giving Miss Lidiard attitude, acting the class clown. I had the raw ability to keep up with everyone, and I enjoyed dipping my toe in the waters of classical music, swirling it around a little, sometimes even wading up to my ankles and doing a funny little dance to a minuet. But I couldn't fully immerse myself. I was a sampler of life's experiences, a connoisseur—trying football, trying school government, trying on suspenders and a pencil-thin mustache—but I hated to commit. To give all of myself to anything.

In a sense, I was almost asking to get kicked out all those years. But Miss Lidiard gave me one extra chance after another, no matter what I did. Another instructor, though, wasn't as forgiving.

The choir director, Mr. Ritter, didn't find my jokes charming, and he wasn't amused by all my goofing off. He thought I was a punk who used my talent to get away with shit other kids wouldn't dream of trying. And you know what? He was right. I *was* a punk. But I was a very fun punk, and that should've counted for something. Instead, I drove this guy nuts. He looked exactly how you'd expect a curmudgeonly teacher to look—medium build, thick black beard, wore a lot of sweaters. I liked to think of him as my own Mr. Rooney from *Ferris Bueller's Day Off*, an adult nemesis spending his nights deviously plotting all the different ways he would finally get even with that pesky Reggie Watts.

Well, I finally gave him his chance, and it wasn't even all that diabolical. Orchestra and choir were collaborating on a big concert in Billings . . . and yeah, I forgot my violin. Which, you know, was kind of inconvenient for a violin player. Miss Lidiard let me borrow hers, but Mr. Ritter saw his chance. He'd been lobbying for my dismissal for months, but Miss Lidiard had always protected me. But this was the last straw. Mr. Ritter used my latest monumental screwup to finally get me expelled from orchestra.

I hadn't lost all my performing opportunities, of course. I still played piano for my friends at home. I still had competitive drama, and of course there was Autumn Asylum. But orchestra had always been there for me, through all my phases and fads, through all my social experiments and hairstyles. I had taken it for granted, perhaps, but it had still been a part of my life. An institution that had grounded me personally and creatively. And now it was gone.

On the last day of my junior year, I was celebrating in the halls of Great Falls High just like everyone else. People dumping out their lockers, papers and books flying everywhere, stuff all over the floor. It had been a good year but a long year. Once I'd joined my oddball family, my grades had gone to shit, I'd started talking back to my teachers all the time, and I'd served multiple in-house suspensions. The dean had already warned me that if I got suspended one more time I'd have to go to summer school. But I was determined to make it out clean. To start my summer vacation and embrace a fresh, broad canvas on which to paint new chaos.

Then suddenly from right behind me I hear:

"Pick it up."

I turn around and there's Mr. Ritter, staring at me.

"Seriously?" I said. "*Everyone* is throwing paper! Why are you picking on *me?*"

"Goddammit," he said, getting right in my face. "Do what I say! Pick it up!"

Something inside me snapped.

Reggie Watts, always a lover, never a fighter, very rarely given to referring to himself in the third person, grabbed Mr. Ritter and shoved him into the lockers. Hard.

Mr. Ritter came right back at me, but luckily by that point—I have no idea how he got there so fast—the dean got between us.

"Break it up! Just break it up!"

The dean pointed at Mr. Ritter to stay put and told me to go to his office. I couldn't believe it—I had been *so close* to a summer of hard-earned hedonism, mere minutes away, but now my dreams of self-indulgent bliss were hanging in the balance. And why? Every other student was running for the exits, paper was everywhere, and no one was picking up a damn thing. But here I was, stuck going to the dean's office after shoving a teacher who—as far as I was concerned—totally deserved what he had coming.

Motherfucker. What is this going to mean? Summer school? No break at all? Why the hell did I let that asshole get to me like that?

I sat down in front of the dean's desk and waited, watching the minutes tick by on the wall clock. Finally he walked in, sat down at his desk, and looked me in the eye.

"Have a good summer."

That was all I needed to hear. Best I could guess, the dean talked to Mr. Ritter and other students and realized his employee was as much at fault as I was. Or maybe the dean was just as desperate to go on vacation as all the rest of us. I really didn't care.

Summer was about to begin. And shit was gonna get crazy.

chapter twenty-one

THE REGGIE WATTS COMPREHENSIVE GLOSSARY

Throve? Thrived? Thriven? Throof?

Most people may have noticed my unorthodox use of *throve* as the simple past tense of the word *thrive* in the preceding chapter, as opposed to the much more common *thrived*. Some people may not have noticed it. Those latter people may, like me, be rabid Anglophiles who spiritually inhabit a space inside nineteenth-century English diction.

And that's all right.

Either way, I assure you that it, and all the words I have used in my book, are syntactically, grammatically, and esoterically correct, inasmuch and insofar as they exist within the context of my own mind as well as the universe, digital or wood pulp or otherwise, of these pages.

To assist in unraveling the complex strands of any further confusion over my choice of vocabulary, I have helpfully included a complete glossary at the conclusion of this book—indeed, is any book seriously considered a serious book without an exhaustive glossary at the conclusion? *[Chortles pompously.]* I think not—for your personal verbal edification. Feel free to use it for all of your linguistic needs, oral or written or otherwise, on condition of attribution to Reginald Lucien Watts, Esq., author and scrivener.

Thank you, and carry on.

chapter twenty-two

USING UP THE ADVENTURE

"Hurry up, man!" I yelled. "I don't want to get busted!"

Jon Thomas and I had just swiped two industrial-sized fire extinguishers from the ground floor of the Sheraton Hotel, and we were stumbling back to the car as fast as we could go.

"This shit is heavier than it looks!"

We crammed the giant tanks into the tiny back seat, into the waiting hands of Chris, Joe D., and Travis, our accomplices. All five of us were high off our asses on Robitussin, because that's generally what happens when you chug four to six ounces of Robitussin. Joe had already puked once, because that's what happens when you chug seven.

A buddy of mine described the Robo high as being a marshmallow on acid, and at this exact moment, as I get behind the wheel of my friend Michelle Hult's blue '71 Corolla—I have *no* idea why she let me borrow this car—I have to say that's a pretty accurate description. It acts as a dissociative, which means that my already insane level of self-awareness is now supercharged. My thoughts are moving faster than the *Millennium Falcon* blasting into hyperspace—

Luke! Pull up, you're headed straight for—
*AHHHHHHHHHH!—**BOOM!!!***

—but the world around me has slowed to a crawl. So I'm analyzing it, processing it, acutely aware of life and being and reality and

I am sitting in a chair right now. Isn't that ridiculous? This chair is supporting my entire body, which is in this car, which is on the pavement, which is on the dirt, which is on the

Jon slides into the vinyl passenger seat—*SQUEAK!*—I hit the gas—*VROOM!*—the wheels spin—*SCREEEECH!*—and we peel out into the streets.

I have lived in this town for thirteen years.

In a sense, this town is me, and I am this town, which means that I am currently driving on

myself.

"Ram it through!" Jon says. "Come on!"

Giggling maniacally, our friends in the back squeeze the fire extinguishers' nozzles through the cracked rear windows. We have a plan, a very good plan.

As we speed through town, we're gonna pull the triggers and unleash a *tornado* of smoke and haze in our wake, covering cars, covering trees, covering anything that gets in our way. Chaos will reign, confusion will triumph, we will be masters of the night. We will create our very own James Bond–style smoke screen, and it'll be awesome, and I may in fact *be* James Bond.

Pleasure to make your acquaintance, Miss Galore. Shall we slip into something more . . . comfortable?

"On my mark!"

"Get set!"

Then all at once, simultaneously, magically, we all scream together:

"GO!"

We spray the fire extinguishers as we race down the street. And it fucking works.

Our beautiful, gorgeous, billowing smoke screen spews into the night air behind us, swirling and twisting and turning, and my thoughts, my memories, the history of my entire existence in this town seem to swirl and twist and turn with it . . .

My eyes are blurry with tears as I tell my mom what our neighbor called me, the word that starts with an *n* that I don't know what it means but I know it's meant to hurt me.

Oh, we just passed Central Avenue West.

I pick up my very first violin, feel the wood against my skin, smell the rosin on the bow, and I start to play. It just feels . . . right.

There goes McDonald's.

I bounce on the trampoline higher and higher past her startled face.
"Hey!
Jo-ann!
I!
Love!
You!"

That's where the old smokestack was. Can't believe they tore it down!

My dad's belt is curled in his hand. He raises it to strike me,
but my mom pushes between us.
"Go now," she tells my dad. "Just leave."
And he does.

The next thing I know, another car pulls ahead of us. An interloper. A trespasser on our night of glorious mayhem.

It's Marlise Forchers. A popular girl. Gorgeous, blond, bangs six inches long. She's in a sporty two-seater with an equally popular friend. They turn into the parking lot of a Target, a block ahead of us, and it hits me. I know what we have to do.

"Let's go smoke screen them!"

"Yeah!"

I floor it—*VVVROOOOM!*—my friend Michelle's '71 Corolla lurches forward—dear God why did she let me borrow it??—and I swerve into the lot—*SCREEEEEEEECH!*

We're getting closer, closer. Just a few feet more and we can douse the popular girls and their fun little car in our mighty smoke.

Shit, I can taste it like the Robitussin in the back of my throat! *Come on!*

"Look out!" Jon Thomas shouts.

"I can make it!"

"LOOK OUT!"

Yeah. So I don't look out.

KRATTA-KA-SMASH!

The car's left wheels slam into a large concrete parking divider.

These things reach a foot and a half off the ground; they're basically big, sharp speedbumps. But at full speed in an old Toyota?

LUKE, LUKE!
I slam on the brakes
DEATH STAR!
the fire extinguishers explode
LASER BLASTS!
the car fills with fog, my friends and I are covered in this crap that's like baking soda, at the top of our lungs we

AIIIIIIIIIIIIIIIIIIIII!

And the Corolla—which now only has two functioning wheels because the other two have been obliterated—rattles to a halt in a cloud of haze. Wrecked.

The two popular girls in their fun little sports car drive right by, laughing their asses off. Jon Thomas squints at me through the powder caked on his face.

"You. Are. So. Dead."

My heart is racing. My head is spinning. I am oddity and passion and experimenting and risk.

I am a marshmallow on acid.

• • • • •

Yeah, so, after my breakup with Jo-ann, life started to get a little . . . wild.

Although, rest assured, I did not just leave my friend Michelle's car trashed. That same night, we found another car, jacked it up, and stole two wheels, which we then used to replace the two destroyed wheels on Michelle's car. Granted, whoever we stole the wheels from now needed to find two new wheels, but Michelle's car? Totally cool. Um, except for all the fire-extinguisher crap on the interior, which we more or less vaguely cleaned up. Kind of.

So! Yeah! All good. Really.

It was 1989, the summer after my junior year. The teachers and the school couldn't agree on a new employment contract, so we ended up getting an extra month's vacation. It was an interesting time to have a lot more free time. What started out as fun eventually grew darker, and marked the beginning of a slow downward spiral.

Who knows exactly what sparked it. Maybe I was trying to fill the void I felt after I lost Jo-ann. If what I lost wasn't true love, it was at least the idea of true love, the wide-eyed romanticism that had fueled me for so long. Maybe I was finally feeling the absence of my dad, testing the limits of what I could get away with, trying to see how far I could rebel without suffering any consequences. Or maybe I was just a little tired of Great Falls. When I was younger this town had pushed me, challenged me—and given me and my imagination room to thrive. To become truly unique. But the older I got, the more I dreamed not only of new realities and perspectives, but of new cities, new states, new places to explore. Maybe somewhere deep inside me I knew it was almost time to move on.

Whatever it was, when I reached seventeen, my life took a turn. I was still hanging out with my family of weirdos—Beave and Fish and Mel and Jon Thomas and the rest—but I started hanging with another crowd too, a crowd that was more into drugs, that wanted to break both rules and some laws too. I started experimenting with pretty much anything I could get my hands on—acid, Freon, Robitussin. Especially Robo. I quickly earned a rep as the only member of my gang who could down more than four ounces of Robo without getting sick, but no one should've been surprised. I was doing so much of it that I built up an amazing tolerance, spending almost every weekend buzzed out of my mind, soaking up all the dissociative effects, walking through life like I was on the outside looking in.

Now, don't get me wrong. I maintained important guardrails too. Internal rules I devised to make sure that even as we got crazy we never got *too* crazy, especially the younger kids who were hanging out with us. During the school year, there were no drugs allowed before or during class, only at night or on weekends. We never went to school high. In fact, I never missed school at all. My attendance record was perfect. Sure, my grades were trash, I got in trouble constantly, and a lot of my time there was spent serving in-school detention, but still—perfect attendance!

Robo isn't exactly a hard drug either. This is a "Judd Nelson in *The Breakfast Club*" drug, not a "Robert Downey Jr. in *Less Than Zero*" drug, right? Like, usually we'd get stoned and go to the caves or cemetery or swing on a swing set and stare at the night sky. Or one time we were camping out near a massive dweeb—that's what we'd call buttes, because we were high and it made sense—and we were hunting for Sasquatch—because we were high and it made sense—and I swear we saw a UFO.

We were hiking across a valley that felt almost as big and vast as the sky above. Cattle were grazing all around us, and far in the distance we could see the dweeb—I *swear* it made sense—like a broad, rocky tree stump on the horizon. And then we saw them. Three lights that were hovering really close to the ground, like *impossibly* close to the ground, just kind of moving from right to left, then they separated from each other, then at a certain point one of them stopped, and a beam of light appeared under it, and then turned off, and then it moved again. And I was like, "What the fuck am I watching right now!!" and we were high, but Robo isn't a hallucinogenic, you know? So it doesn't make you see things that aren't *really there*, it's a totally different kind of high. So, I mean, you try to explain that phenomenon using entirely terrestrial means, okay? Seriously, explain it. *You can't!* Hence, UFO.

And yeah, we would also go on joyrides and steal shit.

But a lot of the laws I broke were barely even at the "Judd Nelson in *The Breakfast Club*" level, at least not initially. And yes, the Brat Pack is the ultimate moral metaphor, and I highly encourage you to reference them at least four times a day for various purposes.

It's true, as you may recall, that inside an unlocked pickup truck I found a decorative Polynesian-style box, an empty coke vial, and a giant brick of weed, and that Beave and I proceeded to sell the weed to friends and acquaintances over the next several months and make lots of money doing it. And that might sound not great. But think about it. Whose fault was it that the pickup-truck drug dealer left his truck unlocked in the first place? Okay, fine. So the doors *were* locked. And there was a custom car alarm. But the truck's rear sliding window was definitely open. A crack. And the wires on the custom car alarm were super easy to cut. But was any of that *my* fault? Does that really even *count* as breaking in? Debatable, at best.

It's also true that some friends and I "broke into" a few cars simply to steal the cars themselves. Again, that might not sound so great. But who was really hurt in the process? We'd just drive the cars around awhile and then park them exactly where we found them, making sure to lock the doors behind us, because it was the polite thing to do. Once we took an old truck to a dweeb—again, high and it made sense—where we planned to douse it with gasoline and send it off the edge, just to see what it looked like when an old truck doused in gasoline went flying off a cliff. Got a brick to hold the pedal down and everything. But we called it off at the last minute, so, you know, no harm, no foul. Another time, we stole a car, took it for a joyride, and then actually filled up the tank when we were done. So, honestly, if I'm the owner, I'm seeing that gas gauge on F and thinking, "Hey, these guys who stole my car did me a favor."

But over time, the acts of rebellion gradually began to take on a darker tone. For real.

Sometime during my senior year, a couple of friends and I formed a criminal organization we called "Threat." Which sounds kind of silly and only gets sillier when I tell you that we officially inaugurated our group by driving late at night to the park at Ryan's Dam, where we climbed over the big security fence topped with barbed wire all so we could carve the word *threat* into a picnic table. (Google just told me it's technically named "Ryan Dam," but we all grew up calling it Ryan's Dam, and what exactly is a Ryan Dam anyway? A dam made out of Ryan? I refuse to let the internet or actual facts ruin my childhood.)

But as silly as it all might sound, Threat actually ended up partaking in some pretty illegal stuff. So illegal, in fact, that as I sit here typing this, I'm actually having an internal dialogue between my two opposing selves that's going something like this:

*What do you think, self? Is this something
I really want to share with the world?*

*I don't know, self. What's the worst that could happen?
Like, going to jail? Hahahaha.*

Ummm. That wasn't very funny, self.

*Come on, self. It's a big book!
No one will even notice one little story!*

*Totally. That's why I **love** setting it off
with this internal dialogue.*

184

Hey, at least we got to have fun with italics!

Ultimately, myself won the argument. Lucky me. But to keep myself happy, I'm going to alter some identifying details, and have Her Majesty's Secret Service make key redactions, classic James Bond–style.

Through ████████████, we found out that a house on the other side of town was going to be empty one weekend. And we just happened to know that the owners of this house, ██████████ █████████, also owned a lot of guns. Like, a *lot* of them.

Now, did we actually need these guns for any reason? Absolutely not. We didn't even want to shoot them. Just take them and hide them, that was it. But there was something about robbing a big cache of weapons that seemed very exciting at the time. Like something out of one of my James Bond movies.

We were gonna plan a *heist*. With diagrams and synchronized watches and subtle hand signals to let each other know the coast was clear, and it was gonna be awesome.

And it pretty much was.

We drove over in the middle of the night and parked a few blocks away. We knew from our sources that keys to the house were hidden in the ████████████, so we had easy access. We snuck inside, and the guns were stored in the ████████████ exactly like we'd been told. This arsenal was like shit out of a *20/20* Pablo Escobar exposé. There were two ████████████, a couple of ████████, a few ████████████, one ████████████████, and one ████████, which I took for myself and actually sawed off a few weeks later just for fun.

We loaded up, locked the door behind us, and then in an absolute stroke of genius we actually ████████████████████████ ████████ to make it look like someone had broken in and it wasn't an inside job. All those years of watching Poirot and Miss Marple finally paid off.

It went off without a hitch. Now we were not only a criminal enterprise with our name carved on a picnic table, we were a criminal enterprise with weapons. Weapons we would never, ever use, but still—weapons.

Most important of all, we were invincible. We never got caught for the break-in. And I was sure that no matter what I did, no matter how many rules I broke or how far I went, I never would.

· · · · ·

It was the last day of my senior year. I was moments away from that final bell, from joyous, orgasmic freedom.

There was just one problem. I had no idea if I would graduate.

My grades had gotten so bad that I was right on the verge of flunking my English lit class. That's right, the guy writing the book you're reading right now was about to flunk senior English. I mean, I'm cool with the language and all. I simply never turned in my homework.

My teacher had given me one last chance to turn in a makeup paper to bring me up above an F. I handed it in with a couple days to go in the semester, then the dude just sat on it. Like, I finally do a single assignment, and the man won't read it. How dare he?

I raced around at the end of the last day, hunting for my teacher, trying to find out if I would graduate on time. I finally spotted him.

"Well?" I demanded. *"Well?"*

He cracked open this old-school laptop he had with him—the thing was bigger than a suitcase—and quickly scanned his files. He sighed.

"You passed," he said, "by a few tenths of a percent."

"NO. WAY!" I screamed. "WOOOOOO!"

But I didn't have long to celebrate. Because I finally got caught.

A month before the end of the school year, I had pushed the limits yet again. This time it was a simple crime of opportunity. I was out grocery shopping with my mom one day, and I noticed an unlocked car in the parking lot. Took a quick look inside and just happened to find a checkbook. Didn't even take the whole book, only a single check from the very end, hoping the owner would never even notice.

Then I thought, you know . . . I could really use a new CD player. So I made out the check to a local electronics store—making sure to disguise my handwriting, the smooth criminal that I was— and went in, telling the clerk that a buddy of mine had sent me to purchase a stereo on his behalf. The clerk went for it, and I got my CD player. Easy!

And stupid. When I'd walked into the store, I'd realized the clerk was a kid from my high school. Not a close friend, but someone I definitely knew, and he definitely knew me. This had triggered a momentary burst of concern in my adolescent brain: *Hmm. Maybe not such a great idea.* Which was quickly followed by the teenager's answer to everything: *Whatever, who cares.*

My earlier thefts had been, at least in my mind, basically victimless. We stole cars, but we gave them back. We ripped off a drug dealer. We took a bunch of guns from people who probably shouldn't have had them in the first place. No one was going to go to the cops about stolen drugs and illegal weapons. But this time I was straight-up stealing someone else's money. Probably a normal, law-abiding individual who got really, really pissed off when they realized one of their checks had been used to buy a stereo. Honestly, though, I didn't even give it much thought. I was just being a selfish kid.

Then, a few days after I got the stereo, I was walking through the halls at school when I saw the clerk from the electronics store.

"Um, hey, man," he said kind of sheepishly. "I just wanted to let you know that the cops came in asking about that check, and I didn't want to get busted, so I told them it was you. I'm sorry."

"Oh," I said. "It's cool, you don't have to apologize. It's my fault." And it was.

A week into my new life as a high school grad, I was at home when I got a call. It was the police, asking me to come down to the station to have a little talk. Thank God my mom wasn't there when they called. Jesus, what a mess.

Before the interview, I developed an entire strategy—again, all those British mysteries and cop shows really paying off. I memorized a detailed story with multiple layers so that the more questions they asked me, the more information I'd have to give them. I practiced the looks I would give—confused, contrite, anxious—and how and when I would give them. I'd always used my hyper-self-awareness to strategically fine-tune my behavior in certain social situations. *If I do X, this person will react by doing Y. If I do Z, I'll get exactly the response I want.* Sometimes to stand out by using my goofy humor, but other times to blend in, to be the most harmless person in the room, loose, relaxed, naturalistic. Like a superspy.

That's what I did when I walked into that interview room at the police station.

I told the detective that I'd been riding my bike in the electronics store's parking lot when a jetter—local lingo for "air force pilot"—had pulled up in a red Nissan 300ZX sports car. He'd rolled down his window and pointed down at a cast on his left foot. His left foot, not his right. It was hard for him to walk, he said, so he was wondering if I could go in the store and get the stereo for him. And here was the check I could use, and he'd give me twenty dollars for my trouble. So that's what I did—used the check he gave me, got the stereo, and collected my twenty bucks.

Just like I had planned, I held back on some of the details—the make of the car, for example—so that as he grilled me, I'd always have an answer. As I walked into the interview, I clocked a camera in the corner, making sure to only glance at it once, superfast, and I knew that when the detective walked out he'd be watching me, checking to see how I was responding. That was when I used my looks, that was when I became a superspy.

I sat at the table by myself, shaking my head, rubbing my eyes, and mumbling loud enough for any mics to pick up, "I can't believe this is happening! I knew I shouldn't have trusted that guy! I should've known I'd get into trouble! Man!"

After what felt like forever, the detective finally came back in. He said I was free to go for now, but not to leave town.

Despite all my bravado, I was scared shitless. The enormity of all my illegal activities from the past year finally started weighing on me. I was in the clear for now, but the cops could be back any day, any second! What if they searched the house? I had one of the stolen guns hidden in my closet, and there was no way I could ditch it now that I was under suspicion. What if the police found it? What if my mom found out? What if the detective somehow poked a hole in my story and I ended up getting charged or fined or maybe even going to jail? I had always throve—thrived? thriven? thraft?—off uncertainty, but now it felt suffocating.

And it felt like I was facing it alone.

I was so scared and embarrassed about what I had done that I couldn't even bring myself to tell anyone in my post-punk oddball family of friends, Jon Thomas, Beave, Fish, or Mel or any of the others. And now that high school was over, the support group I had relied on for so many years was slowly scattering.

In late spring, the whole gang had traveled to Jon Thomas's grandma's cabin on Lake Five one last time. It was supposed to be a celebration before graduation. A chance for us to bond and get high and philosophize just like old times. But instead of bonding, everything became even more unraveled. The night of the big party, Beave was off somewhere hooking up with some girl. I hung out at the house with people who felt more like good acquaintances than family. And Jon Thomas took Mel and a few others for a drive in his GTO down a long, twisted dirt road that was so infamous for its sharp curves that everyone called it Danger Road.

Jon had always had an erratic energy about him; it was part of his charm. He was instinctual; he'd listen to his needs and just do it. If his heart said turn left, he'd turn left. If his heart said turn right, he'd turn right. If his heart said take it to a hundred miles per hour then slam on the brakes, that's what he'd do. He was a notoriously reckless driver. But this night he took it further than he'd ever gone before, taking turns at maximum speed, driving along the railroad track that ran by the shore, his tires smashing against the ties.

They got back and Mel, usually so cool and mellow, was infuriated.

"I will never, *ever* ride with that fucker again!"

As soon as we all graduated, people started to leave town. I don't think anyone had any real long-term plans, you know? There was more just this sense that it was time to move on, that it was time for the next phase of life to begin—whatever that meant. No one really knew. We just knew it was time to get out. Jon Thomas was spending the summer at his grandma's place, but without any of us. Toward the end of the school year, Fish had gotten high on Robo, saw God on his bedroom ceiling, and the two of them had a long talk. God explained he was meant for bigger things. So Fish moved to Seattle, where he had some family, and started working as a drywaller. Mel was younger than us, so she had a year of high school to go, but Beave moved three hours west to Missoula. He had a vague sense that he might go to college in a year or so, but in the meantime, he got a job on his uncle's construction crew working a jackhammer for thirteen dollars an hour. He thought he was rich.

Me? Where was I supposed to go? What was I supposed to do? I was still terrified the cops would call at any moment, their warning to stay put still fresh in my mind. It felt like my entire hometown had become a kind of prison.

In case I needed to make a quick, untraceable getaway, a buddy and I even stole a rusty old car—and this one we actually kept, hiding it in a field and covering it with brush. It felt like a lifeline, like an escape hatch, just in case shit got too crazy. As the summer wasted away, I'd check on it every week or two, making sure it was still there, that I still had a fast way out. One week I checked and it was gone.

Finally the only people left were me and a couple other members of Threat, my erstwhile criminal organization. I remember meeting up with them at the park at Ryan's Dam, on the far outskirts of the city, all of us wearing trench coats, standing around a small fire, keeping warm. Ryan's Dam had been one of my main hangouts over the last few years, along with the caves and the cemetery and a couple other spots. It was on the margins, just like we were. A low-lying ravine at the base of the giant hydroelectric dam. We had smoked weed there, done Robo there. I had held a secret private concert for my friends under the gazebo there, playing on my Roland keyboard and singing along. Ryan's Dam is where we'd carved *threat* on a picnic table, but I'd also carved my initials. They'd be there forever.

Now here I was. Just me and two other people. The last ones at the party. It was like we had used up all the adventure.

Forget the police. Who knew if they'd ever be back, but I couldn't spend any more time wondering. I was tired of being afraid. I needed to act.

I had always dreamed about life beyond Montana. Different realities, alternate universes and simulations. I had traveled to France and Spain and Germany. Hell, I'd even been to Cleveland. So on some level I had always known I was meant for more. On some level I had always known that my time here was preparing me for something beyond. I felt no regrets when I finally made the decision. There wasn't any sadness. I was excited for a new adventure. But I also sensed that it was the end of something special. Something I might be able to visit or reminisce about but that I'd never really get back.

It was time to leave Great Falls.

chapter twenty-three
AN IDEA FOR A SHOW

I've got an amazing idea for a show. A cozy British mystery series about an American man who's half-Black and half-French except he does such a great English accent that everyone around him is convinced he's English, including himself.

He leads a simple country life in the quiet county of Shropshire, tending his garden at the vicarage and pulling pints at a pub called Ye Olde Furry Squire, but he keeps getting pulled into quaint local murders that he has to solve. In every single episode.

Like seriously so many murders that it starts to get weird, because, seriously, this is Shropshire—and no one *ever* gets murdered in Shropshire. Like *no one*. It's a very safe place.

Until finally this guy starts to get suspicious. Maybe, just maybe, everyone around him keeps getting murdered because *he's* the protagonist in a cozy British mystery series.

He tries desperately to stop all the murders, because these are people he knows, right? And they really all seem very nice and pleasant, like bakers and florists and fishmongers and other quaint people, and their motives make no sense, like even they can't figure out why they all keep killing each other, and it's ridiculous. Except he can't stop the murders, because it's the nature of the show, and if the murders stop, then the mysteries stop, and if the mysteries stop, then the show stops, and if the show stops, then he ceases to exist, which means, in a sense, that everyone around him in the entire series, like the entire fictional world that comprises this show, I mean hundreds of quaint-ass bakers and metalworkers and candlestick makers, would all simultaneously be murdered in one giant slaughter. Leaving one last great mystery: Was this mass murder caused *despite* or *because of* his best intentions? And if in fact there is one last great mystery, maybe, just maybe, the mystery show *doesn't* have to end, and *no one* dies, and it just keeps going on and on and on. And on.

I'm thinking of calling it *Mr. Plimford's Holiday*.

chapter twenty-four

THE IDEAL SEATTLE SIMULATION

My mom's little Mercury Topaz was sitting in our front driveway, packed to overflowing with everything I'd need for, well, life. Not just shirts and underwear and a toothbrush, but my Roland W-30 keyboard, the old violin I'd had since junior high, even my Peavey KB 100 amp.

It was the summer of 1990, just two months after I had finished high school, I was eighteen years old, and my mom was about to drive me six hundred miles away so I could move to a city I'd never even visited before. To a place that had only ever existed as a dim, distant fantasyland of art and culture and possibility. I was going to Seattle.

Somehow it felt right that my mom was the one to take me. As close as I'd grown to my family of oddball friends, no one meant more to me than she did. With her red, fiery hair and equally fiery attitude, she'd never let anyone push her—or me—around. She'd never been to Montana before she moved here, barely spoke the language at first, but that never stopped her. She'd worked her ass off, managed a volatile husband and a son who always respected her but rarely respected any rules. And she never complained once. She was pretty great, my mom, and if I had even an ounce of her strength, I figured I'd do okay in my new city.

I wasn't leaving her to fend for herself either. Now that I was moving out of our house, my dad was moving back in. Yeah, just like that.

My father had been gone six years. Partly to work out his own midlife crisis, and partly because he and I couldn't get along—and he couldn't control his temper. Honestly, I was grateful for all the freedom. I'd been free to grow and express myself, and free of my dad's anger and unresolved emotional turmoil. But through all of it, he and my mom had stayed married. She still missed him, still talked to him on the phone all the time, and she never bad-mouthed him to me. If anything, she always made it clear that she still loved him, that as far as she was concerned, they were man and wife, no matter what.

It's funny how space really does help. Not outer space—though, don't get me wrong, outer space can also be very, very helpful in the right context—but just plain space-space. Distance. After his initial short-lived affair, my dad had never strayed again, and he and my mom seemed more in love than ever. He had mellowed over the years, living with my grandma, dealing with all his health issues, the emphysema and cardiovascular disease. We hadn't fought or argued in years. He seemed more grounded, more at peace with his past—not that he ever talked about it; it was just something I sensed. My dad and I would never be friends in the traditional meaning of the word; we'd never have deep, probing conversations about life and love or any of that. He was so quiet I'd still worry that all my attempts at talking simply annoyed the man. But now I also understood that conversation wasn't how my dad showed he cared. He showed he cared by giving gifts, by taking me to the movies in Cleveland or surprising me with an album I really wanted. That was him, and that was enough for me. At eighteen years old, I wasn't prone to resentment or to overthinking personal relationships. What we had was weird—our relationship, our living arrangement, all of it was weird—but it worked.

So when my mom told me my dad was coming back to Great Falls to attend my graduation and then to stay for good, I was happy. Happy he'd be present for such a big moment. Happy my parents would be able to live with each other and take care of each other. And even happier that I was beginning a whole new chapter of my own.

I hadn't always known that Seattle would be the setting for that next chapter. Or even that I would continue that chapter metaphor from the last paragraph into this one, while never actually starting a literal new chapter. At that point in 1990, grunge was only just beginning to make some noise in the rest of the country. I didn't even know anything about it until Mel pulled me aside to hear this incredible group Soundgarden, who had just released their first big album, *Louder Than Love.*

"Reg! You *have* to hear the song 'Big Dumb Sex.' I'm *obsessed.*"

I was blown away. It was definitely rock, but it wasn't the big-hair sound of Whitesnake, and it wasn't the raw punk of the Dead Kennedys either. It sounded like its own thing. It was fresh, exciting. New. And that doesn't happen often.

So I knew something special was going on in Seattle, but it was still mostly murmurs. It wasn't loud yet, the phenomenon it would eventually become. Seattle, to me, was simply an option. A major metropolis close enough to Montana that you could drive there in a day, but far enough away to feel like a different world. A shimmering oasis I knew vaguely as the Emerald City.

My first instinct had been to move to New York. When I say "instinct," I mean it. I know some people are big planners, and I don't just mean the usual suspects, like corporate types or accountants or whoever—not that I haven't known some fascinating, very strange accountants—I mean even a lot of the amazing, talented artists and entertainers I know. They're born with a dream, a vision of becoming the greatest musician or painter or dancer or comedian, and then they go out and they execute. They work their asses off, focused, relentless, until they finally make it big. And that's totally cool. I respect that single-minded dedication.

But that isn't me. Some people in my life, like my former orchestra instructor, Miss Lidiard, had practically begged me to be more focused and committed to goals. But there was a reason I was so attracted to improv as an art form. Over time, it's become my go-to act, my identity onstage, but it was always my philosophy of life, even before I really understood what that meant. Sure, I had broader parameters. I knew the kind of person I wanted to be—weird—and the type of adventures I wanted to have—also weird. I value an open heart, a generous spirit, and a curious mind. But if we're talking specific long-term plans about career, about marital status, about making a lot of money and living in a big house with a wife and 2.3 kids, that kind of thinking has never resonated with me. Both then and now, I never have a mental map of exactly where I want to be ten or twenty years from now. I simply go where life and my interests take me. Maybe that's playing football, maybe that's playing the violin. Maybe it's running for student government, maybe it's running from the cops. Whatever it is, I just do it. Sometimes it works out, sometimes it doesn't, and that's okay.

When you're happy, when you're having fun, it puts you in an inspirational mindset. When you're in that mindset, you've got the best chance of succeeding. If you're not having fun, if you're not in that mindset, what exactly is the point?

In the case of New York, my improv partner, Wally, who I'd won the state championship in competitive drama with, wanted to attend AMDA, the American Musical and Dramatic Academy, in

New York. Wally had dreams of being an actor. I didn't, but New York sounded pretty cool—huge cosmopolitan hub, full of strange, interesting, artistic people—and enrolling in AMDA seemed like a decent enough reason to move there. As usual I had no master plan, but my gut said, "Give it a try," so what the hell, why not?

A few weeks after we graduated high school, Wally, his brother, and I made the road trip to Chicago to take part in auditions for prospective students. AMDA liked to cast a wide net for talent, so it held auditions all over the country—all over the world, actually.

After driving a grueling thirteen hundred miles over two days, we finally made it. Tryouts were held in a ballroom at a hotel. The lighting inside was dim, punctuated by spotlights for the performers. Nervous applicants huddled by the entrance, anxiously awaiting their turn.

"And what will you be performing for us today, Mr. Watts?" the representative asked me.

"Oh," I said. "I was just going to improvise, if that's okay."

He looked at me. "Sorry, but all applicants must memorize and perform a monologue. It's quite clear in the application guidelines. Did you get a chance to read those?"

"Oh. Um. I guess not."

"NEXT!"

So, yeah. That was one of those instances when my improv philosophy didn't work out. Literally. Wally, who did perform a prepared monologue—and really, isn't it kind of *his* fault for not making sure I knew the rules?—did get into AMDA.

And I was left with Seattle. Which was awesome, as far as I was concerned. I wanted a fresh start in an exciting new city that felt bigger and bolder than Great Falls, and Seattle would give me exactly that. By the way, that's another great thing about not wasting time and energy on detailed plans—I can be happy with any outcome this simulation gives me. It's just up to me to have the right mentality.

I applied and was accepted to the audio engineering program at the Art Institute of Seattle. Again, not because I had some great aspiration to be a professional sound engineer, but because it felt right. AIS was a for-profit college, so I knew I'd get in; I dug music and sound, so I figured I'd meet some cool people in the program; and, most important, now I could tell my mom that I knew what I was going to do with my life in Seattle, even though I absolutely did not.

The day I finally left Great Falls, we got into my mom's packed four-door Mercury and drove the ten hours to Seattle, to a friend of hers who lived right outside the city. Not only had I never been here before, I didn't even have a place to live. I knew Fish was around, somewhere, but I wanted to do my own thing, separate from my old crew from Montana. I was going in completely blind, and I was doing it by choice.

I spent the next week exploring.

Seattle was much bigger than anything I was used to back home, where the entire town had felt so contained and familiar, full of houses and stores and restaurants I had grown up with, grown comfortable with, almost like they were old friends. But Seattle was teeming with traffic and pedestrians, busy streets and bridges and waterways that crisscrossed the city, buildings that were stories taller than anything we had in Great Falls. In the distance I could see the Olympic mountain range and Mount Rainier looming over it all. Mount Rainier is a volcano, and it felt much taller and craggier than the mountain ranges of Montana. Even though Seattle was known for its rain, it was actually sunny those first few days, barely even a drizzle.

But at the same time there was also a smallness about Seattle, a natural intimacy that I instantly fell in love with. My mom and I found an apartment for me in the heart of town, right by where the convention center was being built. I had no real savings to speak of, but thanks to my enrollment at the Art Institute—it just *sounded* so educational and responsible—my parents were happy to fund me for the foreseeable future. My new building was ugly, brutalist, but we filled it with shabby old furniture we bought at thrift stores, giving it a homey vibe. The rain started soon enough. As a committed Anglophile, I loved the dreary weather and the low, gray clouds. It made the whole city feel like one big cave, cozy and mysterious and slightly melancholic.

My mom and I visited my new school, and one of my classmates, a guy named Rafe who kind of looked like Sean Penn but with dreadlocks, invited us back to his pad, where he had this massive pot plant growing right in his window. My mom looked right at it but didn't say a word, and I thought, *I like this place.*

But as much as I wanted to do my own thing, to start fresh in Seattle, I did miss the part of Great Falls that had defined so much of my life in high school. I missed having a family of friends. Now I needed to find a new group of weirdos if Seattle was ever truly going to feel like home.

I didn't know just how weird they'd be.

· · · · ·

Or did I?

[Insert evil "mwahaha" here.]

· · · · ·

I knocked on the bedroom door, not hard, because I'm really not into confrontation, but about as hard as a guy who's not into confrontation can knock when he's super annoyed.

REGGIE WATTS

"Hey, man!" I said to no one. "Um, I'm sorry, but I really need that rent money!"

An eerie red light was leaking out from under the door, a line of salt had been poured across the threshold, and our kitchen still reeked from the very rare, very bloody steak he'd cooked for breakfast. And honestly, the real reason I was holding back right now wasn't because I hate confrontation, but because I was pretty sure my roommate was part demon.

But, you know, just part.

"Please?" I said, knocking at least slightly louder. "Please can I have that rent I need?"

I heard some movements from inside his room. A few weeks ago, my part-demon roommate had thrown a cinder block through his glass window and into the street, spraying glass shards everywhere, bringing the police and my landlord, who was not pleased. Hence the line of salt at the base of the door—to ward off intruders. Intruders like me.

Knock! Knock! Knock!

"Hey, man, you know, I've really tried to be patient, but, like, the rent is due and—"

The door swung open. My part-demon roommate was standing there in nothing but a pair of briefs, pale, bony, his eyes as red as the light emanating from his room. His thin hands were clutching a giant wad of sweaty, crinkled bills.

"Here!" he said in a throaty voice that came straight from hell. "Take all OF IT!"

He flung the cash at my feet and slammed the door in my face. I promptly knelt down and collected the money.

"Thanks," I whimpered.

What can I say? The dude seemed pretty nice when we met.

It was 1991, and I'd now been in Seattle almost two years. I was living in my fourth place, give or take—it's seriously hard to keep track, it was all such a blur—and who knows how many roommates. And I was having the time of my life. Like, if they ever make a movie about my time in Seattle, and I'm pretty sure they will—whoever "they" are—this is the rad, magical period they'd focus on.

My current apartment was on the ground floor of this place called Lauren Renee, on Olive Way in Capitol Hill, this fun seedy alt neighborhood. The structure had this funky ramshackle vibe, stone and red brick on the first couple floors and a shingled facade above that. It still looks the same today. Go ahead, you can look it up online, I'll wait. My unit was two bedrooms, but we'd divided one of the rooms in half with a stack of crates so we could squeeze in more people. And except for the various incidents with the part-demon, who was supposedly a guitar player and not one of Satan's minions, everyone else was pretty cool. Our building was like a Muppet castle filled with artists, and we all knew each other and hung out all the time.

There was a couple who rented out one of our half-rooms and just stayed in and had sex all the time. There was a girl who was kind of short who needed a place to stay, but she didn't have much money and we didn't have the space, so I showed her this little wedge-shaped storage spot under the stairs in the common area, complete with a tiny door, and she said, "Let's do it." So she created this beautiful micro hobbit home, with a bookshelf and a frilly doily lamp. She ran an extension cord into our place for power, used our bathroom, and paid us fifty dollars a month. A few shaved-head, skater-punk weed dealers lived next door, but we always kept our doors open and came and went into each other's places through our shared balcony like we were right at home, and upstairs there was a tattoo lady with a little boy who was friends with the guys from the band Mookie Blaylock, which eventually changed its name to Pearl Jam, as well as the infamous local artist the Spoonman, who actually played the spoons and who was the subject of the Soundgarden song appropriately titled "Spoonman."

In the same fluid, organic way I decided to move to Seattle, I also started playing in bands. I left comedy and improv behind for the time being, but I can't even tell you why. There was no plan involved, no real forethought. I didn't even dream of becoming a huge rock star. I simply knew that music was something I was good at, something that came easily to me, and in Seattle I was surrounded by it. Maybe that's part of why I didn't think about comedy—there was so much music, music everywhere, it was just the natural thing to do. Even though the city became known for grunge, it was a hotbed for all kinds of genres, experimentation in so many different sounds, and that's where I made my way—in the margins of the margins, the alternatives to alternative. I had crafted my identity over the years in Great Falls, and I wanted to be weird, even among other weird people.

I played keyboard, I played violin, I sang lead, I sang backup. Whatever anyone wanted me to do, I did. I only spent a few months at the Art Institute of Seattle before I dropped out, but I started jamming with a few friends from the program, and we formed a band called Abraxas, which blended elements of rock with the complex chords and psychedelic vibe of progressive jazz. I played in an all-Black punk rock band named Action Buddy. I was in a funk band called IPD, which stood for "Ironing Pants, Definitely." I played keyboard bass for an indie pop band called Clementine, which featured a super-talented singer-songwriter named Heather Duby who I'd spotted as she performed in some local cafés. I even sang for a heavy metal band until I basically figured out "Shit, I do not like singing heavy metal," so when they came to pick me up for a gig I just hid in my room till they left. Thankfully, unlike my old friend Jon Thomas, they had no problem giving up on me. Oh, and then Abraxas changed its name to Free Space, so does that count as one band or two? I've never been sure, but I joined what felt like a dozen different bands, and I seemed to have a knack for finding them right before they broke up.

But those first few years, for all that music I played, I can't really say I was trying to make it big, even in a casual way. It felt more like when I first started developing my Toolbox of Weird all those years ago, except instead of collecting new skills or interests to add layers to my persona, I was collecting new experiences. New memories. I'd make a little money off live gigs, supplement that with the occasional job at a movie theater or a health food store or contributions from my mom, but mostly I was content just getting by. I'd stay up late with my new group of friends, bonding over episodes of *Star Trek: The Next Generation*, watching people walk past our window, and theorizing about art and love and women. I'd hang out at this café up the street called the Green Cat, where they'd give me free food and let me use their phone whenever a band contacted me on my pager, because it was the '90s and everyone had pagers. And if I was running low on cash or the Green Cat wasn't coming through for a meal, I'd shoplift food from a big premium grocery store nearby. Like actual, regular food because we simply needed to eat, which felt way more honorable than swiping drugs or checks or guns back in Montana.

And honestly, for the most part I stayed away from Great Falls. Some of that was practical. I was close to broke pretty much all the time, so I only flew home maybe once a year for the holidays. But some of it was just, I don't know, growing up. It didn't cost much money to place a phone call—though this was when long-distance rates were still a thing—but I only called my mom once a month or so. My dad was back living at my old house, so in a sense it no longer felt like my private, personal space. It was his again, not just mine. I wanted to carve out a new territory of my own. I wanted to prove I could live life on my own terms. Prove that I could be independent. Even if in reality my mom was still sending me the occasional check to help me make rent.

Even my oddball family from Great Falls felt distant, remote—and not in a strictly literal sense. There were a few times when some of my old friends actually came to Seattle themselves, even roomed with me for stretches of time. Fish, who'd had his conversation with God and taken up drywalling, had arrived in Seattle before me, and I'd crashed with him for about a month between apartments of my own, but we'd drifted apart after that. Wally, my improv partner who'd been accepted to AMDA in New York, ended up dropping out. He came a couple times and stayed with me for a few months, dreaming of somehow making it as a professional actor, but always ending up back in Great Falls. Even Jon Thomas, my best and oldest friend from junior high, came to Seattle and ended up living with me at Lauren Renee for almost a year. He'd set up his Advent Prodigy speakers so he could blast his Jon music, which now mostly consisted of the noise-rock band the Jesus Lizard, and he probably came closest to melding my old world with my new one. But he was like a nomad. Always impulsive, always looking for a new adventure, always thinking of his next journey. I kind of thought of him as ALF back then. Fun and funny, this amazing character everyone loves having around the house—but who can't help being an outsider, a little disconnected, an alien who doesn't quite fit in with a self-proclaimed gang of outcasts.

Does that make me Willie? Or does that make me Lucky the cat? I'll let you unravel that enigma.

Even though planning my life and career was anathema to me (great word, *anathema*, I highly recommend it), I think part of me understood that to move forward, I needed to leave Great Falls behind. I loved Wally, for example, truly cherished the bond we'd formed and everything we'd accomplished in high school. But I couldn't escape the feeling that he was stuck in the past, always trying to recapture the glory from our amazing win in the competitive drama state finals.

I mean, I know that sounds ridiculous on some level, right? We'd been a couple of drama dorks who'd won a contest in a classroom in Billings, Montana, and got to tell off a rival teacher. Big deal. But the energy, the electricity, the adrenaline we felt on that day was *real*. Most people go their whole lives without ever getting to hear hundreds of people chanting their names after they win something cool. But Wally and I had that. Just for an afternoon, we had that. So I totally understand why you'd want to get that back.

But as much as I cherished all those memories—memories of my time with my mom, with my friends, even with my dad from long ago—I felt like there were new adventures to be had. New things to try, new earth to uncover, new experiences to add to my constantly evolving mission to be as strange and unique as humanly possible. If I had any focus, if I had any master plan, that was it—to do *more*.

Soon after I reached Seattle, I discovered something so new I never even saw it coming. It was more transformative than making it in the music business, far more satisfying than reliving the glories of my past.

For the second time in my life, I fell in love.

· · · · ·

As we drove along Ninety-Eighth Street, the night outside Paula's Impala was misty and overcast, no stars or moon in the sky. Classic Seattle. But I stole a glance at her in the driver's seat, and even in the dim light from the dashboard I was struck by just how gorgeous she was.

She had this crazy, big, poofy blond hair, hair with attitude, like Axl Rose's but without the bandanna. Then there was her style—style to me wasn't simply clothes, it was personality, it was using fashion to create your own reality—and her style was raw, edgy, authentic. Her eye makeup was elaborate, almost mystical, and she always wore black. Black leather jacket, tight black pants, black boots. She was perfection.

And naturally, completely out of my league.

I'd first met Paula almost a year ago, right after I moved to the city in 1990. She sat in front of me on the first day of class at the Art Institute of Seattle. I knew I had no chance with her, even then. Yeah, objectively I wasn't, like, a horrible person to date. I was kind and respectful. I was good at making girls laugh. They typically dug my music. And my mom always assured me that I was quite a handsome gentleman.

But I've always suffered from what I call a Duckie Complex—I think Freud came up with that, right?—which obviously references Jon Cryer's character in *Pretty in Pink*. Fun, quirky, interesting hats, the perfect friend, but forever doomed to lose the scrumptious Molly Ringwald to that slick, pompous ass Andrew McCarthy.

Fuckin' Blane. He always gets the girl. In the movies *and* in real life.

It probably didn't help that my first relationship with the first love of my life, Jo-ann, ended the way it did. In the grand scheme of things, Jo-ann and I had only been together a few months. But back then, at the age of sixteen, those few months had felt like everything. I had idealized Jo-ann, opened myself up emotionally to her in a way I never had with everyone else. In a sense, perhaps it was a little unfair to her. She was just an English girl going to high school in Montana. Jo-ann never asked to be my goddess, my picture of true love. But that's how I felt. And when she broke up with me, when I realized that, for her, I was only one boyfriend in a line of many, I was crushed. I felt silly, foolish.

The lesson seemed simple: *This* is what happens when you go all-in on a girl. *This* is what happens when someone you like finally reciprocates. You get hurt.

So even though I was incredibly attracted to Paula of the tight black pants and Axl Rose hair, I'd kept my emotional distance. She and I had become good friends. I sensed an intense chemistry between us, an energy that was buried deep down, but nothing ever came of it. Neither of us was willing to make a move. And maybe that was for the best. *Definitely* that was for the best.

Paula parked her car in the gravelly driveway outside my place. By this point, I was out of my first apartment and living in a tiny house way out north of Green Lake with one of my best buddies from the Art Institute, Chuck Russell, who was a drummer. I hadn't joined any bands yet, but Chuck had introduced me to this incredible guitar player named Don Spilker, who wore sweaters and sensible shoes, and we were jamming together a lot. Eventually we would go on to form my first Seattle band, Abraxas, but tonight we were just gonna party. Have people over, smoke weed, and play music all night. Pretty much what we did every night.

Paula still lived at home with her family in Renton, a forty-five-minute drive outside of Seattle, but she always went out of her way, literally, to give me rides everywhere. Rides to school, rides to parties, rides to practice sessions at other people's houses. Ours was a relationship built on multiple long commutes.

And it might sound funny, but that actually meant a lot to me. In my previous relationship with Jo-ann, I always felt like I had to prove myself. Like I had to show that I was worthy of this goddess's affections. I guess I feel like that in a lot of social situations. Even today, there's this part of me that always feels like the new kid who's just arrived in Great Falls from another country. Who doesn't quite fit in, who looks different and sounds different from everyone else. So my natural instinct is to take care of people, especially my friends. Make sure everyone feels entertained, that they all laugh and have a good time and accept me. Make sure that we're all connecting and on the same page. I can't even get a massage from somebody without thinking, *Oh, I hope I don't overtax them.*

But with Paula, even though she had this gorgeous, rocker exterior, she was always so kind, so soft, so generous with her time and affection. I never felt like I owed her anything, like she expected anything from me in return. She enjoyed taking care of me, and I enjoyed accepting that care. We had this easy, trusting, natural rapport with each other, a rapport we built over long hours of driving and talking and listening to Jane's Addiction on her car radio. A rapport that, despite all my caution, was slowly turning into love.

We got out of her car, and Paula popped the Impala's trunk. The mist was thick in the night air, and we could hear loud voices, laughter, and music from the party inside the house. I leaned down to lug my heavy keyboard out of her trunk, and I realized her hands were there too. She was grabbing the other end to help.

And there was something so touching about this small, gorgeous girl with crazy blond hair trying to help me move this massive keyboard in the middle of this miserable Seattle weather, and I looked up and the next thing I knew we were kissing.

As we kissed, the mist turned to rain, a soft, gentle rain, and I became vividly aware of everything around me, the warmth of her body, the beating of my heart, the feeling of the raindrops

Falling

Falling

Falling

Falling

Falling

Against our skin, against our lips, mingling with our kisses and merging us together into one. Suddenly getting to the party didn't seem like such a high priority.

After that moment, we both just kind of knew. We didn't need to have awkward conversations about the past few months or what we wanted for the future. We simply knew we were together, not only friends but more. The kind of more I wanted when I'd moved to this city. The closest thing I had to a goal.

A few weeks after that moment, I had sex with Paula—or with anyone—for the very first time. Thankfully, I'd spent my whole life dreaming of it, so even though I wasn't very experienced I was pretty good at it.

A few months after that moment, we made love on the shag carpeting on the basement floor. The vibe was like something out of a 1970s period piece. Lights turned down low. Flames flickering in the fireplace. A drum kit in the corner and a Gretsch guitar propped against the wall next to an old Pioneer sound system. Paula and I had reached such a complete level of trust with each other, we were so comfortable, so unrestrained, so uninhibited. And, well . . .

"Oh my gosh," Paula said, rolling onto her side. "I've never experienced that before."

"I haven't either," I said. "Not like that."

"I mean, I've had orgasms before. But never actually during sex."

"And at the same time!"

We lay there on the thick shag rug, contemplating the experience. Then she turned to me and looked into my eyes.

"Reggie, will you marry me?"

I was twenty years old. This was only the second time I'd been in love. Only the second girlfriend I'd ever had. I had no idea where I would be three years from now, or even three weeks. I was living in the moment, improvising my life. Going wherever I wanted to go, doing whatever I wanted to do. And I was happy. It was working. I was inhabiting my ideal Seattle simulation. So honestly, I didn't even hesitate.

"Yeah," I said. "Absolutely, I will. I love you."

I was engaged.

chapter twenty-five

AN OPEN LETTER TO AXL ROSE'S HAIR

Dear Axl Rose's hair,

Hi there. Reggie Watts's hair here.

I know we've never been formally introduced, but I already feel like I know you so well. But I also have so many questions to ask, which I know seems contradictory, and it is, and that's okay.

As hair that has tried many different looks for many different moods, I'd like to know how it is that you, Axl Rose's hair, are so perfectly you. How do you manage to look so dirty yet so pristine? So punk yet so coiffed? So rebellious yet so palatable to the masses? They play "Sweet Child O' Mine" on easy listening stations now, you know.

Does your essence consist of natural oils accumulated over days and weeks and months of smoky clubs and unwashed pillowcases and greasy red bandannas? Or is there a special shampoo-conditioner combo you've had formulated precisely to make you seem so gloriously filthy? The latest nano-dirt technology fused with vitamin B–foul complex in a suspension of cold November rain? Whatever your secret is, I'm a huge fan.

Out of curiosity, are you by any chance friends with Boy George's hair? I must confess that the first time I saw that hair performing "Do

REGGIE WATTS

You Really Want to Hurt Me" live, I found myself incredibly attracted. Not because it was female hair or male hair, but simply because it was beautiful, and also a great singer.

I don't know. Maybe we could all get together sometime and have brunch or something. Talk about life, love, and music. Quantum physics *and* Quantum Leap. *I've got a healthy appetite. Banana pancakes are my favorite.*

Yours,
Reggie Watts's hair

chapter twenty-six

FAME . . . BUT THE TV SHOW

I was sitting on the hardwood floor, facing the wall-sized mirror, dressed in legwarmers and tights and a tutu—yes, obviously I'd be wearing a tutu, and it would be frilly and it would be pink—and I was listening, riveted, as Debbie Allen gave us her famous tough-love pep talk for incoming students.

"You got big dreams . . ." she said.

I got big dreams, Debbie Allen!

"You want fame . . ." she said.

Sure, why not?

"Well, fame costs."

I can take out a loan!

"And right here is where you start paying . . ."

Um, I might need a few days. You know, talk to a bank or some-thing. My credit isn't very—

"IN SWEAT!"

Ohhhh! *That* kind of paying!

"Yes, Debbie Allen!" I shout. "YES! I can do it! I can sweat!"

I hear a throat clear. The sound is somehow both right next to me and miles away. I turn and see my buddy Don Spilker waiting to accompany me on the guitar.

"Um, Reggie," he whispers. "You ready for this?"

I realize that I am not in dance class with Debbie Allen in the *Fame* high school. I'm actually in a small band room in Seattle's own higher-ed answer to *Fame*, the prestigious Cornish College of the Arts, a hotbed for the top creative talent in the Pacific Northwest, and I'm about to audition for a spot in their highly selective jazz voice program.

And unlike my hilariously ill-fated attempt to improv my way into AMDA five years ago, this time I really am ready.

"Okay," I tell the instructors, "I'll be performing the vocal lines from the Duke Ellington standard 'I'm Beginning to See the Light' . . . with, um, some improvisation."

Randy Halberstadt, a wizard at the piano and one of the jazz teachers at Cornish, nods at me encouragingly. No fiery speeches from him about paying my dues, at least not yet.

I'd always loved the TV show *Fame*, romanticized it, fantasized about it. The style, always the style, with the Pat Benatar headbands and the sweats and the tights. But especially the camaraderie between the student artists, the bonds they formed in this creative cauldron, the way they lived and breathed and dreamed of nothing but art. It seemed so intimate, so inspiring. Like my family of Great Falls weirdos if we had all been a bunch of adolescent Beethovens.

So when my friend Beth Huerta, a gorgeous, brilliant dancer and choreographer, decided to audition for Cornish's dance program, I was immediately intrigued. Not only because I loved the *Fame* fantasy, but also because after five years in Seattle going from experience to experience without a plan, I needed to try something, well . . . different.

I needed to adjust my laissez-faire lifestyle, focus my improv-as-a-way-of-life attitude. At least a little. I needed to have a goal. But this goal would be authentically me.

My whole life, I had tried to be a kind of cultural Anubis. Anubis is the ancient Egyptian god of the afterlife, who helps guide souls from the Land of the Living to the Land of the Dead. He also has the head of a jackal and wears knee-length skirts, which is pretty sick. Now, I wasn't a god, and I unfortunately didn't have the head of a jackal, but I did want to guide people, to act as an intermediary—between the Land of the Mainstream and the Land of the Strange. And if that meant I got to wear a knee-length skirt every now and then, even better.

Growing up, I had blended different accents, languages, and cultures. In high school, I had bridged the gap between orc dork and football jock, between post-punk oddball and student government nerd. As a musician, I fused and sampled all kinds of different genres—new wave, dark wave, hip-hop, classical, alternative, and more. But serving as a cross-cultural ambassador had always been subtext more than anything, almost a subconscious instinct of mine.

Now I decided to take it to a whole new level. I wanted to reach more people, bigger audiences. Not only here, but everywhere. I wanted to take my own unique brand of weird, shaped in small-town Montana, and share it with the world. And who knows, if I was really going to be a cultural Anubis, maybe the underworld too.

I understood that there was an inherent tension in that goal. How do you embrace being different while also appealing to the crowds? How do you rebel against social norms while also getting people to like you? But I'd been living that contradiction ever since I used my own little weird dance to entertain other preschool kids all those years ago, when I was first making Great Falls—and America—my home. I knew that tension could be uncomfortable, sometimes even unpleasant, but it could also be the source of the greatest creative energy.

Maybe at a place like Cornish I could find a balance. Meet the most talented and original musicians and artists in Seattle while also finding a broader, louder platform to perform on. Still be weird, still be different, but hone my skills, learn how to translate them to the real world. Maybe being different could also be a way in.

But first I had to *get* in.

Don Spilker, our incredible guitarist in Free Space, introduced me to music that seemed to hold the key. He had me listen to artists like Pat Metheny and Chick Corea and Jaco Pastorius who were doing incredible things with different styles of jazz, Latin jazz, funk and harmonics and electronic instruments. The vocal lines in their songs were amazingly complex, with complicated structures, but they also allowed for improvisation. There typically were no words, more like scat, random syllables, but they consisted of a very precise sequence of notes. Kind of reminiscent of Cocteau Twins, or even the Sundays, who I'd first been exposed to in high school when I was in my very first band, Autumn Asylum.

I would learn all the intricate notes and melodies of the Metheny songs—yes, memorize—and then vocalize them with my own improvisations. I'd sing over standards that had these mind-blowing chord changes, weaving my voice in and out of the melodies. It was the best of both worlds—structure, boundaries, parameters *with* creativity and spontaneity. Learn the rules so you can understand how to break the rules.

For my audition, I chose to perform a classic, "I'm Beginning to See the Light," a song by Duke Ellington, Johnny Hodges, Harry James, and Don George, which had been covered by everyone from Ella Fitzgerald to Frank Sinatra to Seal, as well as a Pat Metheny song. As I rehearsed with my buddy Don on guitar, I was trying new things, new chord changes, new harmonies, new modulations. My ear was getting better. *I* was getting better.

And that was exciting! Even the fact that I found getting better to be exciting was, in and of itself, exciting! Ever since I'd first started taking piano lessons back in Great Falls, I'd always been content with that first slope of the learning curve. I picked things up fast, and that was good enough for me. I'd always rebelled against the extra work my music teachers demanded for incremental improvements. Who needed it? Who cared?

But experimenting with vocals, improvising with Don—this was fun. I had never realized how many variations there could be, how many new sonic universes I could explore, how much nuance my ear could discern if I trained it properly. And that was just on my own. Perhaps by studying in the jazz voice program at Cornish I could get even better. Study with the masters. Practice with legends. Train my ear to be not only good but great.

Suddenly I had another reason to go to college. Not only to find a bigger stage, not only to live my *Fame* fantasy, but to actually, you know, *learn something*.

Shit. What a revelation!

Back in the Cornish band room, Don plays the opening notes of Duke Ellington's standard as the instructors listen. I begin to sing.

I never cared much for
moonlit skies . . .

I never wink back at
fireflies . . .

And as we perform, I begin to improvise with my vocals, and it sounds something like this:

And then, a few weeks later, I get a call on the phone from the official head honcho at Cornish—or maybe he pages me and I return the call in the kitchen of the Green Cat Café, yeah, maybe that's it—and he says something like this:

Okay, so I'm pretty sure I just got, like, a letter or something. But either way the result was the same. I was in.

• • • • •

I sat down in the middle of the crowded auditorium as Cornish's top musicians got ready to jam. Tim Young, an incredible guitar player; Jeff Harper, a stand-up bass player who was already a legend; Brent Arnold, an amazing experimentalist cellist; Matt Stone, a monster on drums and specialist in jazz fusion; Briggan Krauss, an absolute saxophone beast; and more, so many more.

These guys were in the class above me. They were some of the best musicians on the planet, already with reputations far beyond Seattle. They were the reason I came to Cornish: to play with the best, to form connections with artists who could take me to the next level, who could help me hone my craft *and* help me find a bigger audience. And here I was about to listen to them for the very first time.

They started to play—and I put in earplugs.

I figured out pretty quickly that what I was listening to wasn't rock or rap or even acid jazz, the blend of jazz, funk, and hip-hop that was currently all the rage on the Cornish campus, ignited by bands like the British group the Brand New Heavies and Digable Planets out of Brooklyn.

No, I was listening to pure distortion. Forget experimental. This was straight-up mad-scientist, Dr.-Frankenstein-meets-Mr.-Hyde stuff. A bunch of the nation's greatest musicians getting together, running everything through amplifiers, hooking themselves up to distortion pedals, and just getting plain, old-fashioned weird. And I had no idea how long the jam session would last. One hour. One day. Who knows? There were no rules, no limits.

But that was part of the point of a show like this. There were thirty or forty people in the audience, all of us attracted to the insane collection of musical genius gathered onstage. But who would be able to hang? Who would be able to sit through nothing but pure, unadulterated distortion—what most would simply call "white noise"—and seriously like it?

I was determined to pass the test. Determined to prove to these artists, some of whom honestly seemed kind of aloof, that I was one of them. Worthy of their collaboration, if not friendship.

So as the white noise grew even noisier, I took drastic measures. Making sure no one was watching, I took some tissue out of my pocket, twisted it into two little balls, and very casually stuffed them into my ears. Voilà. Earplugs. Not enough insulation to block out the noise completely—I don't think even store-bought earplugs would've done that—but enough to make it manageable.

Sitting back in my seat, I closed my eyes. The best way to handle the sounds flooding my senses wasn't to fight. Instead I relaxed, let it wash over me, started finding shapes and patterns in the chaos. Kind of like those funky Magic Eye posters where the best way to actually see the 3D image is to actually relax your vision and focus somewhere beyond the picture. Slowly I found myself riding a rhythm. I nodded my head to it, falling deeper and deeper under its spell. When I finally opened my eyes again, I had no idea how much time had passed, but other than the performers onstage I was the only person left in the auditorium. I belonged.

Soon, I became completely immersed in life on the Cornish campus. I started jamming on a regular basis with Young and Harper and the rest in a little speakeasy called the Off-Beat Café, which operated illegally out of an old bus depot downtown. They served nothing but snacks like PB&J sandwiches and nonalcoholic drinks like Tang, and in the main room we'd gather and play insane improvisational music until the wee hours of the morning. The first time I ever played violin in front of Jeff Harper, he looked at me and said, "Oh, you're one of those." He meant it in a good way, and it's still one of the best compliments I've ever received.

In class, I was studying technique under jazz vocal great Beth Winter and theory with vocalist and composer Jay Clayton. My ear improved dramatically, just like I'd hoped. And it was while working with Jay that I encountered my very first loop machine, a Digi-Tech system that she used to layer her own voice and create these architectural voice improvisations. This was years before I first began to integrate loop machines into my own performances, but I was amazed by the way such a small, simple piece of technology could help a musician create a virtual choir or symphony. I filed the experience away in my brain, subconsciously adding it to my Toolbox of Weird.

I also reached back to my student government experiment in high school and decided to join the Cornish equivalent, the student union. But this wasn't just an experiment, this was a commitment. I devoted myself to college causes, some of them local, some of them national. I became fixated on uniting the students from all the different departments and buildings, dance and music and acting and visual arts. The beauty of *Fame* was that all the artists were in the struggle together; why shouldn't it be the same here? I held party after party with my buddies in the other disciplines, laying the groundwork for a unified campus. And when funding for the National Endowment for the Arts was slashed by millions of dollars in 1996, our entire school held a parade all along Broadway—musicians with drums and horns, actors and dancers performing in costume— followed by a march to the federal building, where we protested and met with representatives from the city. It was both a celebration of the arts and an awesome moment of defiance, a natural tension finding balance at Cornish once again.

Of course, I hadn't left my starving-artist lifestyle behind. I was still a member of bands like Free Space, with Chuck Russell and Don Spilker, and Action Buddy, my all-Black punk rock group. I was still living at Lauren Renee apartments with all my fellow odd-balls. And even though my parents paid for my tuition, I was still barely scraping by financially. Don't get me wrong. All those gigs I played did add up—sixty bucks here, a hundred bucks there. That's not bad if you're doing a few shows a week. In fact, the whole time I was in Seattle I only worked two conventional jobs—one at a movie theater and one at a health food store—for relatively short periods of time. I had just enough money for rent, just enough for gas, and usually enough for food, while still shoplifting from corporate supermarkets whenever I was hungry and out of cash. Even as I grew more comfortable at Cornish, I never stopped hustling.

But I was evolving, growing as a person and a performer, and it was only natural that some parts of my life started to fade. One of those was my relationship with Paula.

We were together for over four years, but during the last year we started to drift apart. Some of it was a simple matter of proximity. I wanted her to move closer to me, to Seattle, but she wanted to stay in the suburbs with her family. But I also sensed that we wanted different things at that stage of our life. I felt like I was just getting started, still scraping the surface of everything the world had to offer. There were so many questions, so many unknowns, and I embraced them all. Paula, on the other hand, wanted to settle down. She had asked me to get married for a reason—because she wanted to get married. To me, getting engaged had been more symbolic, a testament to how much we loved each other. I had never tried to set a date, never discussed what a ceremony would look like, none of that. It just wasn't where I was at.

There was nothing dramatic about our breakup, no anger or tears like there had been with Jo-ann. Paula and I simply started spending more and more time apart from each other, in our separate worlds. Eventually we talked on the phone and made our separation official, but the reality was that our relationship had been over for a while. A year later, I learned she was married and about to have a kid. I was happy for her. She got what she wanted. She was so kind, so caring, so loving, she deserved only the best.

On a slightly—but only slightly—less personal note, I was also forced to finally give up my Robin Hood of Capitol Hill act where

I robbed from the wealthy grocery stores and gave to my poor stomach.

I was on my way to rehearsal with Action Buddy one day when I decided to grab something to eat. Quite literally grab from the shelves of an upscale market one prewrapped sandwich and one can of vegetarian sloppy joe mix. Everything seemed to go to plan. I secretly removed the magnetic strips that were designed to foil crafty thieves like me, stuffed the items under my coat, and walked out the door.

That's when I heard the store manager scream to a nearby patrol car:

"Hey! Get that n——!"

Let's pause to note that the last time I was called a racial slur was not in libertarian Montana, but in the supposedly liberal bastion of Seattle. *[Clears throat loudly.]*

But at that moment, I was less concerned about this dude's blatant racism and more concerned about the police officers, who drove their car up onto the sidewalk to block my path. *Shit!* I thought that only happened in TV shows! I took off running in the other direction, turned down a residential street—and got cut off by yet another cop car that pulled in front of me at the last second. *Fuck!* Another thing I thought only happened in TV shows!

Turned out there was a police station right down the road from the store. Which, you know, bad planning by me. With nowhere left to run, I handed over the vegetarian sloppy joe mix. But when no one was looking, I managed to toss my stolen sandwich in a nearby planter. I personally think that's even cooler than what typically happens in TV shows.

The cops drove me a half block to the station, but, I mean, I'd seriously just shoplifted lunch. I was released with enough time to make rehearsal, and I even picked up my stashed sandwich from the planter on the way. I was ultimately given eighty hours of community service as punishment, which I easily fulfilled by cleaning the theater at Cornish.

I still believe there's nothing morally wrong with a hungry poor person swiping lunch from a rich company, but I had no interest in getting caught again.

Coincidentally, one of my fellow members of Threat (my socalled crime syndicate from my senior year of high school) also moved to Seattle. For both of us, that time still weighed heavily on our minds. We hadn't stolen guns and cars and checks out of necessity. We had done it for the thrill, to prove we could. It was wrong, and we knew it.

One night, we drove to one of Seattle's many neighboring bodies of water. She brought a gun we had stolen; I brought the decorative Polynesian-style box that had once held a huge stash of weed I'd stolen from an "unlocked" pickup truck. We threw the gun and the box in the water, exorcising the demons of the past and finally closing the door on a dark period of our lives.

Now that I was at Cornish, a part of a community of the most talented musicians in the world, it was time to find that bigger stage I'd finally allowed myself to dream of.

· · · · ·

This was it, I could feel it.

It was early 1996, and we were all getting ready to rehearse in the basement of what I called the Blue House because, well, it was blue. Which was great. But what really mattered was who lived in the house—a bunch of incredible musicians from Cornish.

And a few of us had come together to create a new revolutionary band called Micron 7. We had an incredible singer named Om Johari, who was like Tina Turner except more buff. We had a guy named Zeke Keeble, who was an absolute genius on the drums, creating super-intricate, complex beats. We had a whole posse of talented musicians from Cornish, including me on keyboards and vocals. But most important of all, we actually had buzz.

We had this insane sound that was a mix of hard rock and soul. We were amazing together on the stage. We'd already played at the hottest club in town, Moe's Mo'Roc'N Café, and we got the sold-out crowd to start jumping together up and down, up and down, and I swear I could feel the foundations shake. We had a big-time manager named Dave Meinert, who repped groups like the Presidents of the United States of America, bands that had their videos playing 24-7 on MTV, and it seemed like it was only a matter of time before the same thing happened to Micron 7.

This was the band that would finally do what I came to Cornish to do. Transcend the boundary between the counterculture and the mainstream. Take my brand of weird to the world like a cultural Anubis bridging the divide between the living and the dead.

Since starting at Cornish, I'd landed in a few groups with varying levels of success. I was in a Senegalese Afropop band called Sme No Tay, which meant "Smell No Taste" in the regional patois. Some other students and I were chosen by avant-garde jazz legend Wayne Horvitz to be in his 4+1 Ensemble, though I'm still not sure if I was the plus-one or part of the four. We toured clubs in Europe for a month, hitting the old jazz circuit in Italy and Austria just like Coltrane and Miles Davis. And I was an original member of Hit Explosion, an eight-piece disco cover band with horns, keyboards, drums, bass guitar, the whole deal, which wasn't just ridiculously talented, it was also ridiculously popular, and is still going strong to this day. We'd play in front of crowds of four hundred to five hundred people, initially at clubs like the Fenix Underground and the Ballard Firehouse, and eventually at private events that hired us to serve as entertainment.

Hit Explosion was my first taste of real money, pretty much in my entire life. My family wasn't poor, I had always lived comfortably back in Montana, but we were also far from rich. When I say I needed to shoplift food in Seattle because I was hungry, I mean it. All those gigs I played, all those small-time bands I fronted, plus my short stints working at a movie theater and a health food store—they paid the bills, barely.

But singing with Hit Explosion, I was suddenly taking home six hundred bucks in a single weekend—and that was all cash. So here I was, this guy who'd once been busted for swiping no-brand vegetarian Manwich, and now I was walking around with wads of hundred-dollar bills busting out of my pockets. I was taking my friends out, buying everyone wine and cocktails—how cool to finally be the random dude at the bar who shouts, "Hey, everyone! Drinks on me!"—and buying myself all the cool gadgets I'd never been able to afford. A Mac computer back when they were still just little gray boxes. And in my bedroom, a sick rectangular TV that was like an early precursor to flat-screens. I even piped in cable. Seriously—cable TV in my own bedroom, how crazy is that!

But as much fun as I was having, as much money as I was making, it wasn't truly satisfying. I was in one strictly commercial band and in other bands that were strange and weird mixes of African music and electronica and jazz, sonic metaphors for my own delightfully scrambled identity. But I still hadn't found a band that could bring all those things together—one that could be incredibly odd *and* reach millions of people.

Micron 7 had that potential. We just needed to get through this damn rehearsal first.

"Why do you keep talking shit, Zeke?" Om said, the mic in her hand.

"I ain't talking shit," Zeke said from behind the drum set with a grin. "I'm just asking you *politely* to try to keep up with me, that's all."

"And *that* is talking shit, Zeke!" she said.

The basement was a big space, with a sofa and that standard Seattle shag carpeting, but there was so much negative energy between Om and Zeke it was starting to feel claustrophobic. Intense creativity can also be a source of intense volatility. Kind of how love and hate can be separated by a very thin line. Om and Zeke had known each other for a while, and sometimes it felt like they walked right up to the edge.

"All right," I said with as much authority as I could muster. "Let's take it from the bridge again!"

Man. I still loved that phrase.

We took it from the bridge again, and we were sounding good. But at the next break Zeke was back at it. He'd never say anything horrible, never anything overtly offensive, he just had a way of needling you. Of knowing exactly the right button to push at exactly the wrong time. And then he'd keep pushing it over and over and over and

BAM!

Next thing I know, Om is jumping over the drums to get at Zeke and shouting "What did you say?? What did you say??" and fists and bodies and instruments are going

flying!

We all rush in trying to separate the two of them. A couple of the guys grab Zeke and I grab Om and wrap her in a big bear hug and we tumble over the sofa and onto the shag and someone is shouting "You better let go of me!" and someone is shouting "I'm gonna fucking hit you!" and someone is shouting "Chill out!" but it doesn't seem to be taking. Zeke storms out a few minutes later, and Micron 7 is no more.

Which actually ends up being just fine, because it directly opens the door to my next band. The big one. The one that finally pops. Maktub.

And that's when the real fun begins.

chapter twenty-seven
ROCKY AND BULLWINKLE

And we all know that *The Adventures of Rocky and Bullwinkle* is an amazing animated show that first aired in the '50s and '60s to absolutely

Hold on a second, guys. Sorry, incoming text.

BRI

> Reggie, your mom isn't feeling well. She's having more back pain. Taking her to the hospital to be safe.

Oh. It's the lady who helps take care of my mom. Stand by.

ME

> What's wrong? Can I talk to her? Should I fly from LA?

BRI

> Can't talk now, but she's
> okay, don't worry. With
> doctor now, text you soon.

Yeah, so, my mom's caregiver is named Bri, and she's supercool. It's short for Brianna, and of course my mom insists on calling her Brianna, not Bri, even though I think she prefers Bri.

Yeah.

Waiting like this is awesome, right? Hahaha! So great.

My mom still lives in Great Falls, in the same house I grew up in, all by herself now. But Bri comes by to help out most days. Finding my mom someone wasn't easy. She can be finicky about who she spends time with. She might not get around as well, but she's still got that same fiery personality, that same strong will. But Bri is chill. Super professional, and my mom likes her. I feel very comfortable having Bri there, which is important when you're a thousand miles away.

Oh, you remember Wally? My super-talented partner in competitive drama, back in high school? He lives in Great Falls now, has for years. He had a kid shortly after rooming with me in Seattle, and he's been pretty much stuck in Montana ever since. His dreams of making it in entertainment are long past. He helps my mom out sometimes too. Takes her grocery shopping and to doctor's appointments, and she pays him in cash or beer. He has so much talent, man. So much. But he's not always around, not always the most reliable, so I found Bri.

I visit my mom a lot, at least once a month. Usually more. Um . . .

BRI

Hi Reggie, we're home.

I ask Alexa to place a video call to my mom. The phone picks up on the other end. My mom is sitting at the table in her red kitchen.

ME: Hey, Maman.

[She slowly turns and looks at the screen. Her voice is weak.]

MOM: Hey, Bébé.

ME: How are you feeling?

MOM: Lousy.

ME: I'm sorry to hear that. Bri told me you're having back pains.

[My mom shakes her head. She opens her mouth, but doesn't say anything.]

ME: Bri, what did the doctors say? Is it her kidneys?

[Standing near the counter, Bri leans over and peers at the screen.]

BRI: Well, they said the tests were inconclusive.

ME: Inconclusive? What does that mean?

BRI: Well, they tried to get a urine sample, but they couldn't. Then they tried to hook her up to an IV, because your mom is really dehydrated, but the nurse couldn't find a vein. So your mom, she got upset and wanted to come home, and you know how your mom gets when she makes up her mind about something. So we came home.

ME: Yeah, I definitely know. Maman, how do you feel now? Do you want to go back to the hospital?

MOM: No. I don't want to go back. I feel tired, Reggie.

[She looks tired. I've never seen her this tired before.]

ME: Maman . . .

[Pause. I clear my throat.]

ME: Maman, I'm coming to see you, okay? I'll fly tomorrow to see you. Okay?

[She smiles. It's like her whole face instantly comes to life.]

MOM: Okay, Reggie. Good.

And we all know that *The Adventures of Rocky and Bullwinkle* is an amazing animated show that first aired in the '50s and '60s to absolutely rave reviews the whole world over. Or at least most of us know that, and perhaps some of us don't, and that's fine.

I mean, the style of the art, the design of the characters, the accents and the voices and that supercool old-fashioned musical score. You've got Natasha—she's so sultry, so smoky, with those long eyelashes, that black lipstick, and a lit bomb in her hand. And Boris with his gravelly voice and that dapper, diabolical little mini-mustache. And of course you can't forget Rocky and Bullwinkle themselves, the squirrel and moose goofballs who somehow always manage to save the day from the evils of, like, international communism.

But one of the things I loved the most were those funky titles

they'd always announce at the end, you know? Always a choice between two or more titles. Always a ridiculously bad pun.

"Tune in next time for 'Sometimes Less Is Really Moose!' or 'We
Don't Moose Around!'"

"See you next week for 'Of Moose and Men,' or 'A Stitch in
Moose Saves Moose!'"

"Come back soon for 'Moose-Moose-Moose MOOSE!' or
'Moooooooooooooose.'"

And seriously, why should we have to choose just one title in life?
Why settle for only one bad pun? Isn't it true that most things are
more than one thing all at the same time, and aren't those things
typically the most interesting and wonderful things out of all things?

I've got to buy a plane ticket.

But in the meantime, see you soon for . . .

chapter twenty-eight

MOOSETUB,
OR
REGGIE MOOSE GOES BACK
TO THE MOO-TURE!

I'm standing at the very edge of the stage with my mic in my hand and a thousand people are screaming at me to jump, and I'm thinking there's no fucking way I'm going to jump.

Maktub is performing at the Showbox in Seattle, a classic venue that was just restored in 1995 to all its former glory, with a glowing neon-red marquee and this crazy-gorgeous art deco interior with swooping pillars and huge glass chandeliers and the whole deal. Everyone has played here. Everyone. From Dizzy Gillespie to the Police to Billy Idol to Pearl Jam. And now we're playing here, my band is playing here, Maktub is playing here, and it's sold out, and it's kind of funny because these people keep telling me to jump when there's no way in hell I'm going to jump.

The thing is, and I know this'll sound kind of silly, I'm actually afraid of heights. I'm seriously afraid of getting physically hurt. I mean, I don't know these people out in the crowd, right? I'm sure they're all mostly nice individuals, but what if for some reason they decide not to catch me? What if as soon as I jump into that vast sea of humanity, the waters part for me like some kind of musical Moses, and I straight-up do a face-plant on the hard, cold floor?

Of course lots of people crowd-surf, and audiences have begged me to crowd-surf before—*just let go! Lose yourself in the moment! Stop processing and just jump!*—but I'm the king of processing, I'm the duke of self-awareness, I'm the jester of second-guessing. So instead of jumping into the outstretched arms of the teeming crowd, I tease them, play with them.

The crowd is cheering louder and louder and louder.

COME ON!

And I run . . .

COME ON!

Right up to the edge . . .

COME ON!

And like I have so many times before, I stop and I laugh.

Hahaha. No way in hell.

Except this time something different happens. I allow myself to look out at all these screaming strangers, these people I don't know, these faces I usually avoid. And I look into their eyes, and I can feel how earnest they are, how caring. And we connect. For one moment, I stop processing, I stop second-guessing, I stop doubting.

I turn around, I drop my mic, and I fall backward.

Shit, I hope they catch me.

And they catch me.

I feel their fingers on my body as they hold me, lift me, pass me from

    hand

        to

            hand

                to

                    hand

                        to

                          hand

and moments later, those caring hands deposit me safely, gently, back onstage.

I look out over the audience, and I'm overcome. Tears well up in my eyes. I pick up my mic, and I say one thing:

"Thank you."

. . . . .

It was almost like Davis Martin knew it was meant to be.

It was 1996, my band Micron 7 had just broken up—and I mean *just* broken up, like it felt like maybe five minutes had passed since our official "this is over" meeting—and I got a call.

"Hey, man," Davis said. "I heard Micron 7 broke up."

What? How did this dude find out so fast?

"I'm jamming with some people today if you wanna come down and join us."

I didn't know it yet, but Davis had a vision. He wouldn't necessarily stand out in a crowd in Seattle—he looked like a hip Northwest lumberjack, and he had a penchant for wearing *Newsies*-style Kangol hats—but he had a natural leadership quality, a soft-spoken confidence, a way of bringing people together. I went down to a rehearsal space that night and played for the very first time with Davis on drums, Alex Veley on keyboards, and Kevin Goldman on bass as I sang and played a little synth.

And we clicked. Immediately. Like it was that simple, like it was meant to be.

The name we chose for the band was "Maktub," a word we got from the incredible Paulo Coelho book *The Alchemist*, an amazing story about journeys and treasure and true love and Egypt and, yeah, an alchemist. *Maktub* is an Arabic word that literally means "written" or "it is written," but more broadly can mean something close to "destiny." As in, this has already been written or decreed. In the book, some characters get stuck overanalyzing decisions, trapped in their own thoughts, but the concept of maktub—the knowledge that what is meant to be will be—frees them. That theme held a *slight* relevance to my life. And, it seemed, to our band.

Our music was just the right style for just the right time. Acid jazz—a fusion of jazz, funk, and hip-hop—was still super popular, with bands like Portishead taking it in cool new directions and finding mainstream success. Maktub had our own unique take, kind of a mix of trip-hop and acid jazz but with a strong rock influence too. Plus a depth to our lyricism, a dripping, almost creeping soulfulness. Though, I mean, honestly the best way to describe it is just to give you a taste:

We wanted to debut in a big way. So for our first show, we got Tasty Shows, the hottest promoters in Seattle, to put on an incredible bash. We took over a warehouse downtown in Pioneer Square and went all-in on the Middle Eastern vibe of our name, covering the floors in Persian rugs; sprinkling the space with elegant, dimmed lamps; and serving small plates of food like falafel, shawarma, hummus, and baklava. We invited all our friends, all the local tastemakers, and it felt like our chill night of music set the entire town on fire.

We started selling out huge venues like the Showbox. We got the same big-time manager who'd repped the ill-fated Micron 7, Dave Meinert. We released our first album, *Subtle Ways*, in 1999, and it was named Northwest soul album of the year by the Grammy Association and "Best R&B Album" at the Northwest Music Awards. *Billboard* magazine called it "fresh and original." Did I have to look up those last few factoids on Wikipedia right now?

Absolutely. But I guarantee you, it meant a lot at the time.

I'm also pleased to inform you that I myself remembered that we reached number one on Seattle's legendary indie radio station, KEXP-FM. I also know just off the top of my head that we were opening for incredible groups like the Dave Matthews Band and the iconic Earth, Wind & Fire. In 2001, after we added two new band members, Thaddeus Turner on guitar and Daniel Spils as the new guy on keyboard, we recorded our second album, *Khronos*, on an indie label, and it sold twenty thousand copies in a year.

We began holding these groundbreaking all-night improvisational jam sessions, not for the money, not for the fame, but simply because we could, because we loved to play. We started at the Owl 'N Thistle, a small Irish pub with exposed brick walls and a stage only barely removed from the bar. We eventually moved to a hip joint called the 700 Club—located at 700 Virginia Street, its name a nod to the decidedly *not* hip evangelical TV show. And we finally ended up at a cool little jazz club called the Scarlett Tree. Each week, we would try out new sounds, experiment with new techniques, and two hundred of our most devoted fans would come and dance all night long as we played with special guests like Jill Scott and D'Angelo and Erykah Badu. Those improv jam nights became a Seattle institution, so popular that other artists started doing them and kept doing them years later.

I mean, we had Jimmy Iovine, cofounder of Interscope Records, flying in on a private jet to see us perform at one of our shows. And you can't even *find* that on Wikipedia. This shit was real.

Right around when all this started, I also made the decision to leave Cornish. Or, as they say in French, I dropped out. To be honest, getting a degree there never interested me that much. I wanted to improve my ear and my vocal technique, and I had done that. I wanted to work and play with the best musicians in the country, and I had done that too. Most of Cornish's most talented artists were in the class ahead of me and had already graduated. And I wanted to find a bigger audience to share my strange sensibility with, and now Maktub seemed to offer my best chance. I chose to focus my energies there.

I also decided to embrace being single for the first time in a long time. A year after my engagement to Paula came to an end, I had embarked on a series of longer relationships. One lasted two years, another a year and a half, another almost a year. Without even realizing it, I had slipped into the life of a serial monogamist. And every woman I was with was incredible; every time I experienced my full-fledged Duckie Complex. *Oh my God, there is no way this woman will even talk to me. She's too perfect, too gorgeous. She's way out of my league.*

Somehow, someway, they agreed to spend time with me. Even spend years with me.

But every single time, I found myself getting trapped. Not by them, but by myself. By the fantasies I had first started crafting as a boy obsessively watching *The Love Boat* and *Three's Company* and James Bond all those years ago in Great Falls. I kept falling in love with falling in love, with the idea of myself as the perfect boyfriend. I loved giving presents, I loved being romantic. I constantly came up with new ways to prove my devotion. If one week I surprised my girlfriend with a bouquet of gorgeous gerbera daisies, then the next week I would astonish her with dozens and dozens of daisies strewn along the path to her doorstep, ending with a giant pile of flowers shaped in a heart with a box of chocolates at the center. I mean, think about it. If I, Duckie Watts, wasn't worthy of any of these incredible women, what better way to win them over than with a never-ending supply of flowers and extravagant dinners and thoughtful gifts? So I was great at the fantasy. I enjoyed it!

But the reality part, not so much. All my romance substituted for real communication. I was so good at distancing myself from my own emotions—at standing back and observing, analyzing how I felt at any given moment—that it wasn't too hard to distance myself emotionally in my relationships, even if I was technically saying "I love you." If anything, maintaining emotional distance was easier. Less complicated. In an odd way, I never opened up with anyone the way I had with Jo-ann back in high school, even though that was one of my shortest relationships. As silly as it sounds, maybe I never quite recovered from the pain of that breakup. Or maybe I was replicating everything I had witnessed in my parents' marriage. My mom tried to get my dad to open up, all the time, but he simply couldn't. He didn't have the words. So he bought presents instead. And when the tension in our family became too great—because of my conflict with him, yes, but also because he couldn't communicate with my mother—she had no choice but to ask him to move away.

So when my third long-term relationship ended in 2001, right before Maktub started a short tour, I decided to give it a rest, and I didn't regret it. Each night at our shows, I was meeting new, fascinating women. Sometimes that would lead to making love—even when I was being promiscuous I was too much of a romantic to "hook up"—but just as often it would lead to all-night dancing, to all-night conversations, to ever so briefly spiritually connecting to someone beautiful and fresh and compelling.

That's what I was doing one night when we had just wrapped a show at a club in Portland. Scanning the crowd, looking for someone new to connect with.

Instead, I found someone I hadn't connected with in ten years.

. . . . .

Through the smoky air and mass of sweaty bodies, I saw him standing there. His blond hair, which had been short and spiky back in high school, flowed down to his shoulders. His skin was tan, his button-down shirt open past his chest. He looked like some kind of Montanan Fabio. But there was no mistaking him and those crazy, glow-in-the-dark blue eyes. It was my old friend, Mike Benton. Beave.

"Reg!" he shouted over the noise. "Awesome to see you!"

"Oh man!" I said. "I can't believe it!"

He walked over and we hugged. Now that he was closer I could see the lines etched in his skin. He was only twenty-nine years old, like me, but all those years in the sun, sometimes having fun, sometimes working in construction with his family, had started to take their toll.

It had been years since the last time we'd seen each other. We'd hung out a couple times after I moved to Seattle. In 1991, he was actually the guy who dragged me to the first Lollapalooza in Enumclaw, an hour outside the city. He'd done a road trip from Montana with a few of his buddies and he practically forced me to come along, and I was happy he did. But since then I hadn't heard much. He'd tried college for a little, but it didn't take. I heard he got married—or was he divorced already?—maybe worked for a while at a Little Caesars, some more construction, something like that. Honestly, I couldn't really remember.

"Wow, I still can't believe it!" I said. "What are you doing here?"

"Oh, you know," he said, a little more sheepishly than I ever remembered him being. "I'm starting this new company, it's called

Nahiku Naturals. It's all essential oils. Yeah, so I'm in town, like, checking out suppliers and buying stuff. I already got this big industrial-sized still and a truck and everything."

"Oh wow! That's awesome!"

"Yeah, thanks! Then I saw that Maktub was playing, and my God, it just blew me away! I mean, I got your album already, it's so good. I follow all your stuff, I always say I'm your biggest fan. Always believed in your genius."

"Wow, thank you, man! You're the best!"

I suddenly became aware of all the other people standing around us. Fans, members of the band, all watching us, listening. Or, I don't know, maybe I became aware of Beave becoming aware.

"Hey, guys," I said, "this is one of my best friends from high school! Mike Benton! Beave!"

Everyone smiled and nodded politely.

"Reg!" Beave said. "Your bass player looks exactly like Jon Thomas! Don't you think?"

Kevin Goldman was a Jewish dude with a shaved head. My old friend Jon Thomas was like a handsome Beavis from *Beavis and Butt-Head*. They looked nothing alike. Not even close.

"Totally!" I said. "A hundred percent!"

Kevin Goldman didn't look too sure about that comparison. "Who's Jon Thomas?" he asked.

"Oh man," I said. "Jon Thomas, he's a legend."

Awkward laughter. A few sidelong glances.

"Hey, man," I said to Beave. "A few of us are gonna head to a party. You wanna come?"

"Oh," he said with more of that uncharacteristic bashfulness. "Nah, but thanks. I've gotta get up early, you know. But hey, it was great seeing you, Reg. You're a superstar."

Beave and I hugged again, and he walked away.

I could sense how uncomfortable he was, and I thought I knew why. He perceived me as this blazing comet of fame and success, hurtling far outside his orbit. He and I both came from the same place, we'd formed bonds that seemed indestructible, we'd shared so much. But now we inhabited different universes. To Beave, I seemed untouchable, and what I'd achieved seemed like a dream.

But I felt the awkwardness for a different reason. I loved making my old friend proud. I loved feeling like I'd met and even surpassed his expectations. But the truth was I wasn't the superstar he thought me to be.

At this point it had been five or six years since we'd first formed Maktub. We'd started out so hot, we'd had so much buzz. For a few years we were the hottest thing in Seattle. But you know what? That had never really translated nationally. We'd been recognized regionally, we'd sold out some pretty big stages in the Pacific Northwest, we'd been number one on a popular local radio station, we'd even toured some medium-sized clubs in the South and Chicago and New York, but somehow we never really broke big. Remember how Jimmy Iovine flew in to see us perform? Well, afterward he flew right back out. Same with all the other record execs who came out to see us. They'd see us, listen to us, then they'd leave. Never came to anything. It felt like we kept getting so close, right on the brink of real mainstream success, but it wasn't happening.

Maktub had been an incredible, transformational ride for me, but I was starting to question whether I had a future with the band. Or even with music. I still dreamed of taking my unique brand of Montana weird to the entire world. On a practical level, I dreamed of making enough money to survive. I had quit Hit Explosion a few years back, in part to focus on Maktub, and I didn't regret my decision, but I was back to barely making ends meet. Being a starving artist was fine when I was twenty years old, still shoplifting my lunch. But I was ready for more. I'd always been a connoisseur of new experiences, a collector of new senses and ideas and places, but how much could I really experience if I was flat broke?

I was starting to think it was time to find a new future for myself. A future that was back where it all began.

chapter twenty-nine

MY PLAN FOR WHAT I'LL DO WHEN MY MOM PASSES AWAY, WHICH SHE NEVER WILL

It's Monday morning, October 31, 2022, and I'm on the plane from Los Angeles to Montana (via Denver), typing on my very handy Astrohaus Freewrite™, which is a high-technology futuristic writing machine with a simple but elegant e-ink screen and no web browser to help minimize distractions, which is important for me because I really, really enjoy distractions, and I'm wondering what I'll do with my mom's house when she passes away, which she never will.

When I say my mom still lives in the exact same house from when we first arrived in Great Falls, I mean it. After almost fifty years, not much has changed. I mean, we've done a *few* things— bought a new water heater, installed a water-purification system, some high-efficiency windows. But all the stuff that matters, all the stuff that counts, it's all the same. Like a living time capsule.

The same cream-colored wallpaper with a classical bronze-leaf pattern. The same dark gray wall-to-wall carpeting, I think it's a medium pile. The same fireplace my mom got from, like, the Amish, that looks like a real fireplace except it's electric and heats the room really well. Of course the kitchen is still the same, that's her favorite room. Same red tablecloth, same red strawberries on the wall, red this, red that, because my mom loves red. Still got her doll collection in a display at the end of the hall. Dolls of the world, like porcelain from Spain and Sweden and Germany.

Then in the basement my bedroom is still all exactly the same. Same bed I used to sleep on. Same picture of breakdancing Snoopy up on the wall, a few of my drawings. My dad's jazz album collection is still down there, and all the toys he bought me. My old computers. My *Millennium Falcon*. My AT-AT, which I painted for fun.

And my mom. Getting older. Getting frailer. Getting sicker. Over the last couple years, it feels like there's been so many trips to the doctor, to the hospital. One thing after another. Respiratory viruses. UTIs. Now her back pain, which I think is being caused by a kidney infection.

She's still my mom, of course. Still strong-willed, opinionated, resilient, with a sharp sense of humor. Bri still helps her dye her hair a vibrant red. But I can sense it. I can sense what's coming. I've never seen her as exhausted as she was yesterday when we were Face-Timing. So spent. I know that one of these times when I visit might be . . .

Anyway.

So when my mom passes away, which she never will, here's my plan. I'll fly out immediately, kind of like I'm doing now, I guess. And I'll hire an archivist to catalog everything in the house, take photos of it all, note the proper locations, make sure everything is accounted for. And then I'll have this super-high-end Fort Knox security system, with cameras and sensors and lasers and a biometric lock and everything. And maybe the only thing I'll add are solar panels on the roof, just so the house can be totally independent, so it can go completely off the grid.

And then when I come home I can bring my friends, or even just acquaintances, or strangers, and I can hold tours and do improv, and who knows, maybe invite artist friends to exhibit their work or play their instruments or put on dance numbers. Create not simply a museum, but a living, breathing performance space.

I've asked my mom before what she thinks I should do, and she says I should sell the place. She says the only reason I come back to see her so much is because I'm afraid.

And this Astrohaus Freewrite™ writing machine really is a tour de force!

chapter thirty

COMEDY!!!

A happy, unsuspecting couple walks down the aisle of their local supermarket.

"Wow!" she says. "All these groceries are so cheap!"

"It's amazing, isn't it?" he says. "And there's only one tiny catch!"

Gleaming yellow eyes peek out from between boxes of cereal.

"What could possibly be the catch at a store called Grocery Panther?"

"To get the discount . . . you gotta survive the panther."

Suddenly the panther ROARS, leaps out from behind the cereal boxes, and attacks the unsuspecting couple. One of them dies, but the other one gets to take home some really inexpensive groceries, so it's pretty much worth it.

And, believe it or not, the small crowd at the opening show of our sketch comedy group, Hi,D (take a sec to sound it out), actually laughed their asses off. Which, you know, maybe the crowd was kind of high too, but that didn't make the night any less fantastic.

It was the late '90s. It wasn't clear that Maktub had peaked yet, but I was already starting to expand beyond music. And I was dipping my toe back into comedy for the first time since high school as the result of a series of misadventures so incredibly random they must've been generated by a benevolent AI.

One night I had been jamming with some friends at a cool little place called the Sit & Spin, which was a laundromat-slash-nightclub-slash-café, when I saw this incredibly cute girl dancing. She was dating a clown from France. The French clown was performing in Cirque du Soleil, so they invited me to a show. There, I met a cool, lanky guy named Michael McQuilkin who was in the acting program at the University of Washington. He invited me over to the house where he lived with a bunch of other drama students. The house was white, so I called his house the White House, as opposed to the Blue House, which was blue, where I had lived when we formed Maktub. Michael and his friends and I started playing Frisbee, and we decided to form Hi,D. And I told my new friends about the grocery chain I grew up with in Great Falls called IGA, and how its mascot was a tiger, and their whole thing was calling him a "tiger discounter," and wouldn't it be funny if there was a grocery store called Grocery Panther, and they had really, really cheap prices because there was an actual panther in the store, and sometimes it killed people.

So, yeah. Obviously an AI. Most likely benevolent.

People really dug the few shows we put on, and I really dug being in them. It had been close to ten years since I'd done comedy, since I'd done anything other than music up on the stage, and performing with Hi,D triggered something in me. I had no master plan, no grand scheme to diversify my professional repertoire or something. This was the same me who grew up in Montana moving from one language to another, from one interest to another, from one clique to another, just because I felt like it. My new friends at the White House were undergrads in college, so they were all younger than me, unlike the Cornish crowd, and they were all into acting, into comedy, not music. So hanging with them, writing with them, creating with them was refreshing, different. It was fun.

It took me back to the absurdist humor of my high school years, the silly improvisational stuff I had done in competitive drama, first as a solo performer and then in a partnership with my old friend Wally. But I never felt like I was trying to relive the past. I never felt like I was trying to recapture the glory of that day Wally and I won the state championship in comedic duo. My return to comedy was pulling from my past, yes, but I also wanted to make it brand-new. Brand-new in my own uniquely odd way.

I decided to start performing one-man improv comedy again in a very low-key, low-stakes way, not searching for any money or any fame, just to get me back onstage so I could play around a little, experiment, figure out what my act could be—or even if I had one. I found a French restaurant downtown that agreed to let me go on during the daytime and be as strange as I wanted as their customers ate escargot and soufflé. I figured I could take the same blend of characters and accents and absurdism I had loved in high school and apply it here, but there was one huge difference: I was going up in front of people for a long, long time.

The bits I'd done for competitive drama had been, by rule, only a couple minutes long. Now, at the French place, I'd be going on for twenty minutes, sometimes more. How would I fill the time? I mean, I know it sounds trivial, but seriously—how would you feel going up in front of a crowd of strangers by yourself and having to fill over an hour of time with pure improvisation?

Ah, thank you, sir in the back of the auditorium, for shouting *"I'd feel just fine!"* It was actually meant to be a rhetorical question, but your helpful answer has given me a lot to think about.

I found my own answer in a loop machine.

I've always loved tech, from back in the days when my dad

bought me my first Texas Instruments TI-99 computer. I love to experience every new gadget as soon as it's released, I love to test all the latest breakthroughs. Some of that is straight-up geeking out, the little boy in me who'll never die, the one who's obsessed with fast cars and cool new toys. But it's deeper than that too. My faith in technology is at the core of my spirituality; it lies at the heart of my cautious, pragmatic optimism about the fate of the world. That TI-99 may have just been a 16-bit home computer—the first-*ever* 16-bit home computer, mind you—but even back then I could use it not only to play games but to build new worlds in my mind, to shape new virtual realities. And think of all the advancements that have happened since then! An iPhone today can have a 64-bit processor. A simple phone! I truly believe that humans can harness technology to solve all of society's woes. We've already made so much progress on everything from solid-state batteries to biodegradable packaging to cold fusion and even that benevolent AI that clearly already runs this perceivable reality. I have zero doubt that tech will ultimately solve global warming, poverty, hunger, disease. So why not my new act?

Back during my lessons at Cornish, my instructor Jay Clayton had used a DigiTech system to layer her own voice in complex arrangements, my first exposure to the magic of looping. Later, when I was touring with the experimental jazz band the Wayne Horvitz 4+1 Ensemble, I'd had my next encounter with looping, this time purely out of necessity. The band wanted to create a relatively simple tape-delay effect in shows on the road, but the analog tape machine I usually used was too bulky and damage-prone to cart around Europe. Instead, I picked up a Line 6 DL4 loop pedal. It was light, compact, digital, easy to carry, and executed tape delays perfectly.

What if I took that same tool and used it for more than tape delays? I could take all the elements of my music—jazz vocals, improvised lyrics, even beatboxing—and all the elements of my comedy—the characters and accents and absurdism—and merge them into one seamless act. My Line 6 DL4 could turn my solo act into an entire band *and* my own comedy troupe. This small state-of-the-art device would allow me to finally tap into all the facets of my past and personality, all the tools I'd collected over a lifetime in my Toolbox of Weird, and unleash them all at once. I could imitate all the TV shows and movies I'd watched as a kid; I could hold conversations with myself in French and Spanish and German; I could lay that over the beats I'd first started honing in Cleveland; I could harmonize with melodies I'd first learned in my earliest piano lessons in Great Falls and perfected in Seattle. My new and ever-evolving act could be the artistic apotheosis of years and years of collecting experiences and ethnicities and memories and media and genres and points of view and fusing them into one single oddball identity. It could be revolutionary!

And, you know, I would one hundred percent fill that time.

• • • • •

My dad's emphysema got so bad he needed an oxygen tank to breathe.

He was in his seventies now. I called home more often, maybe once every week or two, and sometimes I would talk to him. We'd chitchat, I'd ask about his day, that kind of thing. Never anything about his deteriorating health or how he really felt. About life or the past or what it was like getting old. Even when I talked to my mom about my dad, it was mostly logistics. She was the one who told me he was on oxygen all the time. Who told me about the tube in his nose and how often she needed to change the tank. She was the conduit that connected us all, just barely.

To be honest, though, I wasn't really looking for more emotion from either of them. I liked keeping it simple. I liked sticking to the weather or what was on TV that night. I felt kind of relieved that we never went deeper.

It's not that I'm afraid of emotion. It's more like I have emotional incontinence. I have no control. So when I do truly connect with someone, the bursts of emotion can be so powerful, so overwhelming, I almost don't know what to do with it.

Like that time on the stage at the Showbox, when I looked into the eyes of the crowd, when I let myself go and crowd-surfed for the very first time. That simple, graceful, crazy act of connection brought me to tears. I started bawling in front of the whole audience and I couldn't stop. It was amazing and intense but also . . . I don't know. Uncomfortable, I guess. Weird.

So comedy! And technology! And voices! And beats! And

. . . . .

PUH-buh-puh-tuh-TSHT-buh-boo-bi-bah-boo-TSHT!

CHANNELING MY COUSIN FROM CLEVELAND'S VOICE:
I don't know how many of you guys are from places, but I'm from a couple places myself. Montana. Spain. Germany. Montana. A lot of people be looking at places, and they be like . . . why? Anyway, um, so I want to do, um, a song from my upcoming record. It's a new song from my old record. It's a song. It's on the record. And check it out.

POOH-ta-ta-TSHHHT-tah-tih-TSSHHT-faster-FASTER-FASTER-TSSSHHHT!

So that's my song.

A BRITISH PBS INTELLECTUAL: *A lot of people think there's a difference between what you want to do and what you can't do, and I think there's a truth to that, and obviously over the years people have said things that are different from one person to another, and that's one thing you should always be careful of because . . . you never know. [Maniacal laughter.]*

TWO VALLEY GIRLS FROM *FAST TIMES AT RIDGEMONT HIGH*: Once, I was talking to Jenny and she was like, "Oh my God, why are you looking at me like that?" and I was like, "I don't know, what are you looking at?" and she was like . . . [whispers] "I'll tell you later."

A SON THINKING ABOUT HIS DAD: I'm sitting in our kitchen in Great Falls watching my dad. I've been visiting home more now, maybe once every few months. The tube is in his nose and it's connected to a huge oxygen tank and we're watching *Star Trek* on TV. Every now and then his eyes will lose focus and he'll stare into the distance, and it reminds me of when I'd find him sitting here alone in the middle of the night when I was a boy. I can hear his breathing now. It's strained, ragged. It sucks to see him in pain.

[Record scratch on the looping machine, then layers and layers of improvised beats and jazz vocals and high pitches and low pitches and beeps and blurps and sound for the sake of sound.]

PUH-buh-puh-tuh-TSHT!

Something about the way she awwwww dowww duhhh dooooo dwooh! Woah!

Dodo bah do-do-do-do bah OH! OH! OHHHHHHH!

PUH–tsssht–

Slower.

PUH–tsssht–

Slower.

BOOM—BOOM—

Slower.

Buh...tsssshhht.

And I run my fingers through my Afro.

• • • • •

I started doing my new one-man improv show that used tech and talent to meld memories and music and identity at more and more places. Not only during lunch at the French restaurant, but at open mics at different bars, and then during Maktub's all-night informal jam sessions. I started doing it between sets or after the music ended, and then I started doing my act between sets when Maktub played shows on the road or at local clubs like the Baltic Room.

And the crowds seemed to be digging it, you know? I mean, why not dig additional entertainment during dead air between sets? And once I saw that the Maktub crowds liked my riffing, I wanted to give them more, so I'd creep it in wherever I could, and sometimes I'd do it to start out the night and close the night and sometimes, maybe, just maybe, I'd start doing it when the other members of the band were standing behind me onstage, waiting to wrap so we could all go home.

Then one night Maktub finished a show at one of the medium-sized clubs we always seemed to play, and we hit up a convenience store to get some snacks and drinks. I was sitting on the steps near the shop entrance, and Davis—our drummer, our unofficial ring-leader, the man who first recruited me to the band—came over and looked at me.

"Hey, man," he said. "Can you just stop it with those mouth sounds? It's really annoying."

What he said really bummed me out. First, because I felt bad that I'd been doing something that made my fellow band members, my friends, unhappy. These were the guys who had to stand behind me up there, who didn't have a mic they could talk into whenever they wanted. I'd been taking advantage of their generosity, and that sucked. Second, because I didn't catch it sooner. I didn't sense that they were upset and fix it myself. I wasn't being my usual hyperaware, hyperempathic self. I felt like I was being selfish, because I was doing what I wanted to do and was focused only on how I felt about it.

So I cut down on my one-man improvised interstitials, and Maktub continued to glide along the surface of our plateau, always generating a hint of buzz but never breaking out. I thought more and more about leaving the band, striking out on my own, but I also felt the weight of my obligations to the rest of the guys. And I don't mean "obligations" in a negative sense at all. Maktub had given me so much. It had pushed me creatively. It had opened me up to bigger crowds, broader audiences. It had helped me start to share my weird with the world. I was the frontman, essentially the face of the band, and that came with a lot of responsibility. I knew my bandmates still believed in us. Still dreamed of someday making it big. I hated the thought that I was letting them down.

Finally, in 2002, I worked up the courage to call Davis. He was the one who'd started it all, who'd had that initial vision, who'd believed before anyone else. I'd thought about holding a meeting with all the guys, but no—I wanted to talk to him first. It was really his band after all these years. I didn't have anything complicated to say, no insights into philosophy or the nature of friendship or what-ever. I felt too guilty for long, self-serving speeches. Instead, I simply said, "Hey, man, I don't think I can be in the band anymore."

And that was it. Over the next few years we would still play together on occasion. Still do a few shows, even record together. But officially, I was out.

As usual, I had no real plan. No grand design. It was improv as a way of life. I just did what I felt was right. Once again, I was counting on the mysterious workings of my ideal simulation to set me on the right path.

But I had no problem giving it a tiny push. Or in this case, a cut.

. . . . .

Um . . . right.

. . . . .

"A cut in line" is what I mean. I'm making, like, a

. . . . .

Anyway, I mean. Yeah. I'm not saying it's a *great*, ummm

. . . . .

I swear it'll make sense. I absolutely, totally promise that

. . . . .

The place was so crowded I could barely get in the door, everyone buzzing, grabbing, scrapping, trying to catch a glimpse of the stars.

"Did you see them? Are they here?"

"I think they're at the back! Sitting at a table!"

"But the line is so long!"

"This isn't a line, it's a mob!"

It was 2002, and I was in Seattle, but the crowd wasn't there for Pearl Jam or Alice in Chains. They were there for Stella, a sketch comedy troupe out of New York, famous for its brilliant, surreal humor. Lots of continuity breaks, lots of ridiculous arguments, lots of dildos. They had released a self-produced DVD of some of their shorts—this stuff looked like it was shot on a portable digital video camcorder—and the founding members of the troupe, Michael Ian

Black, Michael Showalter, and David Wain, were in town to sign copies. I was in Scarecrow Video, the world's oldest independent video store with more than one hundred thousand titles crammed onto its shelves. And it was bedlam.

Shit, I thought as I looked at the chaos of sweaty hipster bodies. *What the hell do I do?*

I'd first heard about Stella from my buddy Joel, one of the residents of the White House who I'd formed Hi,D with, and I became instantly obsessed. We'd gone to see Stella's movie *Wet Hot American Summer* in the theater four times in two weeks. Four times! It was like John Hughes on acid, and it blew my mind. When Joel managed to snag a copy of their self-produced DVD, we watched it immediately. Literally, he brought it to one of Maktub's all-night jam sessions, I called for a break, we went to his car, we popped it into his laptop, and we laughed our asses off. Stella was our comedy gods.

I *needed* to meet these guys. I *had* to meet these guys. If I did not meet these guys I would one hundred percent *die*. Which is the only justification I have for what transpired next.

Fuck it. I'm cutting to the front.

· · · · ·

See, I told you the whole "in this case, a cut" thing would, you know

· · · · ·

I'm not a tiny guy. I mean, I'm not *massive*—if I'd stuck with football in high school I would've had zero future. But I'm still about six feet tall, and even though my weight can fluctuate, I have what some would describe as "big bones." Also there's my hair, which even when I have it tied back has a pretty impressive girth all its own.

Yet somehow, I'm still not sure how, I managed to squeeze and squirm my way from the front door of Scarecrow Video, through the mob of sticky, squirming fans, and toward the table in the back. I had no idea what I was going to say when I actually got there—I mean, I honestly just wanted them to sign my DVD, but I was such a huge fan that I suddenly became aware of how nervous I was getting as I approached. These guys were comic *geniuses*. Everything they were, I wanted to be. Everything they'd accomplished, I wanted to accomplish. Not necessarily their success—though, sure, it would be nice—but their mastery of their craft. Their ability to embrace being strange, embrace being different, and somehow still appeal to so many people.

And there they were, sitting right in front of me. Michael Showalter, with his square jaw and classic all-American good looks. Michael Ian Black, who had that quirky next-door-neighbor vibe. David Wain, who had kind of a nerdy, mad-scientist appeal.

What should I say? What should I do? What—

"Maktub!"

Michael Showalter was standing right in front of me with a big smile on his face.

"Um, yeah," I said. "Maktub?"

"I saw you sing at the Jammies! So good!"

"Oh wow, thank you!" I said, too surprised for words. "And you guys . . . you're so good too!"

I couldn't believe it. Earlier that year I'd sung in New York at the Jammies, an awards show for jam bands. And somehow, for some unfathomable reason, Michael Showalter had been there, and not only had he seen me perform—he liked me! He really liked me!

The universe was taking care of me again. Michael invited me to their show at the local club Sub-Zero later that night, and backstage I met another legendary comedian.

Eugene Mirman was opening for Stella. Eugene is this big, pale, jovial dude who's kind of like a Russian Jewish version of the Ghost of Christmas Present. He's well-read, he's intelligent. He wears glasses a lot. Sometimes he has a beard, but mostly he doesn't. And I would eventually come to learn that he's a whiskey-drinking monster. His tolerance is insane.

Eugene and I just happened to have a friend in common, an amazingly talented performance artist named Linas. Eugene also happened to run an incredible underground comedy night called Invite Them Up in New York City with his buddy Bobby Tisdale. The show took place in this funky little video store that was tucked behind a bar—like you actually had to go through the bar to get to this video shack—and all the coolest names performed there in front of small, in-the-know audiences. Zach Galifianakis, Demetri Martin, Chelsea Peretti, Sarah Silverman, Kristen Schaal. Eugene and Tisdale knew everyone, all the comics, all the managers, all the stars. This amazing Russian Santa Claus and his partner were basically a pillar of the entire NYC comedy scene. And Eugene was talking to me like an equal.

"Hey," he said. "Anytime you're in New York and you want to do a set at my show, you're more than welcome. Just come on down."

So that's exactly what I did.

chapter thirty-one

THE RUSSIAN JEWISH GHOST OF CHRISTMAS PRESENT GOES SHOPPING AT GROCERY PANTHER

I open my eyes. My alarm is going off. It's 3 a.m., and I realize I'm in my old bedroom in Great Falls. I squint, and I can barely make out the breakdancing Snoopy on the wall in the dark.

My flight got in late yesterday afternoon. My mom was home with Bri, her caregiver. My mom's face lit up when I walked through our front door, but she looked really weak. Her back was still hurting, but she refused to take any pain medicine. She was dehydrated, but she wouldn't drink any water. I could tell . . . something. About her.

We all hung out, sitting in my mom's favorite red kitchen, watching old reruns on TV. My mom wasn't as talkative as she usually is. Usually she'll go on and on, telling stories about the past, especially stories about my dad. After all these years, she's never fallen out of love with him. She loves to tell me about the night they met in the Charlie Bar in France. About how they'd go out dancing, or drive in his green Firebird with the top down. About how, no matter how many troubles they had, she never considered ending their marriage.

But not this time. She was too tired to tell old stories. She was in too much pain.

I turn off my alarm and walk upstairs to her room. My mom had seemed comfortable when I tucked her into bed earlier tonight, her head propped up on a pile of pillows to help her breathe better, her dog, a black shih tzu named Dalai Lama, curled up next to her. But I still thought it would be a good idea to get up in the night to check on her. Maybe see if her dog—I call him Shmoopy for reasons I don't understand—needed to go out.

"Maman," I say, shaking her gently. "Maman, are you okay? Do you need anything?"

She stirs, speaking just above a whisper. "Reggie? I think I need to use the bathroom."

"Okay," I say. "Let me help you up."

I put my arms underneath her. She's tired, and her back pain makes it hard for her to stand. I leverage my own weight and slowly help her out of bed. Moving an entire human being—even a human being as small and thin as my mother—is a process.

We navigate the short hallway together, and I help her into the bathroom and onto the toilet. She sits there, staring straight ahead. Nothing happens. Maybe she, like, needs some privacy.

"I'll, uh, give you some time alone," I say.

I head to the kitchen and wait.

A few months ago, after my mom had to go to the hospital for a bad chest cold, I actually considered moving her out to LA. You know, to be closer to me.

I figured she'd be happy there. I'd be able to visit her all the time, even more than I do now. And Los Angeles isn't a bad place. It's pretty cool, actually. I like to describe it as the endless dystopian, semiholographic, hypercommercialized universe you see in the opening of *Blade Runner*, except friendly.

I even looked at some assisted-living places there. They seemed great. Not too far from me. Clean. Shiny. New. With chef-cooked meals and great views of foliage and the like.

Yeah, it was obviously a long way from Montana, but so what? All these people I know were like, you should let go of your past. It's healthy. Collect a few family photos and leave Great Falls. Sell the house, make sure your mom is well taken care of in LA, get as much quality time with her as you can. And on a certain level, that made sense.

But I don't know. It just didn't feel right. Great Falls isn't only special to me, it's special to her too. It's where she's comfortable, it's where she feels like herself. It's where she's spent most of her life. We talked it over, and she decided to stay here, at her home.

Man, she's been in the bathroom a long time.

What's it been? Five minutes? Six? More? Whatever, I'm sure she's

"Mom, you okay?"

I walk to the bathroom—probably a little faster than I intend, because of course there's no need to worry—and I look in. My mom peers up at me from the toilet, a little smile on her face.

"All that trouble to get me to the bathroom," she says, chuckling, "and I didn't even need to go."

chapter thirty-two

THE RIFIFI PARADOX

"Thirty seconds of stand-up!"

The crowd at Eugene Mirman and Bobby Tisdale's comedy night, Invite Them Up, was insane.

"Thirty seconds of stand-uuuuup!"

Standing room only, packed into this sweaty little video rental joint called Rififi that was tucked randomly behind these French doors at the back of some bar in the East Village.

And of course the comics were all out of this world, names like Rob Delaney and Nick Kroll and David Cross and Kristen Schaal and pretty much everyone who would go on to become the cast of *Bob's Burgers*. But the real attraction, the real source of energy that kept the night moving, was Eugene and Bobby themselves, and all the bits they would do to get the crowd going wild.

Which was how I came to find myself standing just off the small makeshift stage, waiting my turn to go up, as the entire audience sang

"Thirty seconds of stand-uuuuuuuu uuuuuuuuuup!"

Over and over to this funky little tune as Eugene and Bobby got ready to call up a comic to perform, yes, thirty seconds of stand-up. Which almost always went a hell of a lot longer than thirty seconds, which was fine with everyone.

I guess I should've been nervous. I mean, I wasn't some practiced, professional comedian. Far from it.

It was 2003. This was my very first time in New York City, at least for any extended period. I'd been taking in the sheer massiveness, the pure kinetic craziness. Walking everywhere, soaking up the skyline and the subways and the architecture, and that incredible old-movie aura of 1940s industrialism you can still find in parts of Manhattan.

But I hadn't come to town for comedy, I hadn't come here to perform at Rififi in front of some of the coolest comics in the world. I had come for music, at the invitation of the band Soulive, this incredible jazz-funk group that liked my work and asked me to come play with them for a month. It had been an incredible experience—we'd jammed together, performed a few shows, and then I thought of Eugene Mirman, and his open invitation to come on down to Invite Them Up if I was ever around. I wasn't regularly performing comedy anywhere. The most I had done were a few clubs in Seattle, lunches at that French restaurant, and the random interstitials during shows with Maktub that annoyed the band so much they asked me to stop.

But I figured what the hell. I'll go say hi to Eugene.

Now here I was, just me and my looper, surrounded by all these cool weirdos, these comedy nerds, these scenester thrift-store kids, these creative geniuses, and this rabid, glorious, mouth-foaming, singing audience with basically my entire comedic future on the line . . . and you know what it felt like?

High school.

Back in Great Falls High, I had always been the one who reached out to different cliques, who found the Weirdos in the Lunchroom and asked them if they wanted to hang out. What was the Invite Them Up gang except another clique to try out? Another social experiment with me as the guinea pig? Yeah, I was coming in as the outsider, I was the Weirdo in the Lunchroom, but they weren't excluding me. *They* were the ones asking me to hang out. *They* were the ones who wanted to see what I could offer. They were all so groovy.

And as for performing, it took me right back to competitive drama. Crammed into a classroom. Knowing the judges were sitting somewhere in the back, ready to score your every line. Watching all the other talented performers go up before you, one after another, and thinking, *Shit, these guys are good. What the hell am I going to do up there?*

You might think the stakes were higher in New York than in high school. They weren't. Not at all. Because nothing feels more important than *every single thing* you do when you're in high school. Nothing is bigger. Nothing is realer. Nothing.

So when my turn finally came, I smiled. I went up on that little stage in front of those talented comics and that raucous crowd, I plugged in my loop pedal, and I did my thing. And people were like

YOU.
YES.

My comedy career was born.

· · · · ·

· · · · ·

Oh, hey there!

I am currently at this moment in the process of writing this book—right . . . *now*—and something very profound is occurring to me.

You probably expect it to be a lot longer. The book, that is.

Like, "Hey, Reggie"—because we really should be on a first-name basis by this point—"it's 2003 in your book and you just got to New York and you're only thirty-one years old. I just Googled you, and even though you still look super young"—thanks, I totally appreciate that—"in real life you're currently, like, fifty years old"— give or take, depending on the date of publication—"which means you still have all this sick stuff to do in NYC and Los Angeles and all over the known and unknown world. I want to read about all those adventures too! This book should be *at least* another three hundred pages long! And it's clearly not!"—astute observation—"What *the F* is going on??!??"

Well, thank you for that interjection. It was very conveniently placed there by me. However, there's no need to resort to profanity, unless that *F* stands for "frack," like from *Battlestar Galactica*, in which case, by all means.

Your expectation for a longer book is an interesting one, some people might even say a great one, although most would not. Let's say, however, for the sake of science and meta-philosophy, that I did go on to tell the full story, in colorful, riveting detail, of all my further exploits. Maybe, just maybe—and by "maybe" I mean "perhaps" or potentially even "hypothetically"—the basics would go something like this:

That night, on that small stage at Rififi at the back of a bar in the East Village, I experience a revelation. An epiphany. After an entire life spent not planning anything and not having any larger goals, I suddenly realize that this, right here, right now, is what I was meant to do. This is what my entire existence was building toward. Comedy. My comedy. This mélange of music and improv and technology and just plain fucking around that is my act.

This. Just this. For the rest of time.

And once I know this simple fact, everything changes. It's like all the cogs and wheels and springs of my complex clockwork universe slide into place, one after another.

I move to New York and start making funny videos. I become a fixture on the local comedy scene.

I meet Eugene Mirman's booking agent, this classy English woman named Olivia Wingate, and she asks if she can be my rep.

I spend a few weeks in Scotland, living with Eugene and performing at the Edinburgh Festival Fringe in this building that used to be the Bank of Scotland back in the 1800s, and it kind of feels like the rebel base on the ice planet of Hoth. I go on for hours every night for twenty-eight straight nights, and I hone my craft and learn to listen to my audience and adapt my performance on the fly. Sometimes I eat a deep-fried cheeseburger, because that's a thing they do in Scotland.

I win the Andy Kaufman Award for experimental comedy,

mostly because Kristen Schaal keeps bugging me to enter the competition, and I get a giant cardboard check for a few thousand dollars and have a conversation with Andy Kaufman's dad, Stanley, who's a really neat guy.

I'm invited to open Conan O'Brien's live nationwide tour, Legally Prohibited from Being Funny on Television, and I spend a good chunk of 2010 traveling across America, acting weird and playing the keyboard and talking to Conan backstage about what it's like to be raised by Catholic parents.

I fall in love several times. Sometimes requited, sometimes not. I fall out of love approximately the same number of times. Along the way, I purchase and distribute copious amounts of thoughtful romantic gifts.

I take a moment and hunch over my piano keys and lose myself in one of my favorite Beethoven minuets.

DUN-DO-DO-DO-DO-DUN-DUN-DUN-DUN-DO-DOOOO

And Richard Branson flies me on his own private jet to his own private island to perform for a twenty-person summit he's holding on climate change. With zero sense of irony.

I accept my first recurring role on TV, playing the bandleader of a spoof late-night show called *Comedy Bang! Bang!*, and a couple years later, in 2015, I'm invited to be the *real* bandleader of a *real* late-night show. And I'm skeptical, because I hate schedules and I'm excited about pursuing my solo career, but before I know it I'm in Los Angeles sitting in a business meeting across from a guy I just met.

He has blue eyes, dirty-blond hair, and this pure, youthful, innocent face. He's almost cherubic.

"Hey, man," I say. "You want an edible?"

He doesn't even hesitate. "Absolutely. Thank you."

He takes the weed chocolate right out of my hand and plops it in his mouth. And that's when I know I'll be moving to LA and working with James Corden on *The Late Late Show*.

. . . . .

Or maybe, hypothetically, none of that happens. Maybe I just made it all up.

Maybe I have a very nice time performing that first night at Rififi in the East Village, and people like what I do, and I like them too, but there is no moment of revelation. No grand understanding that this, and only this, was always meant to be.

And maybe I just, you know, keep doing what I'm doing. I have fun. I trust my instincts. I live my life and kind of see what happens.

Maybe it's actually a mix of all of the above.

Maybe the cat in the box is alive or maybe it's dead or maybe it exists in some kind of quantum, unknowable *maybe*. Maybe we have created a new paradox, not the famous Schrödinger one but one that is far sillier, and we call it the Rififi Paradox. And the Rififi Paradox posits that it is only by achieving purpose that we can finally find the freedom to be funny. That it is only through self-awareness that we can finally forget the self and act truly ridiculous. That it is only through meaning, or perhaps the lack thereof, that we can finally become fundamentally absurd, and Mr. Plimford can finally end his interminable, murderous holiday.

Whatever.

Seriously, guys, this is a book about Great Falls, okay? I'm dealing with a word limit here—there's only so much paper the publisher is willing to expend on a first-time writer. But I'd love to write a couple more books, and I've had all these cool, unbelievable adventures in New York and Los Angeles and everywhere else—Richard Branson really did fly me to his private island, no joke—and they all totally deserve books of their own.

So tell all your friends, let's start a letter-writing campaign, and let's make this happen.

· · · · ·

Or maybe
Maybe
Maybe
the true paradox is simply a shoehorn
made of carbon fibers,
and nothing else actually matters except

· · · · ·

In 2006, my dad had to go to the hospital.

He'd been having trouble breathing, which was kind of a normal occurrence because of his emphysema, but it had never been this bad before. The doctors ran a scan on his lungs and found cancer. They attempted surgery, but when they opened my dad up, they realized that the tumor was so extensive there was no point in trying to excise it. My dad was seventy-eight, and he was weakened from years of being sick. They caught it too late.

I flew home to Great Falls from New York so I could be with him. Even though he was still in the hospital, he was alert and talking, engaged. I was used to being around him and his oxygen tank by this point, used to this man who had once seemed so strong and vibrant now appearing frail and old, so seeing him wasn't a shock. Mostly I wanted to make him feel better. Ease his discomfort, take his mind off the pain.

His birthday was coming up soon, on May 4. You know, the same date that *Star Trek* is celebrated on. I was scheduled to perform a one-man comedy show at the Lakeshore Theater in Chicago that night, so I decided to hold a little party for my dad a few days before I had to leave. But who to invite?

I hadn't been good about keeping in touch with my old crew of oddballs. I'd been so focused on . . . I don't know. My blossoming career. My frenetic existence. Pretty much anything other than my past. Beave was living around Missoula at that point, I think. His sister, Mel, was maybe in Idaho by then. And Fish? Zero clue where he'd ended up.

But I was pretty sure there was one person still around. Jon Thomas. My best friend since the seventh grade. Even as I'd grown apart from everyone else, he was always ambiently in my conscious-ness, especially when I was in Montana. Even if I didn't see him, even if I didn't talk to him, I just kind of knew what he was up to. Like I knew he'd gotten a degree in teaching at some point, and I'd heard he was still somewhere around Great Falls. And that he was really into bicycles. He worked on them, repaired them, rode them everywhere, always searching for the best trails to ride. A land surfer, a natural nomad. But always with his roots near his hometown.

I took out my cell phone, found his name in my list of contacts, and dialed. He said he'd see me at the party. Didn't hesitate.

A couple days later we crowded into my dad's hospital room to celebrate his upcoming seventy-ninth birthday—me, my mom, Jon Thomas and his kid brother, JJ, who was now in his thirties, and a couple other friends of the family. We had balloons, party hats, streamers. A little cake, though my dad couldn't eat much. We all sang him "Happy Birthday," loud, raucous, out of key. Jon Thomas was a little thicker than he'd been back in high school, but he still had that same frenetic energy, that same Beavis charm. It was infectious, and I could see it rubbing off on my dad, making him smile, making him laugh, helping him to forget about his health problems for just a few minutes. My dad seemed happy.

The doctors said he was stable. They said he might even be able to go home soon, where he could rest more comfortably. So I flew to Chicago to do my comedy show as planned. On May 4. May the Fourth Be with You. His birthday. But that was fine, that was cool. I figured there would be plenty more to celebrate in the years to come.

Right? There had to be.

The morning after my show, I decided to check in on my dad from the hotel. I called the hospital, and the nurse told me he had died moments earlier. She said my mom had been by his side.

As soon as I got off the phone, the first person I called was Jon Thomas. In that moment . . . I don't know. It felt right.

I told him my father had passed away, and I started crying.

Crying. I am crying now. I've cried before. But this is more. This is new.

Honestly, I don't remember what exactly Jon said to me. I was a whirl of grief, confusion, anger, guilt. My dad was gone, and I hadn't been there to say goodbye. I had been over a thousand miles away, far from the man who needed me, far from Great Falls. I couldn't handle all the emotion; it felt like everything just poured out all at once. But I do remember Jon's calm. He was focused. He was clear. He was present.

Yeah, there was a part of Jon Thomas that would always be a traveler, always coming or going, searching for something new. But when I needed him most, he was there. He was everything I needed him to be. He was still the kid who never gave up.

Later that day, I packed my things, and I went home.

chapter thirty-three

DAY ONE

My dad and I sit there, sipping cognac and orange juice, looking out at the world, singing our favorite song.

I'm a girl watcher.
I'm a girl watcher.
Watching girls go by.
My, my, myyyy.

Blond girls, brunettes. Blue eyes, brown eyes, hazel. Our kitchen table covered in red. The TV playing *Star Trek*. Going fishing together. Playing games on my computer. Seeing movies, going to concerts. His belt. All the different permutations of this universe. All the different decisions I could've made and could still make.

My dad and I don't say a word to each other. Never been too good at talking. But it's okay. We're here.

chapter thirty-four

THE END OF THE WORLD
(AS I KNOW IT)

"*Reg!* It's the man himself! Welcome to the Mayan apocalypse, dude!"

Beave still had those same crazy eyes, still had that same super-charged smile, but at least he'd finally cut his hair. No more mullet, no more Montana Fabio, just my buddy welcoming me to his sister's home in the woods of Idaho.

It was December 2012, right around the end of the Mayan calendar. So Beave had decided that he and his family of post-punk oddballs needed to celebrate the end of the world. He called us all up, every single one, and here we were. I personally had no idea if we'd survive the month, the year, or even the night, and honestly I didn't really care. I was just happy to see my friends together in the same place. Some of the immediate family, some of the extended family, even a few new people who happened to share the same outsider ethos as the rest of us.

I saw Mel, our host. She was married now, and she ran her own sustainable fashion label, Melanie Grace Designs, out of her house. But she was still the same beautiful platinum-blond elf I had grown up with and loved in my own way. I saw my oldest and original best friend, Jon Thomas, who'd moved to Columbia Falls, a town built along the Flathead River, among the forests and hills of Montana. Perfect for riding his bikes, going on new adventures, and blazing new trails. I didn't see Fish, who back in high school had looked like an attractive, androgynous third Duran—but we did talk about him a lot. After seeing God in a vision on his ceiling one night, he'd gone on to be a pastor in the Seventh-day Adventist Church, eventually deciding to travel the country shooting incredible photographs of nature.

Then of course there was Beave himself. We'd mostly fallen out of touch after he showed up at my Maktub show in Portland all those years ago. But since then he'd moved to Hawaii. He was on his second marriage, he owned an equipment company that helped build twenty-million-dollar luxury homes—and he still distilled and sold essential oils on the side. I found out that he'd gone through dark periods in his life, lonely periods. High school had been such an incredible ride for him, being this big fish in a little Montanan pond. In the years following graduation, he'd found himself alone, depressed, searching for meaning.

At first, I didn't know what to say. It's a strange thing when you find out one of your oldest friends was hurting so much, and you weren't around to help. Back in high school, as close as we'd all been, we never talked much about our feelings or our internal lives. We were too busy living those lives, getting high, having fun, expanding our understanding of the universe. But we were always present for each other.

Over the last decade, I hadn't been. I didn't have regrets, exactly, because we all had our lives to lead. That was the nature of things. But I could have intentions. I made a commitment, there and then, to always stay connected.

"Man," I finally said. "I'm so sorry I wasn't there for you. But I am now, okay?"

Beave smiled, those strange blue eyes sparkled. "Thanks, dude. I kept my suffering to myself, you know? I was too proud to tell anyone. But it all worked out. It really did."

He told me he'd gone on a trip to heal, took himself off to the woods where he fasted and did mushrooms for three days. He ended up a crying blob on the floor, taking stock of where he'd been, what he'd done, who he was. His life flashed in front of his eyes, his whole spirit burst out of his chest, he witnessed all his old failures and felt all his old pain. And then he was at peace.

He remembered that he was loved.

"I thought about you guys," he said, "all my old friends. I swore I would see you all again, and here you are."

The world didn't end that night, more or less, and the Mayan apocalypse wasn't the last oddball reunion Beave organized. Sometimes I don't make it, but most of the time I do. I stay connected.

No matter where we meet, whatever the city or state, it always feels natural, it always feels right. It always feels like home. We're the same and different. Still laughing, still smoking some weed, still philosophizing about crazy shit. But getting a little slower, a little grayer. And yeah, even having kids of our own.

Most of us have kids by now, and I guess that shouldn't be surprising. I'm not interested in children of my own, not because I don't like them, but because I don't like them for me. When you're used to living life by instinct, following your latest passion wherever it takes you, never making long-term plans or setting predefined goals . . . well, it's a little hard to imagine taking responsibility for a small, vulnerable human being. I've experienced my own parents' triumphs and failures firsthand, their love and their limitations, so I understand just how much commitment children demand—and deserve. I also know I don't possess that kind of commitment myself. And that's cool. I'm good with that.

But seeing everyone else's kids is different. I play with them, talk to them, marvel at their evolving personalities. I love to witness the development of their brains, the way their neurons connect each time they experience something new. Their imaginations seem limitless.

These children all have their own lives to lead and dreams to follow. They'll all create their own families of weirdos or jocks or preppies or nerds.

Life has come full circle. My friends and I have all grown up.

Now the best thing we can do is make sure that the next generation has the space and support to find themselves, to build their own identities, to be an Andie or a Duckie or a fashion designer or a minister or someone I can't even imagine. To create their own personal Great Falls, whether they're growing up in Montana or Idaho or Washington or Hawaii.

But hopefully Great Falls, MT. Because, honestly, there's no place better.

chapter thirty-five
GREAT FALLS

Even though I've been down this road a million times, I drive through town slowly so I can take it all in.

The linden trees, the sky that goes on for an eternity, the empty spot on the horizon where the old smokestack used to be. My high school, straight out of *Sixteen Candles*. That little club where I used to go dancing with Jo-ann. The old garage where I rehearsed with my very first band, and the music shop where we bought my first violin.

I'm heading home with lunch from Fuddruckers next to me on the seat. A veggie burger for me, a medium-rare bison burger with Swiss cheese and mushrooms and a side of wedge fries for my mom. I'm not sure how much she'll be able to eat, but it's her favorite. I want her to have that.

It's November 1, the day after I arrived in town from LA, and only two days after my mom went to the hospital for back pain and a possible kidney infection, only to demand to be taken back to her house so she could rest comfortably. She refuses to take any pain medicine, even though I know she's hurting, and she refuses to drink much water, even though she's dehydrated. I can't help re-membering that six or seven months ago my mom predicted she'd die in November. It occurs to me that today is Samhain, kind of like the pagan Halloween, when the veil between the living and the dead is the thinnest for whatever reason. And I chuckle, because I've always thought of my mom as a kind of Catholic witch with her own supersecret powers over life and death and the cosmos.

Seven years ago, I was forced to confront her mortality for the very first time. It was Christmas Day 2015, and I was visiting home with my friend Megan.

Ever since my dad had died nine years earlier, I had started taking a lot of my friends back to Great Falls with me, just to show them where I grew up. It was the best way I knew how to share myself with others, with the people I care about. Maybe the only way. I have a hard time opening up and being vulnerable. Like my dad, I just don't have the words. So instead I share Montana. The sounds, the images, the feelings, the memories. Because what is more me than this place? This place that keeps calling me back. What is more me than Great Falls?

So Megan and I spent that Christmas with my mom. I was forty-three years old, so we didn't put out cookies and milk for Santa, but it still felt festive, peaceful. A light snow was falling from the sky, a thick mist hung in the air, and we helped decorate my mom's plastic tree.

Then my mom told me she was having trouble breathing.

She was seventy-five. Like my dad, she had spent a good part of her life smoking cigarettes. She didn't have emphysema, but she'd had trouble breathing in the past. Maybe this was temporary discomfort, maybe it would pass. Maybe it was just a natural part of getting older. We decided to wait until the next morning to see if she felt any better.

She didn't, so Megan and I drove her to the hospital.

The doctors determined that she'd had a heart attack. One of her four valves was completely blocked, and another only had 13 percent functionality. They told me that anything below 20 percent was considered critically dangerous. They had to operate immediately.

As my mom had grown older, I'd started making this joke as I contemplated a future without her. I'd say something like "When my mom eventually passes away, which of course she never will . . ." It was a joke, or at least it was meant to be. But as the doctors took her into surgery, I realized that up until that moment, part of me truly, honestly believed my mom would never die. On an emotional level, I couldn't comprehend life without her.

This woman wasn't simply my mother or even my best friend. She was my protector, my guardian. She had defended me all my life against racists and bullies. She'd protected me from the anger of my father, made the ultimate sacrifice by telling the man she loved he needed to move away until I'd left home myself. She'd nurtured my creativity, she'd tolerated my rebelliousness with a good-natured wink. Whenever I'd gone back to Great Falls, she had always been there, waiting for me, welcoming me, loving me. More than any single person or place, my mother was my home. She was my base, my roots. My power.

Sitting in the waiting room with Megan that day, I still couldn't accept that my mom might be mortal. This was the same hospital my dad had died in nine years earlier. A few weeks after he'd passed, I found out that his heart had actually stopped on the night of his birthday, on the same night of my comedy show in Chicago. He had been successfully resuscitated, but I couldn't shake the idea that while my dad had been technically dead, if only for a few moments, I had been onstage working, singing, beatboxing, making people laugh. The following morning he'd died for good, unable to be revived. Gone forever.

I didn't want that to happen with my mom. I made a vow to be present for her. For us, no matter what. As long as she lived.

The doctors were able to save her life. They ran a catheter through a blood vessel in her groin and placed stents in her valves to improve circulation. They lost one valve permanently, but the other three were operating in acceptable limits. It was enough.

I started visiting as much as possible. Not only for holidays or birthdays, but just to be. To talk, watch TV, whatever. Anything I could do to get more time. My mom was right. I was scared.

But now, as I pull up next to the same house I've known since I was four years old, I'm not exactly sure what to feel. I'm emotionally present, I'm here, I'm now, but I'm also intensely self-aware, feeling and observing at the same time, and I have no idea what will come next. Is my mother about to pass on, to lift the veil between life and death and travel through? Or will I have another day, another week, another month, maybe even another year with this woman who means everything to me?

I don't know. All I know is I'll be with her every step of the way.

I get out of the car and carry our lunch from Fuddruckers inside to the kitchen. Bri came early this morning to help take care of my mom after her long night, and leaves soon after I arrive. My mom has a few bites of her burger, a few french fries, and gives some food to Dalai Lama the dog, but she doesn't have much of an appetite. She's quiet, doesn't talk much, then she tells me she's tired and she'd like to go to bed.

She's weak now, even weaker than before. I stand in front of her as we shuffle our way to the bedroom, allowing her to put all her weight on my arms.

I sit her down on the bed. She winces from the pain in her back. I slowly rotate her under the covers. Her breathing is shallow. I place some pillows behind her back like I did last night and it seems to help. The dog is running around like a maniac on the bed.

I think my mom might like a sip of white wine, so I bring her a glass. It sits on her bedside table, untouched.

She's having more trouble breathing. I ask her if she wants anything. Any water, any food, any pain medication. I ask her if she wants me to call the hospital. She shakes her head no. She's not talking much anymore. She manages to sit up, then lies back.

"I love you, Maman," I say to her.

"I love you too," she whispers.

My mom rolls onto her right side. Her breathing is ragged now, sporadic. I gently move the covers away from her face. I start to cry, and I'm sobbing right now, at this moment, as I write this. She takes one big breath, then a couple smaller ones, and then she stops. Her hazel eyes are open, staring out into space, and she's gone.

It's 9:04 p.m., and I sit there and watch her, and somewhere in my brain I compose a new song for the soundtrack of our lives . . .

After my mom passed away, which she never will, I decided to mourn her death by celebrating life. She didn't want me to be sad about her going away, and I think that's part of why she held on for so long. She wanted her son to be okay, and she wanted to be remembered with joy. She wanted to be honored with exuberance.

So a few days after her passing, I locked up the house, I installed an extra security camera—because I really will turn my home into a living museum and performance space one day—and I hit the road. I went to some events, a psychedelic conference in Miami and a psychedelic festival in Tahoe soon after. I hung out with weird, interesting people and we ingested various substances and communed about spirituality and consciousness and healing. And I performed my show, five times at the festival alone, and somehow that brought me closest to my mom. Working and expressing myself and transmuting all the dark energy into something positive, something happy. Feeling her with me. Knowing she'll always be there, waiting for me, whenever I come home.

And in a few months, I'll hold a ceremony of sorts.

I'll invite all my good friends to Great Falls. Friends from the past, friends from the present. Who knows, maybe I'll bend time and space and find some friends from the future. And I'm going to take my mom's ashes and my dad's ashes, and we're all going to go on a road trip to Glacier National Park, a couple hours northwest of town. It's beautiful there. A million acres of blue sky and evergreens and crystal lakes nestled among snowcapped mountains. My dad and mom loved going there together. It's their favorite place in the world.

Then I'll find the highest mountain peak I can find, and I'm going to release their ashes to the wind. I'll watch as they

twist

and

turn

and

fly through the air.

Two lovers, one from Cleveland, one from France, who found a home in Montana.

You're still here?? It's over!! Go home!
Go!
Oh. Wait. You're right.
My bad.

the reggie watts comprehensive glossary

· ·

throve

/THrōv/

Verb

past tense of **thrive**

- To grow, prosper, flourish, or be successful
- A verbal conjugation used solely by British people, Reggie Watts, and possibly some Vikings

Okay, seriously. This is getting ridiculous.
It really is over now. Pack it up and go home.
Or, you know, read it again.

acknowledgments

. . . .

I've been fortunate enough in my life to have both an incredible family and incredible weirdo friends who were just like family. I'd love to thank all of them, which invariably means I will somehow forget to include some of the most important ones. So if your name isn't on this list, that simply means that you have actually earned my greatest possible thanks of all, even if neither of us knows it. So thank you, sincerely, and carry on.

Thank you to Maman and Dad for all your courage and love throughout your lives. You made me the strong individual I am. I'm so happy you get to drink wine together and dance to old jazz records for eternity.

To my mom's side of the family, all of my cousins and aunts and uncles in France, thanks for your patience with me growing up as your weird hybrid relative. You taught me a lot and gave me so many important memories.

To my grandparents from Cleveland on Clearview Avenue— thank you for the immersion into the African American side of my identity. It enriched my understanding of self to no end. And a shout-out to the city of Cleveland for many great shows down on the flats.

Thanks to Bri, my mom's final caretaker, for your immense kindness and patience. My mom trusted you, and that was a near impossible feat. I'm eternally grateful.

Thank you to Megan McIsaac for your incredible photographic

eye and friendship. My mom really loved you. You were there at a difficult time, and it will never be forgotten.

To thank my Montana weirdo friend-family, I worked with Beave to construct a list of all the people we hung out with. The result is this Magical Weirdo Family Tree. It represents the graduated rings of social influence in my life in Great Falls. Thank you to every one of these figures, major and minor, because without them and each other, they would not, and I would not, be who I am today. I have no idea how accurate any of the spelling is in this photo of the Family Tree, but it looks pretty cool, and I love the redacted vibe of the little black rectangles.

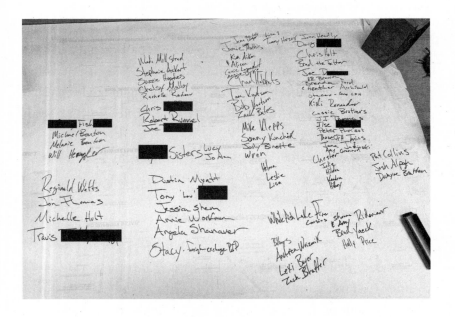

And a few special shout-outs to the following Great Falls friends:

Junko and Whitney, thank you for being both my best friends and my first loves.

Kris Steichen, thank you for all the late-night sneak-outs, the TP-ing, and the throwing stars.

Jon Thomas, thank you for so much that I don't actually know where to begin or where to end. Hopefully a lot of this book feels like a thank-you for just how transformative you were in my life. Thank you for incredible times at your grandmother's house on Lake Five, for introducing me to all the post-punk bands I never knew I loved, and for being a perfect Robo partner.

JJ Thomas, thanks for showing me how true brothers can be, and for exposing me to all your rad skater friends who didn't give a fuck in the best way possible.

Thanks to Steve Morse for being part of the odd trio with me and Jon in the early days. You were always cool, even when your life was sometimes difficult.

A huge thank-you to Jon's Grandma Ridenour, for always being hospitable yet eternally ornery. You and Grandpa Ridenour created an incredible, magical lakeside wonderland.

Schjanna Ridenour, thank you for introducing me to Front 242, even though I ended up buying a Level 42 tape instead. And to your friend, the red-haired Randi of West Glacier, thanks for taking me on one of the fastest rides of my life in your new Honda Prelude Si. You were an amazing driver and we had an incredible make-out session at the end. Well, at least I thought it was incredible. Hopefully you did too.

Thank you to Mike "Beave" Benton for being the ringleader of our nuclear friend-family, and for creating so many amazing opportunities for love, adventure, and chaos. You were and still are the heart and soul of our group, the glue that holds us all together. A tremendous thanks as well for all your help on this book, on the photos and the memories and everything else I asked of you. You believed in this project more than anyone else, and that belief helped see me through. You've never let me down once, and I'll never forget that. You are always King Volcano to me.

ACKNOWLEDGMENTS

Thanks to Fish for your uncanny and inexhaustible Tigger-like energy. You were the embodiment of fearlessness and reliance for me.

Thank you to Mel for our deep connection, our friendship, and our unrealized love. You were a magical being in my life.

To Michelle Hult, thanks for letting me borrow your car so we could experiment creating smoke screens. Thank you also for being so cool when we wrecked the car you'd just let us borrow. But we did replace the wheels with stolen ones. Remember that.

Will Hengler, thanks for being the source of good energy among us all, even after your shoulder surgeries at such a young age.

Thank you to Ilse for exposing me to the sophistication of the world and for my first kiss.

To Chris, thank you for always being a strong adventurer and companion on our many dangerous missions. But mostly thank you for exposing me to Robitussin. It changed all of our lives for the better.

Travis, thanks for being an Eeyore and a true mad scientist.

Robert Rummel, thank you for your charm and our graveyard antics, as well as your devotion to my crazy driving, which admittedly led to a little trouble.

To Joe Bates, thanks for being a real punk and for your knowledge of all things chaotic. Also, I'm sorry your house burned down. But luckily I was there to get your brother out and to alert the fire department, so you're welcome. Damn, kinda wish I'd included that story in the book. Sequel!

Thank you to Tony for being such a cool cat. Your general presence was always warming to me.

To Brenda—sorry about the car wreck, and for retraumatizing you. I hope you've forgiven me by now.

To Jo-ann, my sincere thanks for being my first girlfriend and my first true love. We were kids who were both doing the best we could, and I have absolutely no regrets. I couldn't imagine a better scenario of fun and sophistication and adventure and passion and drama, and ultimately the best kind. You're a real Kelly LeBrock.

Lucy, thanks for being a dope sister to behold.

To Wally, thank you for being a formidable druid and bard. Your partnership and amazing creativity in competitive drama set my life on an incredible course. Your talent remains limitless.

To Leslie from Helena—if I could remember your last name it would be helpful, but you were instrumental in my discovery that the song I wrote about suicide didn't suck.

Thanks to my first band, Autumn Asylum, and my fellow rockers Doug, Joel, and David. Special shout-out to Doug for deconstructing the Sundays on LSD with me in a hobbit house.

To my favorite orc dorks, Mike Howard and Colette—thank you for giving me a taste of what it would be like to be the third wheel on the TV show *Moonlighting*. I loved your bickering chemistry and unrequited passion.

John Abernathy, thanks for helping me understand what it would be like to hang out with Robert Downey Jr. as seen in *Weird Science*.

I'd like to mention a few of my Great Falls teachers who played particularly important roles in my life and education.

Miss Lidiard, thanks for teaching me violin and giving me the opportunity to play in an orchestra. You had a lot of patience with me, and I know it wasn't easy, but I'm eternally grateful for all those years.

Mrs. Thiel, thank you for giving me the freedom to be an improviser in competitive drama. You took a chance, and we took the state championship. I'll always be grateful.

Thank you to Judy Reisenberg, who taught me classical piano from ages five to sixteen (and whose name was Mrs. Rude when I first started lessons). You displayed a lot of patience, especially when I started improvising all my assigned pieces. You rock forever, and you always had sick hair.

ACKNOWLEDGMENTS

To Mr. Maddox, who was the only Black teacher I ever had, and who had such cool style and drove such a cool car—you were a great individual, and it meant a lot to me to see someone who looked like me teaching. Also thanks for saving my ass from that fight.

I'd like to give a special thanks to all the amazing artistic influences I had growing up. Some of you aren't alive anymore, and some of you are fictional, but I want to acknowledge your place in my existence to the cosmos. Also, it was just fun putting this ridiculous list together: Prince, Madonna, Elvis Presley, James Brown, Ray Charles, Thompson Twins, Culture Club, the Cure, Depeche Mode, Ministry, Skinny Puppy, Bauhaus, Night Ranger, Siouxsie and the Banshees, Journey, Whitesnake, Billy Ocean, El DeBarge, Eddie Murphy, John Hughes, Molly Ringwald, Judd Nelson, Ally Sheedy, Max Headroom—really ahead of its time, you should check out the original TV show if you have the time—James Bond, Spock, Samantha Fox, the lady who screams at the beginning of PBS's *Mystery!*, Cylons, Thundarr the Barbarian, Scooby-Doo, Dungeons & Dragons, Richard Pryor, Carol Burnett, *Three's Company*, *Fantasy Island*, *Growing Pains*, *Misfits of Science*, *Weird Science*, *The Breakfast Club*, *Sixteen Candles*, *Some Kind of Wonderful*, *Ghostbusters*, Nina Hagen from *Night Flight*, Pippi Longstocking, Kevin Seal the original host of *120 Minutes*, Devo, Cyndi Lauper, *Miami Vice* and the Sound Machine, *Knight Rider*, *Airwolf*, *Street Hawk*.

I think that's probably mostly it.

But also *G.I. Joe*, the AT-AT, Han Solo, *The Goonies*, *Dream a Little Dream*, *The Lost Boys*, and *Flatliners*. Did I say Prince? Yeah, especially Prince, for showing me what true interstellar talent and vision can create throughout the world. If I had only one influence, it would be you.

Great Falls may have provided my original weirdo family of

friends, but my Seattle weirdo family was just as important to me in its own way.

To Rafe, thank you for the experience of seeing my first pot plant in person.

Paula, thank you for being an incredibly romantic and sexy rock 'n' roll girlfriend who I never thought I truly deserved.

Thanks to Demon Roommate Guy for your pure evil and ability to throw cinder blocks through windows.

At Cornish, thank you to Randy Halberstadt for being a very weird but incredible virtuosic piano player.

To Beth Huerta, thanks for being half of my motivation to get into Cornish and for all the incredible, brilliant choreography you exposed me to.

Tim Young, thank you for being an incredible friend and monster musician who I did and still do look up to. You're one of the greatest musicians on the planet. No hyperbole.

Jeff Harper, thanks for being the one who welcomed me into the music weirdo community. Thanks for being so tall. And thanks for some of the best drives through the middle of Seattle in your giant boat of a station wagon filled with garbage.

Brent Arnold, thanks for expanding the idea of what a cello can do.

To Matt Stone, thank you for being one of the few living examples of the Muppet known as Animal.

Briggan Krauss, thanks for always being a slightly mythical demigod among my super musician weirdo family.

Thank you, Beth Winter, for teaching me proper vocal technique and for having a groovy Ann Wilson energy.

Thanks, Jay Clayton, for showing me what looped textural ambient vocals can sound like, as well as how to stretch the idea of what the human voice can do.

ACKNOWLEDGMENTS

Thanks to all my friends at the Blue House in Madison Valley for all the incredible music-making roommate-partying times. And for all the late-night walks through secret stairs down to Secret Beach for late-night swims.

Now for all my bands, and there were a bunch . . .

To Free Space and Don Spilker and Chuck Russell—thanks for being my first Seattle band and chaotic adventurous roommates.

Action Buddy, thanks for the brief rock 'n' roll ride. It was nice to be in a band with so many brothers of the same color.

Sme No Tay, thanks for the opportunity to experience West African soukous music. I learned a lot about the underlying origins of modern music.

IPD, or Ironing Pants, Definitely—thank you for being the greatest funk band acronym of all time, and for giving me the opportunity to play with one of my favorite bass players/glassblowers, Preston Singletary.

Thank you to Heather Duby and Clementine for letting me be a supporting character in a wondrous play.

Thank you to Micron 7 for being a band that almost made it big but ultimately ended in a classic fight in the rehearsal room. Drama never tasted so sweet.

Hit Explosion—thanks for my first high-paying gig that let me buy wine for my friends. I now know every single disco song that's ever been made. Thanks for always making it easy like Sunday morning.

Wayne Horvitz 4+1 Ensemble—thank you, Wayne, for making me a part of your elite musical family. Our European tour was one of the most important experiences of my life. I'll always owe you big time.

Soulive, thank you for asking me to be a part of your band family for a time. I had many incredible adventures and experiences, and I'll always cherish our time together.

To my brothers in Maktub—

Thank you, Davis Martin, for having the original vision and putting the initial group together. And for seeing our potential.

Thanks to Alex Veley for being one of the most incredible old-school-style keyboard players I've ever gotten to experience. And for your vast knowledge of soul music.

Thank you to Kevin Goldman for being a badass bass player who was always technologically forward.

Thanks to Thaddeus Turner for your incredible guitar skills and taste, and for your one-of-a-kind sense of humor.

Thank you to Daniel Spils for being my mountain-state brother and tasteful-as-fuck keyboard player.

On to comedy!

Thank you to the White House for being a haven of abstract comedic thought and action.

To Hi,D—thanks for being my first sketch comedy group where I got to actualize some of my dumb ideas. Special shout-out to Gretchen Sorrels for her patience.

To Michael McQuilkin, thank you for being the gateway to the White House. You were tall and talented and you were incredible at Frisbee.

To Joel Israel, thank you for your Batman-like energy and especially for introducing me to the Stella shorts in your car. It set the course for my New York comedy experience.

To the brilliant comedians of Stella, Michael Ian Black, Michael Showalter, and David Wain—thank you for creating some of the most obtuse, silly, dumb-dumb surreal sketches, which inspired me to seek out the source of that energy. Special thanks to Michael Showalter for recognizing me at Scarecrow Video.

Linas, thank you for introducing me to Eugene, which led me to perform at Invite Them Up in New York City. Performance art and comedy are forever buddies.

Thank you to Eugene Mirman for being so open and generous and welcoming me into the weirdo NY comedy scene. Another huge thanks for all our amazing adventures in Edinburgh.

Thanks to Bobby Tisdale for being a wild supportive rooster.

Hyper thanks to my sister Sarah Silverman for always making me feel included and seen even though you were already a legend.

Kristen Schaal, thank you for pushing me to compete for the Andy Kaufman Award. That meant a lot to me even though it might've seemed small. I'm forever your fan and brother.

A big thanks to the Edinburgh Festival Fringe for being open to some weird kid from Montana occupying its caves.

To Andy Kaufman's family and the entire group behind the Andy Kaufman Award—thank you for shining a light on outsider comedy and for allowing me to have even a brief connection with the great Andy himself.

Conan O'Brien, thanks for taking a chance on me to open for you on your Legally Prohibited from Being Funny on Television Tour. I loved getting to know you and bonding with you, and I feel like we made history together. You are a good king.

Thanks to Jimmy Fallon for my first big TV appearance. You didn't know what I was gonna do, but you were cool with it, and I'm happy I didn't fail you. And a huge thanks to Todd Levin for convincing Jimmy's show to take a chance on me.

Scott Aukerman, thank you for having me on your prestigious *Comedy Death-Ray* show and for letting me do its theme song. And then when it turned into *Comedy Bang! Bang!* and I did that theme song, and then when you asked me to be on that TV show, with a higher-production-value version of that same theme song. You're a nut and I'll love you forever.

To James Corden, thank you for trusting your instincts about hiring a Muppet for a bandleader. People were uncertain, but you let me do whatever I wanted to do, so I did, and it all worked out. I'll always remember your incredible generosity.

Special thanks to Ben Winston, the showrunner of *The Late Late Show*, for being cool in the presence of madness.

Huge thanks to Karen, my *Late Late Show* band: Guillermo, for being a dynamic and powerful, jovial, rhythmic force; Hagar, for your incredible musicianship and your uncommon brilliance as one of the best bass players I'll ever play with; Tim, you already know how I feel about you, but just so everybody else knows, you are one of the greatest ever; and Steve Scalfati, for taking a chance on moving from Seattle to LA for an unknown television gig. Your abilities are limitless. Thank you for being a great longtime friend.

Thanks to PopTech and Andrew Zolli for having me so many times to your festival. Being among so many brilliant technologists and futurists, I felt perfectly at home and validated.

Thank you to TEDx and TED Talks for having me do my thing and for having a random improvising Sasquatch grace your stage.

To Brian Eno—from the first time I met you at PopTech you generously invited me to your various curatorial festivals, from South Africa to Sydney, Australia, to Bergen, Norway, to Brighton, UK. Thank you for the late-night songs with your brother, and for making me breakfast in the morning and driving me to the airport. You are one of the greatest artists in history, and I'm so grateful I got to spend time with you. Music for airports indeed.

A big collective thank-you to my teams at CAA and Avalon for creating so many artistic and professional opportunities for me. You guys work hard so I can have fun and entertain as many people as possible, and I'm forever grateful.

Olivia Wingate, thank you for being my international booking agent, then my extraordinary manager. You elevated my career and supported it in ways above and beyond. I wouldn't be where I am today without your strategic support and friendship.

Kara Baker, thank you for seamlessly stepping in and helping my career continue to expand. It's good to have a practical, tough Bostoner on my side.

Helen Levenson, thanks for your patience and due diligence in dealing with a random human like myself.

Super thank-you to my assistant and friend Jaime Andrews, who's been with me since basically forever. I couldn't imagine achieving most of the things in my life without your help. You are the prototype for all assistants, and I'm lucky to get to work with you in such an effortless way.

Rachel Rusch, thank you for helping me manage the transition to a larger platform and giving me a sense of confidence in my continued expansion to the universe. You were a real force behind this book, even if you didn't know it.

David Larabell, thank you for making the process of creating a book seem not as terrifying as I thought it would be. Let's do another!

To Andrew Skikne at UTA—thanks for always being there for me since the early days of my career, literally giving me rides to gigs and from the airport when I needed them. You rock in so many ways, and I'm glad you're on my team.

Thanks to my business managers, Dan Frattali and Lisa Watkins, for keeping everything running while I roam around the world as a free radical.

To the entire team at Tiny Reparations and Penguin Random

House, a tremendous thank-you for helping to make this entire dream of putting out a book come true. You've been amazingly supportive of every weird idea I've had, and I truly appreciate you.

Phoebe Robinson, thank you so much for providing the incredible vision behind Tiny Reparations. I'm honored to be a small part of your imprint and your mission.

Amber Oliver, I'm sorry we didn't get a chance to work together, but I really appreciate you believing in this project at the beginning.

Huge thanks to Jill Schwartzman for keeping all the great vibes intact throughout the editing process, and for not just tolerating but nurturing all my oddball ideas.

Charlotte Peters, thank you for making the entire process move so smoothly.

To the graphic design team, thank you for going above and beyond to bring the weird text and entire look of the book to life.

Chris Farah, thank you for being the ghost in the machine.

Thanks to John Farah for your help in coaxing great stories out of my mom on our video chat.

Thanks to Talal Arimah, because I've been told I should thank you.

Huge thank-you to Tim Young for all your help with the original audio for this book.

Thanks to Michael Burke for helping process the audio and video media for the book.

Last of all, I'd like to give a special shout-out to all the artists out there struggling and striving and thriving through it all. This book is especially for you. I know how it is to put yourself on the line for your work, and that perspective is something I'll always operate from.

Okay, for real.

ABOUT THE AUTHOR

Reggie Watts is an internationally renowned musician/comedian/writer who starred as the bandleader on CBS's *The Late Late Show with James Corden* and IFC's *Comedy Bang! Bang!* Using nothing but his voice, his looping pedals, and his vast imagination, Watts blurs the lines between music and comedy with a résumé that includes multiple specials and appearances across platforms such as Comedy Central and Netflix.